D0506776

THE BOOK OF
CHRISTMAS

THE BOOK OF

Christmas

THE READER'S DIGEST ASSOCIATION
CAPETOWN, HONG KONG, LONDON, MONTREAL, SYDNEY
PLEASANTVILLE, NEW YORK

In *The Literature of Christmas*
some of the stories have been condensed, and some poems
are represented by selected verses

Acknowledgments and illustration credits
appear on pages 301 through 303

Library of Congress Cataloging in Publication Data
Main entry under title: The Book of Christmas
1. Christmas—Literary collections.   2. Christmas.   I. The Readers digest.
PN6071.C6B59   394.2'68282   73-84158
ISBN 0-89577-013-X·
Printed in the United States of America

CONTENTS

277   Christmas Around the World

The margins of *The Literature of Christmas* pages contain a number of
old legends and customs of the season, as well as verses from carols and from
poems by Rowena Bennett, Phillips Brooks, Elizabeth Coatsworth, Emily Dickinson,
Eleanor Farjeon, Kenneth Grahame, Washington Irving, Phyllis McGinley,
James Whitcomb Riley, Sir Walter Scott, William Shakespeare, Isabel Shaw,
Robert Southwell, William Makepeace Thackeray, and other authors.

The Birth of Christ

Angel of the Annunciation, part of an altarpiece painted by an unknown French artist, c. 1450

For unto us a child is born, unto us a son is given ...
ISAIAH 9:6

The Birth of Christ

ELISABETH AND ZECHARIAH

There was in the days of Herod, the king of Judea, a certain
priest named Zechariah, of the course of Abijah : and his
wife was of the daughters of Aaron, and her name was Elisabeth.
And they were both righteous before God, walking in all the
commandments and ordinances of the Lord blameless. And they
had no child, because that Elisabeth was barren; and they
both were now well stricken in years. And it came to pass, that,
while he executed the priest's office before God in the order
of his course, according to the custom of the priest's office, his lot
was to burn incense when he went into the temple of the Lord.
And the whole multitude of the people were praying without
at the time of incense. And there appeared unto him an angel of
the Lord standing on the right side of the altar of incense.
And when Zechariah saw him, he was troubled, and fear fell upon
him. But the angel said unto him, Fear not, Zechariah :
for thy prayer is heard; and thy wife Elisabeth shall bear thee
a son, and thou shalt call his name John.

And thou shalt have joy and gladness; and many shall rejoice at his birth. For he shall be great in the sight of the Lord, and shall drink neither wine nor strong drink; and he shall be filled with the Holy Ghost, even from his mother's womb. And many of the children of Israel shall he turn to the Lord their God. . . . And Zechariah said unto the angel, Whereby shall I know this? for I am an old man, and my wife well stricken in years. And the angel answering said unto him, I am Gabriel, that stand in the presence of God; and am sent to speak unto thee, and to show thee these glad tidings. And, behold, thou shalt be dumb, and not able to speak, until the day that these things shall be performed, because thou believest not my words, which shall be fulfilled in their season. And the people waited for Zechariah, and marveled that he tarried so long in the temple. And when he came out, he could not speak unto them : and they perceived that he had seen a vision in the temple; for he beckoned unto them, and remained speechless. And it came to pass, that, as soon as the days of his ministration were accomplished, he departed to his own house. And after those days his wife Elisabeth conceived, and hid herself five months, saying, Thus hath the Lord dealt with me in the days wherein he looked on me, to take away my reproach among men. LUKE 1:5-16, 18-25

Figure of an angel from an 18th-century Neapolitan crèche

Annunciation, by Carlo Crivelli, 1486

THE ANNUNCIATION

And in the sixth month the angel Gabriel was sent from God unto a city of Galilee, named Nazareth, to a virgin espoused to a man whose name was Joseph, of the house of David; and the virgin's name was Mary. And the angel came in unto her, and said, Hail, thou that art highly favored, the Lord is with thee : blessed art thou among women. And when she saw him, she was troubled at his saying, and cast in her mind what manner of salutation this should be. And the angel said unto her, Fear not, Mary : for thou hast found favor with God. And, behold, thou shalt conceive in thy womb, and bring forth a son, and shalt call his name Jesus. He shall be great, and shall be called the Son of the Highest; and the Lord God shall give unto him the throne of his father David : and he shall reign over the house of Jacob for ever; and of his kingdom there shall be no end. Then said Mary unto the angel, How shall this be, seeing I know not a man? And the angel answered and said unto her, The Holy Ghost shall come upon thee, and the power of the Highest shall overshadow thee : therefore also that holy thing which shall be born of thee shall be called the Son of God. And, behold, thy cousin Elisabeth, she hath also conceived a son in her old age; and this is the sixth month with her, who was called barren. For with God nothing shall be impossible. And Mary said, Behold the handmaid of the Lord; be it unto me according to thy word. And the angel departed from her. LUKE 1:26-38

A bronze panel from the north door of the Baptistry, Florence, by Lorenzo Ghiberti, 15th century

A cope fastening showing the Annunciation, from the Treasury of the Cathedral, Aachen

15

The Visitation, by Rogier van der Weyden,
15th century

And Mary arose in those days, and went into the
hill country with haste, into a city of Judah; and entered
into the house of Zechariah, and saluted Elisabeth.
And it came to pass, that, when Elisabeth heard the
salutation of Mary, the babe leaped in her womb; and
Elisabeth was filled with the Holy Ghost: and she
spake out with a loud voice, and said, Blessed art thou
among women, and blessed is the fruit of thy womb.
And whence is this to me, that the mother of my Lord
should come to me? For, lo, as soon as the voice of
thy salutation sounded in mine ears, the babe leaped in
my womb for joy. And blessed is she that believed:
for there shall be a performance of those things which were
told her from the Lord. And Mary said, My soul doth
magnify the Lord, and my spirit hath rejoiced in God my
Saviour. For he hath regarded the low estate of his
handmaiden: for, behold, from henceforth all generations
shall call me blessed. For he that is mighty hath done
to me great things; and holy is his name. And his mercy
is on them that fear him from generation to generation.
He hath showed strength with his arm; he hath scattered
the proud in the imagination of their hearts. He hath
put down the mighty from their seats, and exalted them
of low degree. He hath filled the hungry with good
things; and the rich he hath sent empty away. He hath
holpen his servant Israel, in remembrance of his mercy;
as he spake to our fathers, to Abraham, and to his
seed for ever. And Mary abode with her about three
months, and returned to her own house. LUKE 1:39-56

Visitation, by Jacopo da Pontormo, 16th century

And it came to pass in those days, that there
went out a decree from Caesar Augustus, that all the
world should be taxed. (And this taxing was first
made when Cyrenius was governor of Syria.) And
all went to be taxed, every one into his own city.
And Joseph also went up from Galilee, out of the
city of Nazareth, into Judea, unto the city of David,
which is called Bethlehem, (because he was of
the house and lineage of David,) to be taxed with
Mary his espoused wife, being great with child. And
so it was, that, while they were there, the days
were accomplished that she should be delivered. And
she brought forth her firstborn son, and wrapped
him in swaddling clothes, and laid him in a manger;
because there was no room for them in the inn.

The Nativity, detail from a Spanish altar frontal

The Nativity, detail from a Spanish retablo

Nativity, a 14th-century Spanish altarpiece

An 18th-century Neapolitan crèche figure

And there were in the same country
shepherds abiding in the field, keeping watch
over their flock by night. And, lo, the angel
of the Lord came upon them, and the glory of
the Lord shone round about them; and they
were sore afraid. And the angel said unto them,
Fear not: for, behold, I bring you good tidings
of great joy, which shall be to all people. For
unto you is born this day in the city of David
a Saviour, which is Christ the Lord. And
this shall be a sign unto you; Ye shall find the
babe wrapped in swaddling clothes, lying in a
manger. And suddenly there was with the
angel a multitude of the heavenly host praising
God, and saying, Glory to God in the highest,
and on earth peace, good will toward men.

Overleaf: *Angels in Adoration*, two fresco panels by Benozzo Gozzoli
for the chapel of the Medici-Riccardi Palace, Florence, 15th century

A 16th-century illumination depicting
the annunciation to the shepherds

Adoration of the Shepherds, by Rembrandt van Rijn, 1646

And it came to pass, as the angels were gone
away from them into heaven, the shepherds said
one to another, Let us now go even unto Bethlehem,
and see this thing which is come to pass, which the
Lord hath made known unto us. And they came
with haste, and found Mary and Joseph, and the
babe lying in a manger. And when they had seen it,
they made known abroad the saying which was
told them concerning this child. And all they that
heard it wondered at those things which were told
them by the shepherds. But Mary kept all these
things, and pondered them in her heart. And the
shepherds returned, glorifying and praising God
for all the things that they had heard and
seen, as it was told unto them. LUKE 2:1-20

The Adoration of the Shepherds, from the Portinari Altarpiece by Hugo van der Goes, c. 1475

THE PRESENTATION
IN THE TEMPLE

And when eight days were accomplished
for the circumcising of the child, his name was called
JESUS, which was so named of the angel before
he was conceived in the womb. And when the days of
her purification according to the law of Moses
were accomplished, they brought him to Jerusalem,
to present him to the Lord . . . and to offer a
sacrifice according to that which is said in the law of
the Lord, A pair of turtledoves, or two young pigeons.
And, behold, there was a man in Jerusalem, whose
name was Simeon; and the same man was just
and devout, waiting for the consolation of Israel: and
the Holy Ghost was upon him. And it was revealed
unto him by the Holy Ghost, that he should not
see death, before he had seen the Lord's Christ. And
he came by the Spirit into the temple: and when
the parents brought in the child Jesus, to do for him
after the custom of the law, then took he him up
in his arms, and blessed God, and said, Lord, now
lettest thou thy servant depart in peace, according to
thy word: for mine eyes have seen thy salvation,
which thou hast prepared before the face of all people;
a light to lighten the Gentiles, and the glory of thy
people Israel. And Joseph and his mother marveled at
those things which were spoken of him. LUKE 2:21, 22, 24-33

The Presentation, a 13th-century illumination

The Circumcision, a 16th-century illumination

Presentation of Jesus in the Temple, by Ambrogio Lorenzetti, 14th century

Herod and the Kings, a 13th-century illumination

THE COMING OF THE MAGI

Now when Jesus was born in Bethlehem of Judea in the days of Herod the king, behold, there came wise men from the east to Jerusalem, saying, Where is he that is born King of the Jews? for we have seen his star in the east, and are come to worship him. When Herod the king had heard these things, he was troubled, and all Jerusalem with him. And when he had gathered all the chief priests and scribes of the people together, he demanded of them where Christ should be born. And they said unto him, In Bethlehem of Judea : for thus it is written by the prophet, And thou Bethlehem, in the land of Judah, art not the least among the princes of Judah : for out of thee shall come a Governor, that shall rule my people Israel. Then Herod, when he had privily called the wise men, inquired of them diligently what time the star appeared. And he sent them to Bethlehem, and said, Go and search diligently for the young child ; and when ye have found him, bring me word again, that I may come and worship him also.

29

Procession of the Magi, a fresco by Benozzo Gozzoli for the Medici-Riccardi Palace, Florence, 15th century

Adoration of the Magi, an altarpiece by Gentile da Fabriano, 15th century

When they had heard the king, they departed; and, lo, the star, which they saw in the east, went before them, till it came and stood over where the young child was. When they saw the star, they rejoiced with exceeding great joy. And when they were come into the house, they saw the young child with Mary his mother, and fell down, and worshipped him : and when they had opened their treasures, they presented unto him gifts; gold, and frankincense, and myrrh. And being warned of God in a dream that they should not return to Herod, they departed into their own country another way. MATTHEW 2:1-12

Sleep of the Magi, by Gislebertus for the Cathedral of St. Lazare, Autun

Joseph's Dream, an 11th-century illumination

Ａnd when they were departed, behold, the angel of the Lord appeareth to Joseph in a dream, saying, Arise, and take the young child and his mother, and flee into Egypt, and be thou there until I bring thee word : for Herod will seek the young child to destroy him. When he arose, he took the young child and his mother by night, and departed into Egypt : and was there until the death of Herod : that it might be fulfilled which was spoken of the Lord by the prophet, saying, Out of Egypt have I called my son. Then Herod, when he saw that he was mocked of the wise men, was exceeding wroth, and sent forth, and slew all the children that were in Bethlehem, and in all the coasts thereof, from two years old and under, according to the time which he had diligently inquired of the wise men. Then was fulfilled that which was spoken by Jeremiah the prophet, saying, In Ramah was there a voice heard, lamentation, and weeping, and great mourning, Rachel weeping for her children, and would not be comforted, because they are not.

Slaughter of the Innocents, a 13th-century illumination

The Flight into Egypt, detail of a stone carving by Gislebertus for the Cathedral of St. Lazare, Autun, 12th century

Rest on the Flight into Egypt, by Pieter Bruegel the Younger

Wood sculpture by Adriaen van Wessel, c. 1510

But when Herod was dead, behold, an angel
of the Lord appeareth in a dream to Joseph
in Egypt, saying, Arise, and take the young child
and his mother, and go into the land of Israel:
for they are dead which sought the young child's
life. And he arose, and took the young child
and his mother, and came into the land of Israel.
But when he heard that Archelaus did reign
in Judea in the room of his father Herod, he was
afraid to go thither: notwithstanding, being
warned of God in a dream, he turned aside into
the parts of Galilee: and he came and dwelt
in a city called Nazareth: that it might
be fulfilled which was spoken by the prophets,
He shall be called a Nazarene. MATTHEW 2:13-23

35

And the child grew, and waxed strong in spirit, filled with wisdom; and the grace of God was upon him. LUKE 2:40

The Virgin and Child near a Window, a drawing by Rembrandt van Rijn, 17th century

The History of
Christmas

In the beginning was the Word, and the Word was with God . . . In him was life,
and the life was the light of men.   John 1:1, 4

The History of Christmas

by Rumer Godden

AMONG EARLY CHRISTIANS there was a custom of saying a blessing when the household lamps were lit: "Praise God who sends us the light of heaven."

The Jewish Sabbath observance begins with the ritual lighting of candles by the woman of the house, a reminder that light was one of the first acts of creation. The Sabbath ends with the father saying a prayer, his hands spread towards a lighted candle, towards the light, as if longing for it.

When the light of the first Christmas came, however, its glory shone not, as the Jews had expected, over all Israel, but around a few simple workingmen in the watches of the night, when most people are asleep. It led them, curious as all simple people are, to see for themselves if those extraordinary words that had been told them from the sky were true.

The shepherds would have taken their lanterns and held them up to see the "sign"—a baby, newborn by its swaddling clothes, lying where longed-for babies are not expected to lie—in a manger. But this was the Child of whom Zechariah, priest of the Temple, had sung: *"The dayspring from on high hath visited us, to give light to them that sit in darkness and . . . to guide our feet into the way of peace."*

39

Light has always been the symbol of good, of knowledge and understanding, darkness of ignorance and evil; but a dayspring? The dictionary says it means a beginning of day, or of a new era, and that it is an almost discontinued word, now used only figuratively. Yet how badly this troubled world needs a dayspring: something fresh, utterly pure and unstained.

Nothing can be more natural and good than the act of love if it is not debased. Yet there has always been something else, not natural, an ideal that has haunted minds in almost every civilization on this earth—the ideal of a miraculous or virgin birth.

In nature there have always been inexplicable "appearances": for a long time it was believed bees procreated their own young. Wrote Virgil:

> *Most you shall marvel at this habit*
> *   peculiar to bees—*
> *That they have no sexual union: their*
> *   bodies never dissolve*
> *Lax into love, nor bear with pangs of*
> *   birth their young.*
> *But all by themselves from leaves and*
> *   sweet herbs they will gather*
> *Their children in their mouths, keep up*
> *   the queenly succession*
> *And the birthrate, restore the halls*
> *   and the realm of wax . . .*

which is why bees have remained symbols of purity—and independence. There have been instances of spontaneous generation in insects, plants, fish. But for a woman thus to beget a child? Impossible—yet the ideal obstinately stayed.

The Incas believed that after the sun created the earth, his rays shone on a mortal woman and she gave birth to a son who was divine.

Fu-Hsi, a legendary Chinese emperor, was thought to be the child of a virgin who ate a flower, while in Finland's epic *Kalevala*, the virgin Ilmatar was fructified by the east wind; and it was the wind, too, this time the west wind, that quickened

Bees Flying to Hives, an English manuscript illumination, c. 1200

Wenonah, royal maiden of the Algonquin Indian tribe; she gave birth to a son, Michabo, known to the world as Longfellow's Hiawatha.

All these were impregnations by nature, but a Mayan maiden, Chimalmat, was breathed on by the Lord of Existence and so conceived. This is the story nearest to the overshadowing of the Virgin Mary by the Holy Spirit.

Ironically, Christian writers and artists have often tried to explain this supernatural ideal in physical terms, sometimes sweetly comical. "God spake by the Angel and the Virgin was impregnated through the ear," wrote one of the early doctors of learning, and there is a painting of this with the Holy Spirit in the shape of a dove, rays streaming from its beak into Mary's ear; another shows the dove entering her side—as the legends tell of Buddha entering his mother, but as a white elephant! One idea was that Christ did not evolve from an ovum in the womb, but arrived in it complete, a minikin who had only to grow in size.

These Christian beliefs are as quaint or naïve as any that had gone before, yet there is a difference. As ancient civilizations disappeared, most of their stories—and gods—faded into myths. But in Palestine, or Israel, in the last millennium be-

The Trinity with Dove and Infant, a Dutch manuscript illumination, c. 1435

fore Christ, the ideal of a virgin birth persisted and grew, though in a different way—not as a telling of something that had happened, but as a *foretelling*. It was as if a thought hazarded in many minds all over the world had come to center on this tiny land that had known, and was to know, such suffering and contention.

It is always a shock to find how small the Holy Land is. It was even smaller at the time of Christ's birth—one hundred and fifty miles from end to end, ninety miles wide in the south, only twenty-two in the north, the homeland of an unimportant "nation"—if one can call them that. Yet no people, no nation, has affected the history of the world as have the Jews.

They call themselves the "chosen people" because, they claim, it was only to them that the divine promises were made. God had made a covenant with Noah and set a rainbow in the sky to seal it; another covenant with Abraham, and then the one with the people of Israel through Moses. It was as if God were preparing the way through the belief and obedience of His people: the New Testament could not have happened without the Old.

When Abraham was "called," he forsook his lands—probably they were in Haran—and, with Sarah, his childless wife, his relatives, slaves, flocks and herds, went, as God told him, into Canaan. This was Abraham's first act of faith, and its reward was that Sarah bore him a son; Abraham was one hundred and she was ninety-one years old!

From the time of Abraham and Sarah the Jews were "God-directed." Abraham's grandson Jacob —called Israel—was told to take his people into Egypt; Moses, to bring them back in the Exodus, about 1250 B.C. The promised land was then divided among the twelve tribes, but some three hundred years later God made it into one kingdom ruled by the great King David, and it became even more prosperous under David's son Solomon. But after Solomon's death, first the Assyrians and then the Babylonians conquered the land, and thousands of Jews were deported to the east. The lament of that long exile comes down to us in the exquisite psalm:

> By the rivers of Babylon,
> there we sat down, yea, we wept,
> when we remembered Zion.
> We hanged our harps upon the
>   willows in the midst thereof.
> For there they that carried us away
>   captive required of us a song . . .
> How shall we sing the Lord's song in
>   a strange land?

Even after the Jews were allowed to come back, the land was conquered and reconquered, and it became a province of the Roman Empire some seventy years before Christ was born.

For generations the Jews had been waiting for the Messiah, who was to give meaning to their long history of wandering and striving. Perhaps, at first, they pictured Him as an earthly king, another David, who would deliver them: yet as time passed a greater conception came. The Christian Church has always seen in the Jewish Messiah an image, dim at first, of a Christ who was not to restore the kingdom of Israel but make a new Israel, a people of God with no limit of nation or race. God had promised the Messiah through men He had called to be His prophets.

The word "prophet" conjures up hoary old men, white-bearded uncomfortable creatures foreshadowing woe and punishment. They did call for repentance, always an unpopular theme, but they were not old; most were young and fiery, with as revolutionary ideas as any young radicals of today. Amos (760 B.C.) was a shepherd who taught that Israel's God was not exclusive to Israel. Micah, years later, dared to condemn rich farmers for robbing poor ones. Of the Messiah, Daniel wrote:

I gazed into the visions of the night. And I saw, coming on the clouds of heaven, one like a son of man.*

Isaiah was the most explicit of the prophets. He was a statesman of Jerusalem, a royal counselor for certainly three or four reigns—may even have been royal himself; he was also a poet of genius, so that in the Old Testament his book stands out in freshness and brilliance. Though Isaiah, too, cried woe, he also cried faith and hope:

> *The people that walked in darkness*
> *has seen a great light;*
> *on those who live in a land of deep shadow*
> *a light has shone.*

Always that light.

> *For there is a child born for us,*
> *a son given to us*
> *and dominion is laid on his shoulders;*
> *and this is the name they give him:*
> *Wonder-Counsellor, Mighty-God,*
> *Eternal-Father, Prince-of-Peace.*

What could be clearer than that? And yet it led to so many not seeing Him when He came. All through history it often seems that the chosen one, one who is to have a great gift, to do a great work, to influence the ages, is the unlikely one: not the sensible choice, but the youngest rather than the eldest, the weak not the strong, the unlettered rather than the learned, often the bad one not the good, the skeptic not the believer.

"Counsellor," "Mighty," "Eternal-Father," "Prince": accustomed as the Jews were to God's unpredictable ways, how could they dream such greatness could be born to an unknown small-town girl like Mary of Nazareth?

---

* In her quotations from the Scriptures, Miss Godden has sometimes drawn on the text of The Jerusalem Bible, and these excerpts are identified by page number in the Acknowledgments, page 301. Otherwise the text is that of the King James Version.   —The Editors.

Top: *King David Playing the Harp*, an Ethiopian manuscript painting, 17th century

Bottom: *Vision of Heaven and the Elders*, a Spanish manuscript illumination, 1220

43

In Jesus' day the town lay farther up the hill, but the present jostling Nazareth is, surprisingly, as it must have been then, with its white houses setting off the slim tall shapes of cypresses, its narrow streets and crowded markets.

It is true that the huge Church of the Annunciation, built in the shape of a rotunda with magnificent picture windows, dominates the little town; true that there are thousands of tourists, of touts offering to show the holy places, children who have learned to shrill for baksheesh; but the little open-fronted shops are still there, still selling grain, fruit, kid flesh. In spite of cars, there are still hundreds of donkeys; men wear Arab robes and the kaffiyeh, the white Arab head covering bound with two black cords. The tiny Chapel of the Annunciation, cluttered with a large altar, seems unconvincing, but the carpenter's clay-walled shop, with its cool underground living room that has niches in the wall for lamps, a trough for a cooking brazier, could easily have been the Holy Family's home.

There is a whole street of carpenters. Women still carry waterpots on their shoulders to 'Ain-sitt Miriam, Mary's Well, as she must have done; its spring is the chief water source of Nazareth.

Surrounded by pleasant hilly farms and gardens, fertile with wild flowers, date palms, fig, olive and pomegranate trees, Nazareth has been called "the flower of Galilee." But in Christ's day it seems to have been a place of some opprobrium: *Can there any good thing come out of Nazareth?* asked Nathanael, speaking of Christ. The pagan Greek influence was still strong in Nazareth—and could any Nazarene be trusted to be as strictly orthodox as surely the parents of the Messiah must be? Again, Nazareth was not in Judea, where, the elders knew, He was to be born. Had not the prophet Micah made that clear?

> *But you, (Bethlehem) Ephrathah,*
> *the least of the clans of Judah,*
> *out of you will be born for me*
> *the one who is to rule over Israel . . .*

How could the elders have guessed the strange way in which Mary of Nazareth would be brought to Bethlehem?

Mary's parents are not mentioned in the Gospels, but, by tradition, they are called Joachim and Anna and venerated as saints because for nine months Anna was the "tabernacle" that held Mary. Anna is the patron of joiners and cabinetmakers, of midwives, even of the useful cupboard.

Their story is told in the apocryphal gospels, which were written later as "embroidery" to the Bible, some beautiful, some naïve. These legends tell us that Joachim and Anna, though married for twenty years, were still childless, and going up to Jerusalem, in orthodox Jewish fashion, for the Feast of the Passover. Joachim's offering of a lamb was rejected by the priest, because he came under the curse laid on those who had not raised children for Israel. Joachim went up into the mountains and wept bitterly, fasted there for forty days, then made a great prayer to the Lord.

Meanwhile Anna was left, as she thought, abandoned and sorrowing, but at the exact time of Joachim's prayer she was moved to put on her wedding clothes and go into the garden. Suddenly an angel appeared both to her and to Joachim and told them they should have a child whose seed would be spoken of in the whole world. In due time the child was born—not, as they had expected, a boy, but a girl.

In gratitude for her birth—the Lord's removal of their "reproach"—Joachim and Anna brought Mary to the Temple when she was three years old and gave her to the high priest, who kissed her, blessed her and told her to sit down on the third step of the altar. But the Lord told her otherwise and, instead of sitting down, she danced—which entranced everyone who saw her.

These "embroidery stories" go on to the Betrothal and Nativity. Most of them say that Joseph was a widower, of any age from fifty to ninety, and medieval theologians seem to have fostered this

The Birth of the Virgin, a detail from a priest's robe, 14th century

Saint Joseph, the right wing of an altarpiece
by Robert Campin, 15th century

belief, thinking Mary's perpetual virginity would seem more likely in the eyes of the world if she were married to an old man; but this belittles her —still more Joseph. His being young makes his restraint, wisdom, unquestioning belief, prompt action and protection of Mary and the Child more unselfish and wonderful.

Probably Mary and Joseph fell in love in the ordinary way of a young man and woman, but the marriage would have been arranged by their parents through a matchmaker. The "tenaim," the Jewish terms of marriage, the dowry—which certainly would have included candlesticks to be lighted by Mary on the Sabbath—the gifts expected of the bridegroom, and the wedding date, would all have been settled at the Betrothal, which was a binding and solemn ceremony.

So Mary gave Joseph her troth, which means fidelity, honesty, loyalty—and then the angel came. We do not know where Mary was at the time, though many paintings show her at her weaving. Did she simply look up and see the dazzling presence?

Angels were of awesome beauty. The prophet Daniel described his as having eyes *like fiery torches*. In the New Testament, at Christ's sepulcher the angel's face was like lightning, his robe white as snow, and the guards were so frightened of him they were like dead men. In fact, it seems that angel visitants usually had to begin their messages by saying, "Do not be afraid."

Perhaps Mary's uniqueness shows in that she was not afraid, though Gabriel's *Hail, thou that art highly favored, the Lord is with thee: blessed art thou among women*, perplexed her; she was obviously modest, but she did not lose her poise, and her acquiescence was not naïve. She said simply, *How shall this be?* She almost certainly had heard the prophecies, particularly Isaiah's, and so her surprise was not that a virgin should bear a child but that she, so lowly and obscure, was chosen to be that virgin.

What must it have been like for a girl, reverent,

46

modest, loving, faithful, as Scripture shows Mary was, to be found with child before she and her betrothed had come together? From the Gospels we can gather that her parents were orthodox Jews who might even have disowned her; for it was Joseph who thought to put her away in secrecy so as not to expose her to shame.

Mary, of course, could not feel any shame, which must have been another puzzlement, nor could she explain; who would have believed her if she had? Was Joseph's bitter disappointment in her the first of those swords of sorrow which were to pierce her heart? Yet it seems she told him nothing. In the whole of the New Testament Mary speaks fewer than two hundred words, Joseph not one, but their acts speak far more eloquently than any words. What must have been Mary's relief when the angel came to Joseph in his turn and, in the words of Matthew, bade him take Mary to himself.

Joseph was certainly God's instrument or, if one prefers, the instrument of providence. It is difficult, nowadays, to realize the risk Mary ran, not only of ignominy, but of death: she could have been stoned, the Jewish punishment for adultery. Joseph's silence silenced that, but in a small town like Nazareth there must still have been curiosity, and perhaps this was why he took Mary with him when he went to Bethlehem for the census.

Every fourteen years the Romans organized a census through their whole empire so that, by a poll tax, they could levy the money that paid for their armies, their luxuries—and the people's

Mary's Wedding by the Master of the Life of Mary, 15th century

47

"bread and circuses." It is probable that the particular census of Luke's Gospel was held between 10 B.C. and 7 B.C., under the emperor Augustus. For this census Joseph was obliged to go back to Bethlehem, his birthplace and the town of the house of David.

To take a young girl, so near the birth of her first baby, on an arduous four- or five-day journey

Voyage to Bethlehem by an unknown artist, 11th century

by donkey seems madness. But to Mary, the coincidence of the census with the birth of her baby must have been another "confirmation"; it fulfilled that ancient prophecy of Micah's about the birthplace of the Messiah.

Centuries later a Roman monk, Dionysius Exiguus, had the idea of dividing history into two eras separated by Christ's birth, but we know now that the calendar year 1 A.D. could not have been the time of Jesus' birth, because He was born in Herod's reign and Herod, a mortally ill man, died in 4 B.C. When the Magi visited him there is no mention of ill health. Probably the Child was born about 7 B.C., which also coincides with one, perhaps two, of the astronomers' attempted explanations of the Magi's star.

Joseph and Mary must have journeyed down the

valley of the Jordan, which was not as hot, dry and craggy as it is now; then, there were still traces of Palestine's ancient fertility and forests. They would have followed the road as far as Jericho, then climbed the hills to Jerusalem, and on to Bethlehem five miles beyond.

It seems too that they traveled alone. Perhaps Joseph wanted to keep Mary hidden from curious eyes, but it was a brave decision—there were bandits in the overhanging cliffs on the way. The donkey has become so much part of the picture that we take it for granted, and Mary, great with child, could not have walked.

Probably at night they rested for safety in one of the inns or caravansaries on the way—perhaps a small one-storied house, a walled-in courtyard, a well in the center, tethering rings for beasts, and places for cooking fires, built of clay or hollowed in the ground.

The donkey would have carried a roll of bedding, and Mary obviously took the swaddling clothes—narrow bands of cloth in which the limbs of newborn babies were bound in those days to prevent too much movement. And so they came to Bethlehem Ephrathah, a hilly little town among the olive groves.

Ephrathah, name of the district around Bethlehem, means "fruitful," Bethlehem "house of bread"; Jesus was to say He was "the true vine," "the bread of life"; and millions of Christians believe He appears again under the guise of bread and wine every day, on altars humble or magnificent in almost every part of the world. But that night in Bethlehem, as we know, there was no welcome for Him, no place in which He could be fittingly born. The stable, possibly the inn's, would have been a cave because, in hilly Bethlehem, that was where household cattle and pack animals were kept.

Mary probably brought forth her son alone; but in another apocryphal story Joseph went to fetch a midwife and suddenly the world stood still:

Now I Joseph was walking, and I walked not. . . . And I looked up unto the pole of the heaven and saw it standing still, and the fowls of the heaven without motion. And I looked upon the earth and saw a dish set, and workmen lying by it, and their hands were in the dish: and they that were chewing chewed not, and they that were lifting the food lifted it not, and they that put it to their mouth put it not thereto, but the faces of all of them were looking upward. And behold there were sheep being driven, and they went not forward but stood still; and the shepherd lifted his hand to smite them with his staff, and his hand remained up. And I looked upon the stream of the river and saw the mouths of the kids upon the water and they drank not. And of a sudden all things moved onward in their course.

. . . and behold a bright cloud overshadowing the cave. And . . . the cloud withdrew itself . . . and a great light appeared in the cave . . . And by little and little that light withdrew itself until the young child appeared . . .

a wonderful picture of the whole world holding its breath.

The presence of the ox and the ass fulfilled prophecy. *In the middle of two living things you will make yourself known,* wrote Habakkuk of the Messiah, while Isaiah said, *The ox knows its owner and the ass its master's crib.* In the East, a manger was made of clay or was, perhaps, a stone trough, and though Mary would have filled hers with hay, it must have been cold. The traditional story is that the ox and the ass kept the Infant warm with their breath.

The Nativity by the Master of Játiva

49

In Palestine one cannot go far without meeting a shepherd, often with a lamb or hurt sheep on his shoulders. He may be wearing over his robes a Bedouin sheepskin coat, its fleece inwards; he carries his staff in his hand as he leads his flock, talking to them in a singsong chant. Shepherds are prominent in the Bible, from Abraham with his flocks, and David, called from his shepherding to be anointed king, to Christ Himself. *The Lord is my shepherd; I shall not want,* is perhaps our most beloved psalm, and over and over again Christ was to say of Himself in the parables that He was a good shepherd. What could be more just than that the first outsiders to see Him newborn were shepherds?

Even this, though, has given rise to endless argument. Some theologians say Jesus could not have been born in winter because Bethlehem in December reaches freezing point and the flocks would have been inside. The birth must have been in spring, say others, because that is lambing time, when shepherds keep watch at night—at other times they would have left the sheep to themselves. Arguments or no, the Gospels say the shepherds of Christmas lived in the fields, from which it seems likely they were Bedouins or other nomads; even now, around Bethlehem, the low black tents of the Bedouins are seen winter or summer, and the glint of their fires in the night.

At Christmas nowadays Bethlehem is crowded with tourists, such thousands of them that the local Christians cannot get into their own midnight Mass. The cave or grotto is below the great Roman church; two flights of steps lead down to the little cavern only a few yards long and wide; it reeks of incense and has ornate trappings—more than fifty lamps; but the floor is inset with a star, its silver worn away by kissings—the spot where Christ was born, a reminder of the line of David and the Magi's star.

What stir the Magi must have made in the Bethlehem streets as they rode to the place where the star stood still! Matthew says it was over a house, so the Holy Family had moved from the cave.

No one knows where the Wise Men came from, but, by the richness of their gifts and the respect they were given at Herod's court, they were certainly illustrious; in popular tradition they were kings. It is obvious they had traveled a long way; if, as is probable, they had had to cross deserts, it would have been by camel. Following a star, they would have done most of their traveling at night.

The Grotto of the Nativity, Bethlehem

Historians and astronomers have argued for centuries as to what that phenomenal star could have been. A comet? One was seen in 17 B.C.—too early; another, taken to be a portent of Nero's death, in 66 A.D.—too late. The Chinese, most precise of astronomical observers, note that a comet was sometimes visible, sometimes invisible, for seventy days in 5 B.C. Or the star might have been a nova, not a new star, but one that has a sudden increase in brilliance as it explodes internally; a nova's radiance can be of colossal magnitude. The Chinese observed one in 4 B.C.; they called these novas "comets without tails"— the language of astronomy is of celestial beauty.

There was another, more likely, coincidence, backed not only by astronomy but astrology—the study of the influence of the stars and planets on

King Baltasar, a detail from a Catalan altarpiece by an unknown artist

human beings and their affairs; planets move through the solar system, sometimes coming so close to one another that they seem from our millions of miles away to be almost in conjunction. In 1603 the great German astronomer Johannes Kepler watched through his telescope a conjunction of Jupiter and Saturn in the constellation of Pisces, and remembered something he had read— that ancient astrologers had long believed that this near meeting of the planets signified the night, even the hour, when the Messiah would appear, because Pisces, those two celestial "fishes" tied by their tails, was His sign; Jupiter was a royal and lucky planet, and Saturn was held to protect Israel.

From careful calculation of his notes Kepler learned that this rare and strange conjunction had happened before, in 6 or 7 B.C. For years his discovery was disregarded, but in 1925 some ancient papers were found in the once famous School of Astrology at Sippar in Babylon; and there, in Babylonian cuneiform, a conjunction was clearly marked and observed for five months in the year 7 B.C.: it was of Jupiter and Saturn in the constellation of Pisces.

It seems irrefutable and yet . . . To wise experienced men like the Magi, could the conjunction, however close, have seemed one star? Would they not have said, "We have seen His stars," in the plural? Again, whether explained with planets, the Chinese comet or nova, there is still one flaw:

52

Voyage of the Magi, a mosaic by an unknown artist

all were visible in Babylon and over the East as far as China, yet no one in Palestine seems to have noticed them, not Herod's chief priests and scribes, nor anyone in Jerusalem. Even when the Magi told them, they were mystified. Why?

In The Jerusalem Bible, the commentary on the Gospels is careful to scotch any fantasy, scrupulously separating truth from legend, and yet the relevant note says, "Obviously the evangelist [the careful historian Matthew] is thinking of a miraculous star; it is futile to look for a natural explanation." And is it not the essence of a vision that it is seen only by those for whom it is intended? There is no record that anyone but John the Baptist saw the dove descending at the Baptism; on the road to Damascus no one but Paul saw anything, yet Paul for a while was blinded by the light. It has been the same with all visions.

So it might have been that the true wonder of the star was that no one but the Magi saw it. To Mary, their homage too would have seemed unearthly, these great visitants from countries far beyond her ken, kneeling before her Child—but then there were those earthly gifts, strange gifts for most babies, but the Wise Men were seers: they offered this one gold for His royalty, frankincense for His divinity, myrrh for bitter death and sorrow.

The sorrow came almost straightaway. In all history there can have been no more horrible monster than Herod, of whom Flavius Josephus wrote, "He was no king but the most cruel tyrant that ever ascended to a throne. He robbed his own people, tortured whole communities; almost every day someone was sentenced to death, even among his friends, his priests and family, including his wife and sons." But nothing seems more terrible in his terrible life than the murder of those hundreds of babies, the Innocents, every male child under two years old, in and around Bethlehem. Jesus was saved by Joseph's quick action and obedience to the words of the angel of the Lord,

not even waiting for daylight; but what must it have been like for Mary, that flight into Egypt, leaving such pitiful carnage behind?

The journey under this shadow of horror was long, far longer than from Nazareth to Judea, two hundred and fifty miles, a caravan route south to Hebron, west to Gaza and along the coast, most of it through rocky or sandy country—the donkey is said to have died on the way.

Over the border and a few miles north of Cairo is the village of El Matariya, standing now in fields

The Sinai Desert between Israel and Egypt

of sugarcane, and this is where Joseph is supposed by some to have taken Mary and the Child. Pilgrims still go there to see the Church of the Holy Family, also an ancient hollow tree in which, it is said, Mary hid with Jesus when they were chased by soldiers and thieves; a convenient spider quickly wove a web so fine over the hollow that no one could see inside.

When Herod was dead and Joseph was told by the angel of the Lord that the family could go back to Palestine, he returned to Nazareth, where Jesus grew up.

Christmas, in the Bible story, ends here and, what is strange for us to understand now, was not really to be remembered for almost four hundred years. It stayed almost hidden, as most of Christ's life here on earth was hidden; for three short years

53

He taught and healed, stirring hearts and minds, was crucified for it as a dangerous false messiah, and was buried. His only followers were a group of men and women, most of them humble folk who had never been outside Palestine.

His light had burned so low that it seemed extinguished; yet the historian Suetonius tells us that only fifteen years after the Crucifixion there was a Christian faction in Rome. Within three hundred years the Roman emperor himself, Constantine the Great, would put the Cross on his soldiers' shields as a sign of his belief and become the protector of Christendom. The prophet Amos's teaching had come true: God was not exclusive to the Jews.

The chief messengers of Christ were the apostles. Apostle means "one sent out." They taught by word and by letters, but as one after the other died, mostly in appalling ways—Peter and James crucified, Paul beheaded, James the Less thrown from a pinnacle of the Temple, then stoned, Barnabas flayed alive—it became plain there was an urgent need to put Christ's teachings into writ-

Maxentius defeated by Constantine, Battle of the Milvian Bridge, a detail from the Stavelot Triptych, c. 1150

ing, the "good tidings," as the Gospels are called, before they were distorted or lost. The ones to do this were obviously those who had known Him and shared some of His life.

It is suggested that there were rough Aramaic forms of the Gospels as early as 50 A.D., but not as we know them. Matthew, a learned man, seems to have finished his some twenty years later; he wrote trying to convince the Jews, which is why he so often recalls the Old Testament prophecies. Mark's Gospel may have been written in 64 A.D. John, closest of all to Christ, dictated his book at Ephesus, sometime after 70 A.D.

The Gospels are all incomplete, jerky, telling the same happening in different ways; and yet Christ is alive in them all, even in brusque Mark. Mysteriously, only one of the four gives the whole story of His birth—the Gospel of Luke. There must be a reason.

In Luke's day historians did not name their authority, especially if it was a woman—females were almost disregarded among the Jews. "Blessed art thou, O Lord our God, King of the Universe, who hast not made me a woman," is a Jewish masculine prayer. But how could Luke have known those intimate things of Christ's conception and birth, of Elisabeth's and Mary's words in the Visitation, when no one else was present, unless Mary had told him? Joseph, Elisabeth and Zechariah were long dead—and Luke, in the King James Version of the Bible, makes plain these things were secret: *But Mary kept all these things, and pondered them in her heart.* Luke was a doctor and so might easily have been skeptical of the virgin birth, yet his belief shines in every beautifully written line of these first two chapters.

The Fathers made Easter the holiest day of the Church, as it still is—naturally: the Christian faith is founded on Christ's death and Resurrection. Next came Pentecost—again, at that time, naturally; those tongues of fire had to spread across the known world, speaking in every lan-

The Twelve Apostles, a Spanish manuscript illumination, 1220

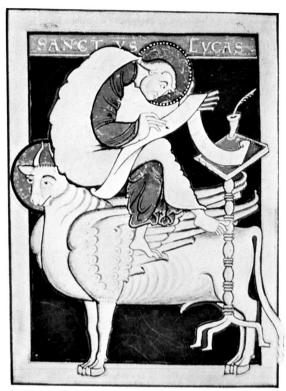

Saint Luke, an English manuscript illumination, 12th century

guage. Last came Epiphany, a threefold "remembering": of the coming of the Magi, of Christ's first miracle at Cana, and of His Baptism by John in the Jordan, which was held to be His real birth. It was a great feast, yet something important was lacking. Christ was spirit, true God, but He was also true man; to ignore His human birth was to take away His double wonder. And, slowly, it dawned on the Fathers that there should be a separate festival—Christmas.

The first question was—when should the festival be held? In spite of the star readings and arguments about the customs of the shepherds, no one knows in what month Jesus was born, but there seemed to be a feeling that Christmas should come in winter—in every religion known to man there had been a winter festival.

Ancient Sumer, for instance, had a winter feast called Zagmuk, to persuade the god who made the world to come down and fight Chaos

in the underworld so that earth could flourish for another cycle of seasons. It was a time of prayer and sacrifice, the chief sacrifice being that of the reigning king, who would die for the atonement of the people's sins. There is more than a germ of the Christian idea here, except that the real king did not die; a criminal, dressed in royal robes, was sacrificed in his place.

Yule, the Norse festival, came in December, the darkest month, when there were perhaps only three or four hours of real daylight. Yule lasted twelve days, and log fires were kept burning to revive the fading sun.

Those early rulers of the Church were astute enough to know, or perhaps had learned the hard way, that rather than fight beloved pagan customs, it was better to accept them and subtly transform them, especially festivals.

Easter was an exaltation of the Jewish Passover, Pentecost of the Feast of Weeks, held in remembrance of Moses being given the stone tablets of the Law on Sinai. There was another great Jewish feast, the Feast of Tabernacles, but that fell in the autumn, which seemed unsuitable. The Church wanted one at the turn of the year or near it. In December came Chanukkah, Feast of Lights; what better name for Christmas? Yet it is likely the Fathers hesitated; by the fourth century the Christian Church had moved far, far away from the Jews; indeed, was already hostile: there had been riots, fights.

Rome had a Feast of Lights, Natalis Invicti; in Rome, the sun in its winter solstice was at its weakest on December 25 and had to be born anew with the help of bonfires, lights, processions and prayer.

It would seem fitting that the birthday of the sun should become the birthday of the "Sun of Resurrection," and one guesses that this was the pagan-Christian blending in the Fathers' minds when they accepted the twenty-fifth of December as the Christmas date, but there was another pair of Roman feasts, far more popular than Natalis Invicti: the Saturnalia, which lasted from the seventeenth to the twenty-third of December, and the Kalends of January, the first three days of the new year.

The Saturnalia had begun as a feast which broke for a few days through all barriers of class and behavior—a memory of a golden time when just and kindly Saturn ruled as king, and all men were happy and good; slaves could tease and mimic their masters, and women, if they were masked, could flirt with whom they chose. The Kalends was more portentous, full of omens, but homes were decorated with lights and evergreens, and everyone gave presents and invited guests.

Everywhere may be seen carousals and well-laden tables; luxurious abundance is found in the houses of the rich, but also in the houses of the poor better food than usual is put upon the table. The impulse to spend seizes everyone. . . . A stream of presents pours itself out on all sides. . . . The highroads and footpaths are covered with whole processions of laden men and beasts. . . . It may justly be said that it is the fairest time of the year. . . . The Kalends festival banishes all that is connected with toil, and allows men to give themselves up to undisturbed enjoyment.

These were frankly holidays—no one could describe them as "holy days"—but Christ Himself had gone to feasts, consorted with ordinary

Actors and Musicians, a mosaic from Pompeii

people. If, thought the Fathers, Advent could be a time of preparation, akin to Lent, and Christmas Eve a vigil, as it still is in a way for those who go to church at midnight, the feasts could be transformed.

Even for the Child's birthday, the Fathers thought of several hours of praise and prayer, of a feast like the at first frugal Agape—the "love feast" of the Apostolic Church, when a group met together, each bringing what food and wine he could, the rich providing for the poor. Men and women sat at different tables and, either before or after eating, one loaf was blessed and broken, one cup of wine, the cup of blessing, passed around. The evening ended with prayers, and this, a first and tentative Christmas, was allowed to be celebrated, almost certainly in Rome. How, over the centuries, the people transformed the Fathers' Christmas is shown in its singing.

As early as 130–135 A.D., it had been ordained that "in the holy night of the Nativity the people should solemnly sing the angels' hymn," meaning the angels' words to the shepherds; but as soon as Christmas began to make its way as a feast, priests and monks began writing their own Christmas hymns. Many of these are still sung in cathedrals and monasteries, especially during Advent, their plainchant making the spirit soar.

> *Creator of the stars of night,*
> *Thy people's everlasting light,*
> *Jesu Redeemer, save us all,*
> *And hear thy servants when they call. . . .*
>
> *Thou camest, the Bridegroom of the Bride,*
> *As drew the world to evening tide,*
> *Proceeding from a Virgin shrine,*
> *The spotless Victim all divine.*

But they were written in old Latin for choirs, few ordinary people could sing them, and there was nothing in their words to evoke the Holy Family or Bethlehem until the poets dared to break in. The first to dare were Italians who wrote their hymns in the vernacular, poets like the scamp Jacopone da Todi, whom the priests regarded as irreverent and yet who was soon nicknamed "the Lord's minstrel."

> *Sweep hearth and floor,*
> *Be all your vessel's store*
> *Shining and clean.*
> *Then bring the little guest*
> *And give Him of your best*
> *Of meat and drink. Yet more*
> *Ye owe than meat.*
> *One gift at your King's feet*
> *Lay now. I mean*
> *A heart full to the brim*
> *Of love, and all for Him*
> *And from all envy clean.*

This was the "carol spirit"—carols, though, were dances and did not become acceptable in churches for another hundred years.

The Saturnalia and the Kalends, run together, could be a fortnight of near riot, of drunkenness, noise and games, naked slaves singing, men dressing up as animals and behaving with less dignity, sex, often with perversion; and though the Fathers and bishops were patient, at last a severe sermon had to be preached, full of forbiddings. At Christmas, men and women were not, repeat not, to dress up or mime; there were not to be auguries, such as superstitions about fire; houses were not to be decorated, no presents given, no well-laden tables, and a strict watch was to be kept on drink. More than a thousand years later, Oliver Cromwell tried to forbid the same things, this time by government order.

What such stern preceptors forgot is that no child could see anything wrong in the forbidden things, and when it comes to festivals, most of us become childlike—not childish, which is something quite else, but childlike—wanting to be natural, even if that means a little boisterous and greedy; to have surprises, secrets, a little fun, perhaps hoping for a touch of magic. No one can be as deaf as a child who does not want to hear, and as if bishops and governors had never spoken, the people kindled Christmas exactly as they chose.

Kindle is the right word because, in any kind of winter, darkness of weather—or of soul—a feast needs living warmth.

Wind and fire are symbols of energy, and one of the sad things of Christmas now is that so few of our houses have that sound of a fire roaring up the chimney, the Yule log back again, its flickering light cheering the rooms, and the smell of wood-smoke making a home incense.

Fire games used to be madcap, men swinging girls high over a bonfire as they danced around it in the open; we still try to catch the excitement of fire, flaming our plum puddings, and at parties we can still play snapdragon, daring one another to snatch raisins from a dish of flaming brandy. If fingers are sure and quick, they really do not get burned—or does one want to get burned, just a little? The best games have a spice of danger.

"The ryghte reverende fader and worshypfull lorde my broder Bysshopp of London . . ." but the voice speaking from the pulpit is not that of a prelate. It is the clear treble of a schoolboy whose chin, above the cope he wears for this occasion, hardly reaches the pulpit ledge. His cheeks are pink with excitement because he is the Boy Bishop, appointed in English cathedrals and colleges for Christmas, and his is the right to give the sermon on Holy Innocents' Day.

Such boy bishops were supposed to say what they liked, but if they were too impudent—this one daring to call the Bishop of London his brother!—they could be birched next day. All the same, on this one day they could make dignified and elderly clergy turn themselves into candle or incense bearers, could demand a supper from the dean and keep the collections from the services.

These church charades were, and are, gay and often clever; the priests had the wit to laugh at themselves and be laughed at, but even priests can

Illuminated page from a Florentine choir book, 14th century

Theatrum Sanitatis: Dancers and Musicians, a manuscript illumination

59

A detail from the biographical portrait of Sir Henry Unton by an unknown artist, 16th century, showing a banquet, masque and musicians

go too far; as in the Feast of Fools of medieval days, when "priests and clerks, wearing masks, danced in the choir and did antics." Once, in Beauvais, France, an ass was actually brought up to the altar; the singing of the Introit, Kyrie, Gloria, even the Credo, the most sacred chants of the liturgy, ended in a bray!

The Nativity plays were all religious, but those that strike the deepest chord keep a human earthiness. There is a song in the American gospel singers' Black Nativity where the women of Nazareth count up the months of Mary's pregnancy, just as gossips do with any girl in trouble—making it vividly real.

These plays, being in church, always exacted a certain degree of good behavior from the congregation; but there is something in most of us that likes now and then to fool, and so charades and masques were soon taken into the home.

At the Tudor courts and every great house of that time, a Lord of Misrule was chosen who gave all the orders for the holiday, even to the king and queen and courtiers. The Lord of Misrule was elaborately dressed and carried a blown-up bladder affixed to the end of a stick; he used the bladder for harmless buffeting, and he could buffet anybody—our balloons are its descendants.

That was for the court, the nobles, but as for the common people—who was to know who they were if they wore masks, the loved old masks of the Saturnalia, but now hiding a farm boy, an apprentice, perhaps the village blacksmith or a shy dairymaid. It was they who became the mummers, who went from house to house, much as children do now at Halloween with trick or treat; the tricks and treats, though, were far wilder, especially as the mummers, at every house, were given drinks.

One Saturnalian custom was to hang little masks of Bacchus, god of wine, on evergreen trees. Bacchus is usually shown as a bloated, fat old man, but the classics describe him as handsome and young, unexpectedly mellow, like one

The Lord of Misrule from The Book of Days

of his own wines. It is true his symbolic bird is the magpie, because in libations people speak with boldness and liberty; but how could they help loving this hero who taught them the use of the vine, the cultivation of the earth and the manner of making honey? Jesus, too, knew the use of the vine—the wine He made from water at the Cana wedding was not only wine, but the best wine.

At Christmas, if the weather is cold and raw, we may serve mulled wine—warmed, and beaten with sugar and spices—or hot punch, a nowadays imitation of the Christmas wassail bowl. The old wassail bowls, usually of silver or pewter, were immense—one, at Oxford, held ten gallons —but Anglo-Saxon for wassail was *wes-hâl*—"be whole"; and it must have been a wholesome drink.

People say the old pagan feasts were gay and innocent. Were they? In Scandinavia and North Germany, when the first snowfall came and the cattle could no longer go out to pasture, the herds were thinned with "a great slaughtering," so that it became a season of eating and drinking, weeks of it, until men and women became almost insensible. Though our markets at Christmas, often with carcasses dressed with evergreens and ribbon rosettes, are a reminder of that, we have nothing like the Roman banquets, when an emetic, probably of herbs and oil, was taken between courses; then there was a hurry to the vomitorium, a throwing up, before the guests came back to gorge again. Hardly anyone now wants to overeat, even at a feast, but all the same, at Christmas one of the first concerns, certainly of the woman of the house, is still a well-laden table.

Jesus was understanding about food—for other people. He made the miracle of the loaves and fishes, and cooked breakfast on the shore for His fishermen disciples after their night of toil; but He often fasted, and we know, from His rebuke to Martha, He did not like a fuss.

Luke wrote of poor Martha, *careful and troubled about many things,* as the housewife is at Christmas. Did she go back to her kitchen and say, "It's all very well, but here is He, whom I love, hungry and worn out . . . and He is our *guest*"? In that word lurks the household pride. Christmas, too, is the time when the family comes home, relatives gather and everyone, it seems to a Martha, has different tastes and, nowadays, different diets. It all has to be remembered.

Usually, too, the good things—parcels and baskets—go far beyond the house; in England's heyday the squire would give a piece of beef to every cottage in the village, and even in poor houses the housewife would put a loaf of bread on top of the roast while it was cooking; the loaf would soak up the nourishing juices and could then feed a family even poorer.

In spite of the hundreds of recipes in present-day magazines and cookbooks, for Christmas most of us do not want something different, but the traditional fare of the country to which we belong. America gave the turkey to England—it was originally wild in Mexico—but the Christmas bird used to be goose, even swan; and in most of Europe the Christmas meat is pig, of which every part is used.

Most households lay in a ham: in Russia, they make a traditional dish of the trotters, while a boar's head used to be an essential part of the feast in England. Its mouth propped open with an apple, the decorated head was brought in on a silver dish, and sometimes there would be a fanfare of trumpets while a special carol was sung:

> *The boar's head in hand bear I,*
> *Bedeck'd with bays and rosemary;*
> *And I pray you, my masters, be merry.*

The ceremony was because, in the Eightieth Psalm, Satan was *the boar out of the wood,* and his head, brought in, showed his defeat by the newborn Child.

Everyone in the household should stir the Christmas pudding and make a wish, to add to the excitement. Some "answers" are in the pudding: tiny trinkets of silver, a coin for riches, a thimble for someone who will be an old maid, a button for a bachelor, a wedding ring.

Besides the pudding, there should be a Christmas cake—different in every country. The French bake huge flat "cakes of the three kings" for Epiphany and, for Christmas, miniature ones called *naulets,* shaped like the Holy Child and often given as presents—rather like the old Polish custom of sending wafers of the eucharistic bread, stamped with patterns, as a sort of Christmas card. It sounds irreverent, but needless to say, the wafers were not consecrated, only blessed by the priest.

In old-time Germany, peasants believed there was a magical power in loaves baked at Christmas if the dough was moistened with the dew of Christmas night: this dew was sacred, mentioned in the antiphons sung at Advent Vespers: "*Rorate, coeli, desuper*—Come down, dew,"—the dew being Christ.

Though nowadays mince pies are made with spiced fruit, chiefly raisins, they used to be filled with minced chicken, neats' tongues—a neat is a bullock or ox. But whether the pies are of fruit or meat, each person should eat at least twelve at Christmas so as to have twelve lucky months in the new year.

The very names of the foods, old and new, are festive: frumenty, syllabubs, velvet cream, cranberry jelly, crystallized fruits, sweet-potato pie, candy canes. And they seem to come in a shower from all over the world: Carlsbad plums, Smyrna figs, ginger in those inviting Chinese jars, tangerines, almonds and raisins. In Italy and Spain a kind of nougat is eaten so that the coming year will be full of sweetness.

With such well-laden tables, it would seem there could be no room on the board for more, but a new passion has come back to Christmas from the Kalends—decoration. Surely decorating our houses is not pagan? Indeed it is, going right back to antiquity, a custom that has brought its double meanings most fittingly into Christmas: the wreaths of holly and streamers of red ribbon on the front doors of every village and little town are festive; yet holly, ivy and mistletoe are all sacred because they bear fruit in winter.

Mistletoe is the "golden bough" that was cut at the winter solstice by the archdruid with a long gold-handled knife. It was supposed to cure all sickness—and it was so powerful in amity that if enemies met it in a wood they laid down their arms until next day, which is why it is hung now over doorways or in corridors where people pass, so that they can kiss in love and friendship.

Our first Christmas trees were small blossom trees: blackthorn, hawthorn, almond, planted in pots or put in water and brought indoors in the hope they might bud or flower on Christmas Day and so bring a fruitful year. This went back to a legend that when Christ was born the rivers ran wine instead of water, and flowering trees blossomed in ice and snow.

These flowering trees forced in the warmth of the house were delicate, and when they failed to

The Bean King's Feast, a detail from a painting by Jacob Jordaens

Winter Slaughter of Livestock from a Flemish manuscript, c. 1515

63

flower, as they often did, the household was filled with dark omen. Northern Europe adopted the evergreen, and soon other countries followed. In Germany, land of forests, the *Weihnachtsbaum* has even more wonder and romance than in other countries, for it links mankind to nature and the perpetual revolution of the seasons: the evergreen stands for immortality. In some parts of Germany, graves are wreathed with holly and ivy, and a little tree with lights is set in their midst.

The popular story is that the prince consort, husband of Queen Victoria, brought the Christmas tree, with other loved Germanic customs, to England—but it was already known in England and France at the turn of the eighteenth century. Now the prettiest signs of Christmas, standing in almost every window, are the little trees sparkling with lights, witch balls, tinsel and spangles.

Presents have become an edict, like the Roman emperor Caligula's when, one New Year's Day, he announced he would stand out on his porch to receive presents of money; if the sum was not enough, the giver was publicly shamed. We, too, are not untouched by this—the richer, more important our friends or relatives, the less they need presents, the more thought and money we spend on the gifts. It is the Kalends again, "the impulse to spend" that "seizes everyone," but now it is not just an impulse.

We send cards, too. These were once handmade and, even when the first commercial ones appeared, were often colored by hand: flowers in a paper lace border, scenes sparkling with silvered snow, very often robins, because "the robin and the wren are God's cock and hen"; or there were motto poems, exquisitely engraved. Then the penny postcard was introduced and the avalanche began. A penny postcard! Now even the stamps are Christmas pictures, costing as much as the cards used to do, but still, each year, it seems there are more and more to be sent: some of us even keep a sort of ledger of "give and got."

Was it when a date was fixed for Christmas that its spirit began to be lost? Easter almost always takes us by surprise, and Jesus Himself seems purposely to have been elusive—His disciples were always having to find Him—so that it seems ironic that He who left no material traces at all, seemingly owned nothing except the coat "without a seam" His mother had woven, for which the soldiers drew lots—and a pair of sandals, perhaps—should have His birthday turned into the trade fair of the year. Father Christmas, innocent descendant of a god and a saint, has become like one of his own blown-up balloon figures, filling our horizon and blotting out the star. Many children think he is God.

He *was* once—the Norse god Odin, lashing his reindeer through the darkness of the northern midwinter, bringing the gifts of spring, new corn and fruit—it does not seem he brought anything else. Then he became Santa Claus, who was really Saint Nicholas, a fourth-century bishop, patron of boys—people believed he brought four of them back to life even though a wicked innkeeper had already pickled them in salt! Saint Nicholas is loved so much that in Russia they used to say, "Even if God dies we still have Saint Nicholas." On the night of December 6, he borrowed Odin's reindeer and visited every house where there were children, who left their shoes in the hearth when they went to bed; in the morning, if they had been good, the shoes were full of sweets; bad children's shoes were empty.

The shoes became stockings, and now, one is glad to think, for good and bad children alike; because nothing can match the excitement of creeping, even before first light, to find that elongated knobby object, left limp the night before, now hanging filled by the hearth.

It is not the giving that has almost driven Christ from Christmas; after all, He taught us endlessly that it is blessed to give. Isn't it rather the quenching of His dayspring, the loss of innocence in greed and grab?

No child ever wrote to Saint Nicholas to give

The Feast of Saint Nicholas by Jan Steen, 17th century

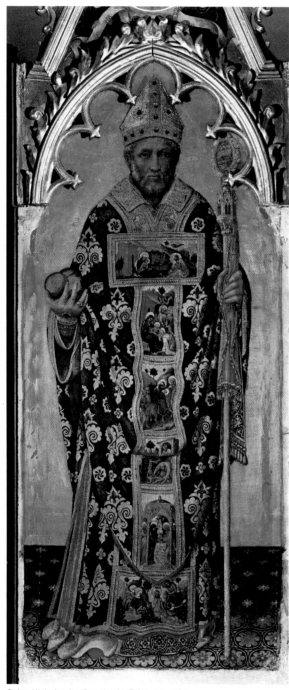

Saint Nicholas by Gentile da Fabriano, 1425

him orders, but though few letters to Father Christmas go up the chimney now in the old magical way, thousands are sent through the post office:

> . . . I want a story about Christ and six horses.

> . . . a swing each (for Natasha and me) so we don't have to fight because we say mine mine mine all the time.

And, far more businesslike, from a boy:

> Father Christmas will you get me two cars and will you get me one road please.

One "embroidery" story says that the five-year-old Jesus played at mud pies, making sparrows out of clay and water, and, as it was the Sabbath, Joseph came out and scolded Him. Jesus did not answer. He clapped His hands, and the sparrows flew away. Joseph must have been disconcerted, but not Jesus, because all children can, in a sense, do this—make believe. But nowadays, what kind of make believe?

Toy guillotines are made, miniature torture sets, and toy guns that policemen, even at a short distance, cannot tell from the real. And here one feels sure that Christ would do again what He did with anger, God's anger, in the Temple—drive the moneymen out. He called them thieves.

Over and over again thinking people have tried to bring Christ back into Christmas. One of them was Francis of Assisi; he did not, like the bishops and Cromwell, use sermons or forbiddings, but something as simple as his own simplicity—the Christmas Crib.

A crib or manger, known as a *praesaepe*, had been in churches centuries before his time, beginning with the veneration in the grotto at Bethlehem, which might not have been the real grotto. In the second century A.D., Hadrian, the famous Roman emperor, deliberately desecrated the Christian holy places; he built a temple to Adonis over the cave, planting a grove on the spot, but Constantine cut both down and built the Basilica of the Nativity in 326 A.D. over the present grotto, which both the historian Origen and Justin the Martyr swore was the very site.

The first *praesaepe* was made seven hundred years later in Rome, in the church of Santa Maria Maggiore; the idea spread quickly to other churches, but all were lavish with silver and gold, precious stones and carving, so far removed from the little cave of Bethlehem that Francis, poorest of saints, decided to make a people's crib in the village of Greccio in Italy.

"I would fain," said Francis, "make a memorial of that Child that was born in Bethlehem and in some sort behold with bodily eyes His infant hardships."

Hardships, not glory. In a wood near the church of Greccio, a manger was made ready with hay, an ox and an ass led in.

"This was simplicity honored," wrote a nobleman who saw it. "Poverty was exalted, humility commended and of Greccio there was made, as it were, a new Bethlehem. The night was lit up as day and was delightsome."

These humble little "Bethlehems" have been made ever since in homes as well as in churches, and not of gold and silver but of wood and thatch, with clay figures that are used year after year. The star may be of tinsel, the ox and ass have lost a leg, a shepherd be inclined to topple over, but the whole Christmas story is there, and often, before the children go to bed, they light the crib with candles and sing carols. The manger, of course, seems empty; but no, it is waiting.

There is a tale about Martin Luther—and how touching if, of this rebel churchman who probably disapproved of all the trimmings of Christmas, it were true—that he, out walking on Christmas Eve, looked up to the clear, wintry sky lit by thousands of stars and suddenly was moved to cut down a small fir tree and set it up in the sitting room for his children; it had no baubles or tinsel or presents, but he lit it with "countless candles as an image of the starry heaven from which Christ would come."

Candles are not usually pure beeswax now, except for church candles—there are not enough bees —but their living flame still means hope. In some Christian churches, for Mary's purification on the last day of Christmas, there is a Candlemas service. As the worshippers enter, each is given an unlighted

Doctor Martin Luther and Family in Wittenberg at Christmas, 1536, a 19th-century engraving

candle. Then, at the close of the service, the priest lights a candle from the altar. The servers light their candles from his and carry them to the congregation, each lighting the candle of the man, woman or child who is nearest. He or she, in turn, lights the next person's until, candle after candle, wick from wick, the whole church is filled with light. Perhaps, being still Christmas, that gentle radiance goes out of the doors and far, far beyond, passing from one of us to another—not as candles, of course, but candles, like angels, have the oddest disguises.

To Luther that Christmas tree must have seemed, as it did to the pagans, immortal, and certainly, if he had gone up now to the winter night sky, as in a way he did, and had looked down, it might have seemed to him as if the stars themselves had come down to earth.

Lights from a *qalgi* fall across the Eskimo snow.

The *qalgi* is a huge snowhouse built for the Christmas games and dancing that have replaced the people's ancient midwinter feast that celebrated the turning point of their long night. There is still a feast, caldrons of stew made of caribou, marrow from caribou leg bones, and rice; and it ends with the famous Eskimo drum dance.

In Australia's sultry summer Christmas night, candles burn in decorations made of those strange flowers, Christmas bells, that carry a cluster of heavy bells, scarlet edged with yellow; if they are shaken, the stamens ring or rattle. Indians light a *deeva* lamp, a wick floating in a leaf-shaped earthenware saucer, and for Christmas they wind its handle with a twist of tinsel. Cities scintillate in every country; faraway little towns have strings of "fairy lights"—gaudy, they are anything but "fairy," but they shine.

It is as if that mysterious pattern were being reversed: from all those lost ages, forgotten civilizations, buried places, this dayspring of a birth came to rest in Bethlehem. Now, in spite of what we, in our ignorance or innocence, or both, do and have done to Christmas, it has spread steadily, *waxed strong*, as the Gospel of Luke says of the Christ Child, and we can be sure that, no matter how small or humble, or how grand and bejeweled the crib, on Christmas morning the manger will be filled.

That was the true Light, which lighteth every man that cometh into the world. John 1:9

The Newborn by Georges de La Tour, c. 1630

68

The Literature of
Christmas

The Literature of Christmas

THIS IS MEETING TIME AGAIN. Home is the magnet. The winter land roars and hums with the eager speed of return journeys. The dark is noisy and bright with late-night arrivals—doors thrown open, running shadows on snow, open arms, kisses, voices and laughter, laughter at everything and nothing. Inarticulate, giddying and confused are those original minutes of being back again. The very familiarity of everything acts like shock. Contentment has to be drawn in slowly, steadyingly, in deep breaths—there is so much of it. We rely on home not to change, and it does not, wherefore we give thanks. Again Christmas: abiding point of return. Set apart by its mystery, mood and magic, the season seems in a way to stand outside time. All that is dear, that is lasting, renews its hold on us: we are home again. . . .

This glow of Christmas, has it not in it also the gold of a harvest? "They shall return with joy, bringing their sheaves with them." To the festival, to each other, we bring in wealth. More to tell, more to understand, more to share. Each we have garnered in yet another year; to be glad, to celebrate to the full, we are come together. How akin we are to each other, how speechlessly dear and one in the fundamentals of being, Christmas shows us. No other time grants us, quite, this vision—round the tree or gathered before the fire we perceive anew, with joy, one another's faces. And each time faces come to mean more.

Is it not one of the mysteries of life that life should, after all, be so simple? Yes, as simple as Christmas, simple as this. Journeys through the dark to a lighted door, arms open. Laughter-smothered kisses, kiss-smothered laughter. And blessedness in the heart of it all. Here are the verities, all made gay with tinsel! Dear, silly Christmas-card saying and cracker mottoes—let them speak! Or, since still we cannot speak, let us sing! Dearer than memory, brighter than expectation is the ever returning *now* of Christmas. Why else, each time we greet its return, should happiness ring out in us like a peal of bells?

Home for Christmas by Elizabeth Bowen

THE HOLY NIGHT
by Selma Lagerlöf

THERE WAS A MAN who went out in the dark night to borrow live coals to kindle a fire. He went from hut to hut and knocked. "Dear friends, help me!" said he. "My wife has just given birth to a child, and I must make a fire to warm her and the little one."

But it was way in the night, and all the people were asleep. No one replied.

The man walked and walked. At last he saw the gleam of a fire a long way off. Then he went in that direction, and saw that the fire was burning in the open. A lot of sheep were sleeping around the fire, and an old shepherd sat and watched over the flock.

When the man who wanted to borrow fire came up to the sheep, he saw that three big dogs lay asleep at the shepherd's feet. All three awoke when the man approached and opened their great jaws, as though they wanted to bark; but not a sound was heard. The man noticed that the hair on their backs stood up and that their sharp, white teeth glistened in the firelight. They dashed toward him.

He felt that one of them bit at his leg and one at his hand and that one clung to his throat. But their jaws and teeth wouldn't obey them, and the man didn't suffer the least harm.

Now the man wished to go farther, to get what he needed. But the sheep lay back to back and so close to one another that he couldn't pass them. Then the man stepped upon their backs and walked over them and up to the fire. And not one of the animals awoke or moved.

When the man had almost reached the fire, the shepherd looked up. He was a surly old man, who was unfriendly and harsh toward human beings. And when he saw the strange man coming, he seized the long, spiked staff, which he always

73

ngels
we have heard
on high,
Sweetly singing
o'er the plains,
And the mountains
in reply
Echoing their
joyous strains.
Gloria in
excelsis Deo!
Gloria in
excelsis Deo!

FROM AN OLD CAROL

held in his hand when he tended his flock, and threw it at him. The staff came right toward the man, but, before it reached him, it turned off to one side and whizzed past him, far out in the meadow.

Now the man came up to the shepherd and said to him: "Good man, help me, and lend me a little fire! My wife has just given birth to a child, and I must make a fire to warm her and the little one."

The shepherd would rather have said no, but when he pondered that the dogs couldn't hurt the man, and the sheep had not run from him, and that the staff had not wished to strike him, he was a little afraid, and dared not deny the man that which he asked.

"Take as much as you need!" he said to the man.

But then the fire was nearly burnt out. There were no logs or branches left, only a big heap of live coals; and the stranger had neither spade nor shovel wherein he could carry the red-hot coals.

When the shepherd saw this, he said again: "Take as much as you need!" And he was glad that the man wouldn't be able to take away any coals.

But the man stooped and picked coals from the ashes with his bare hands, and laid them in his mantle. And he didn't burn his hands when he touched them, nor did the coals scorch his mantle; but he carried them away as if they had been nuts or apples.

And when the shepherd, who was such a cruel and hardhearted man, saw all this, he began to wonder to himself: What kind of a night is this, when the dogs do not bite, the sheep are not scared, the staff does not kill, or the fire scorch? He called the stranger back and said to him: "What kind of a night is this? And how does it happen that all things show you compassion?"

Then said the man: "I cannot tell you if you yourself do not see it." And he wished to go his way, that he might soon make a fire and warm his wife and child.

But the shepherd did not wish to lose sight of the man before he had found out what all this might portend. He got up and followed the man till they came to the place where he lived.

Then the shepherd saw that the man didn't have so much as a hut to dwell in, but that his wife and babe were lying in a mountain grotto, where there was nothing except the cold and naked stone walls.

But the shepherd thought that perhaps the poor innocent child might freeze to death there in the grotto; and, although he was a hard man, he was touched, and thought he would like to help it. And he loosened his knapsack from his shoulder, took from it a soft white sheepskin, gave it to the strange man, and said that he should let the child sleep on it.

But just as soon as he showed that he, too, could be merciful, his eyes were

opened, and he saw what he had not been able to see before, and heard what he could not have heard before.

He saw that all around him stood a ring of little silver-winged angels, and each held a stringed instrument, and all sang in loud tones that tonight the Saviour was born who should redeem the world from its sins.

Then he understood how all things were so happy this night that they didn't want to do anything wrong.

And it was not only around the shepherd that there were angels, but he saw them everywhere. They sat inside the grotto, they sat outside on the mountain, and they flew under the heavens. They came marching in great companies, and, as they passed, they paused and cast a glance at the child.

There were such jubilation and such gladness and songs and play! And all this he saw in the dark night, whereas before he could not have made out anything. He was so happy because his eyes had been opened that he fell upon his knees and thanked God.

What that shepherd saw, we might also see, for the angels fly down from heaven every Christmas Eve, if we could only see them.

You must remember this, for it is as true, as true as that I see you and you see me. It is not revealed by the light of lamps or candles, and it does not depend upon sun and moon; but that which is needful is that we have such eyes as can see God's glory.

BIRD OF
DAWNING

Some say that ever 'gainst that season comes
Wherein our Saviour's birth is celebrated,
The bird of dawning singeth all night long:
And then, they say, no spirit dare stir abroad;
The nights are wholesome; then no planets strike,
No fairy takes, nor witch hath power to charm,
So hallow'd and so gracious is the time.

William Shakespeare

STAR OF THE NATIVITY

It was wintertime.
The wind was blowing from the plains.
And the infant was cold in the cave
On the slope of a hill.

He was warmed by the breath of an ox.
Every farmyard beast
Huddled safe in the cave;
A warm mist drifted over the manger.

On a rock afar some drowsy shepherds
Shook off the wisps of straw
And hayseed of their beds,
And sleepily gazed into the vast of night.

They saw gravestones, fences, fields,
The shafts of a cart
Deep in drifted snows,
And a sky of stars above the graveyard.

And, shyer than a watchman's light,
One star alone
Unseen until then
Shone bright on the way to Bethlehem.

At times it rose, a haystack aflame,
Apart from God and the sky,
Like a barn set on fire,
Like a farmstead ablaze in the night.

It reared in the sky like a flaming stack
Of thatch and hay,
In the midst of Creation
Surprised by this new star in the world.

The flame grew steadily deeper, wider,
Large as a portent.

Three stargazers then
Hastened to follow this marvelous light.

Behind them, their camels with gifts;
Their caparisoned asses, each one smaller
In size, came daintily down the hillside.

And all new matters of ages to come
Arose as a vision of wonder in space.
All thoughts of ages, all dreams, new worlds,
All the future of galleries and of museums,
All the games of fairies, the work of inventors,
The yule trees, and the dreams of all children dream,
The tremulous glow of candles in rows,
The gold and silver of angels and globes
(*A wind blew, raging, long from the plain*)
And the splendor of tinsel and toys under trees.

A part of the pond lay hidden by alders;
A part could be seen afar from the cliff
Where rooks were nesting among the treetops.
The shepherds could see each ass and camel
Trudging its way by the water mill.
"Let us go and worship the miracle,"
They said, and belted their sheepskin coats.

Their bodies grew warm, walking through snows.
There were footprints that glinted like mica
Across bright fields, on the way to the inn.
But the dogs on seeing the tracks in starshine
Growled loud in anger, as if at a flame.

The frosty night was like a fairy tale.
And phantoms from mountain ridges in snows
Invisibly came to walk in the crowd.
The dogs grew fearful of ghosts around
And huddled beside the shepherd lads.

Across these valleys and mountain roads,
Unbodied, unseen by mortal eyes,
A heavenly host appeared in the throng,
And each footprint gleamed as an angel's foot.

At dawn the cedars lifted their heads.
A multitude clustered around the cave.
"Who are you?" said Mary. They spoke: "We come
As shepherds of flocks, as envoys of heaven:
In praise of the Child and your glory we come."
"There's no room in the cave; you must wait outside."

Before dawnlight, in gloom, in ashen dark,
The drivers and shepherds stamped in the cold.
The footmen quarreled with mounted men;
Near the well and the wooden water trough
The asses brayed and the camels bellowed.

The dawn! It swept the last of the stars
Like flecks of ash from the vaulted sky.
Then Mary allowed the Magi alone
To enter the cleft of the mountainside.

He slept in His manger in radiant light,
As a moonbeam sleeps in a hollow tree.
The breath of the ox and the ass kept warm
His hands and feet in the cold of night.

The Magi remained in the twilight cave;
They whispered softly, groping for words.
Then someone in darkness touched the arm
Of one near the manger, to move him aside:
Behold, like a guest above the threshold,
The Star of the Nativity gazed on the Virgin.

Boris Pasternak,
translated by Eugene M. Kayden

THE OX AND THE ASS
AT THE MANGER

by Jules Supervielle

The ass, led by Joseph, bore the Virgin along the road to Bethlehem. She weighed little, being full of nothing but the future within her.

The ox followed, by himself.

On reaching the city, the travelers made their way into a deserted stable, and Joseph at once set to work.

"These men really are astonishing," thought the ox, "the things they manage to do with their hands and arms! Those objects are certainly much more useful than our hoofs and pasterns. And there's no one like our master when it comes to fixing things, straightening what's twisted and twisting what's straight, and doing all that has to be done without repining or getting downhearted."

Joseph went out, and soon returned carrying some straw on his back, wonderful straw, so crisp and glowing that it seemed to herald a miracle.

"What are they preparing there?" said the ass to himself. "It looks like a little bed for a child."

"We may have need of you tonight," said the Virgin to the ox and the ass. The beasts stared at each other for a long time in an effort to understand, and then lay down to sleep.

Soon they were awakened by a voice which, light though it was, had just carried across the whole of heaven. The ox got to his feet, found that there was a naked child asleep in the manger, and methodically warmed him with his breath, all over. The Virgin thanked him with a smiling look. Winged beings came and went, pretending not to see the walls they passed through so easily.

Joseph returned with some swaddling clothes lent him by a neighbor. "It's marvelous," he said in his carpenter's voice, rather loud for such an occasion, "it's midnight, and yet it's day. And there are three suns instead of one. But they're trying to join together."

At dawn the ox got up, taking care where he put his hoofs for fear of waking the child, crushing a heavenly flower, or hurting an angel. How marvelously difficult everything had become!

Neighbors came to see Jesus and the Virgin. They were poor people, who had nothing to offer but their beaming faces. After them came others bringing nuts, or a flageolet. The ox and the ass moved aside a little to let them pass, and wondered what impression they themselves would make on the child, who had not yet seen them. He had only just awakened.

"We aren't monsters," said the ass.

"No, but you see we might frighten him with our faces, which aren't at all like his own or his parents'."

"The manger and the stable and its beamed roof haven't got a face like his either, but he isn't afraid of them."

But the ox was not convinced. He thought of his horns and ruminated: "It really is very upsetting not to be able to draw near those you love best without looking threatening. I always have to take care not to hurt anyone, and yet it isn't in my nature to attack people or things without good cause. I'm neither mischievous nor spiteful. But wherever I go, immediately my horns are there with me. I wake up with them, and even when I'm dropping with sleep and shuffle off in a daze, those two hard, pointed things are there and never forget me. I even feel them on the fringe of my dreams in the middle of the night."

A great fear seized the ox, and he thought how near he had drawn to the child to warm him. What if he had accidentally gored him! "You oughtn't to go too close to the little one," said the ass, who had guessed his companion's thought. "You mustn't even dream of it, you'd hurt him. Besides, you don't keep your slaver in very well, you might let a drop of it fall on him, and that wouldn't be clean. Thinking of that, why do you slobber like that when you're happy? Keep it to yourself, there's no need to show it to everyone."

Silence on the part of the ox.

"For my part, I'm going to offer him my two ears. They twitch, you know, and move in all directions, they haven't any bones and they're soft to touch. They frighten and comfort at the same time. They're just the thing to amuse a child, and at his age they're instructive too."

"Yes, I do know. I've never said the contrary. I'm not a fool." But since the ass looked really too self-satisfied, the ox added, "But don't you go and bray in his face, or you'd kill him."

"Country bumpkin!" said the ass.

The ass stood on the left of the manger, the ox on the right. These were the positions they occupied at the moment of the Nativity, and the ox, who favored a certain formality, set great store by them. There they remained for hours, motionless and respectful, as though they were posing for some invisible painter.

Eager for sleep again, the child closed his eyes. Just on the farther side of sleep, a shining angel awaited him, to teach him, or perhaps to ask him something. The angel came out of Jesus' dream and appeared, a living presence, in the stable. After bowing to the newly born, he painted a very pure halo round his head, another for the Virgin, and a third for Joseph. Then off he went in a dazzle of wings and feathers, ever as freshly white and rustling as the whiteness of the tides.

"There's no halo for us," the ox noticed. "The angel's sure to have reasons why not. We're too lowly, the ass and I. Besides, what have we done to deserve such a radiance?"

"You've certainly done nothing, but you forget that I carried the Virgin."

The ox thought to himself, "The Virgin's so beautiful and so fragile, how did she manage to hide this lovely babe?"

But perhaps he was thinking aloud, for the ass answered, "There are some things you can't understand."

"Why do you always say that I don't understand? I've had a fuller life than you. I've worked in the mountains, on the plains, and by the sea."

"That isn't the point," said the ass, and went on: "It's not only the halo. I feel sure, ox, that you haven't noticed that all about the child there floats a sort of marvelous dust, or rather it's something better than dust."

"It's much more delicate," said the ox. "It's like a light, a golden mist given off by his little body."

"Yes, but you say that to make people think you've seen it."

"And haven't I seen it?"

Jesus our brother,
strong and good,
Was humbly born
in a stable rude,
And the friendly beasts
around Him stood,
Jesus our brother,
strong and good.

"I," said the donkey,
shaggy and brown,
"I carried His mother
up hill and down,
I carried her safely
to Bethlehem town;
I," said the donkey,
shaggy and brown.

The ox led the ass to a corner of the stable where, in token of worship, the ruminant had placed a small branch delicately surrounded with wisps of straw, which gave a very good idea of the rays emanating from the divine flesh. It was the first chapel. The ox had brought the straw in from outside. He dared not touch the straw of the manger; he had a superstitious fear of that, because it was good to eat.

The ox and the ass went off to graze until nightfall. Although stones generally take such a long time to understand anything, there were already a good many in the fields that knew. They even came across a pebble which, by a slight change of shape and color, showed them that it was in on the secret.

There were meadow flowers, too, which knew and had to be spared. It was quite a business to graze in the fields without committing sacrilege. And to the ox, eating seemed more and more unnecessary. His happiness was food enough.

Before he drank, too, he would ask himself, "And what about this water, does it know?"

When in doubt he preferred not to drink, and would go a little farther to some muddy water which was obviously still quite in the dark. Sometimes the only way he could tell was by an infinite sweetness in his throat at the moment when he was swallowing the water. "Too late," the ox would think, "I ought not to have drunk it."

He hardly dared breathe, so sacred and aware did the air seem to him. He was afraid of inhaling an angel.

The ox was ashamed at not always feeling himself as clean as he would have liked. "Well then, I must just be cleaner than before, that's all. It only needs a little more care, and paying attention where I put my feet."

The ass was quite unperturbed.

The sun shone into the stable, and the two beasts competed for the honor of shading the child.

"I daresay a little sun wouldn't do any harm either," thought the ox, "but the ass is sure to say again that I know nothing about it."

The child went on sleeping, and sometimes, in his sleep, he would ponder and frown.

One day while the Virgin was at the door answering the thousands of questions put by future Christians, the ass, with his muzzle, delicately turned the child on his side. On going back to her son, Mary had a great fright, as she kept looking for the child's face where she had left it. When she realized what had happened, she gave the ass to understand that it was advisable not to touch the child. The ox showed his agreement by a silence of exceptional quality. He knew how to put rhythm, and shades of meaning, and punctuation, into his dumbness. On cold days you could easily follow the trend of his thoughts by the length of the column of steam that escaped from his nostrils. In that way you could learn a great deal.

The ox thought he had no right to render any but indirect services to the child, such as attracting to himself the flies in the stable (every morning he went and rubbed his back against a hive of wild bees), or squashing insects against the wall. The ass kept a lookout for noises from outside, and when he thought something was suspicious he barred the entrance. Then the ox would immediately place himself behind the ass to form a block. They both of them made themselves as heavy as possible; while the danger lasted, their heads and bellies were full of lead. But their eyes shone, more watchful than ever.

The ox was dumbfounded to see that when the Virgin drew near to the manger she had the gift of making the child smile. And in spite of his beard, Joseph managed it also without too much difficulty, either by his mere presence or by playing on the flageolet. The ox would have liked to play something too. After all, one only had to blow.

"I don't want to say anything against the master, but I don't think he would have been able to warm the Child Jesus with his breath. And as for the flute, all I need is to be alone with the little one, and then he no longer frightens me. He becomes once more a creature who needs protection. And after all, an ox is aware of his strength."

When they were grazing together in the fields, the ox often used to leave the ass.

"Where are you going?"

"I'll be back in a moment."

"But where are you going?" insisted the ass.

"I'm going to see if he needs anything. You never know."

"For goodness' sake leave him alone!"

But the ox went. In the stable there was a kind of round window—such as was later to be called, for that very reason, a bull's-eye—through which the ox looked in from outside.

One day he noticed that neither Mary nor Joseph was there. He found the flageolet on a bench, within reach of his muzzle, neither too far away from the child nor too near to him.

"What shall I be able to play him?" thought the ox, who dared not approach the ear of Jesus except through this musical go-between. "A song of the plow, the war cry of the brave little bull, or the enchanted heifer?"

Oxen often pretend to be ruminating when in their inmost hearts they are singing. The ox blew delicately into the flute, and it is not at all certain that an angel did not help him to obtain such pure sounds. The child, in his bed, raised his head and shoulders a little, so as to see. For all that, the flutist was not satis-

"**I**," said the cow,
all white and red,
"I gave Him my
manger for His bed,
I gave Him my hay
to pillow His head,
I," said the cow,
all white and red.

fied with the result. But at least he felt sure that no one outside had heard him. He was mistaken. Then he made off in haste, for fear lest someone, and especially the ass, should come in and catch him too near the little flute.

One day the Virgin said to the ox, "Come and look at my child. You warmed him so well when he was still quite naked; why do you never go near him now?"

Emboldened, the ox placed himself quite close to Jesus, who, to put him entirely at ease, seized his muzzle with both hands. The ox held his breath, which had become unnecessary. Jesus smiled. The joy of the ox was a silent joy. It had taken the exact shape of his body and filled it right up to the tips of its horns.

The child looked at the ass and the ox in turn: the ass a little too sure of himself, and the ox who felt himself extraordinarily opaque beside that face so delicately illumined from within, as though one should see, through thin curtains, a lamp passing from one room to another in a very tiny, distant dwelling.

Seeing the ox look so gloomy, the child began to crow with laughter. The animal did not quite understand this laughter, and wondered whether the little one was mocking. Ought he in the future to be more reserved, or even to go away? Then the child laughed again, and his laugh seemed to the ox so luminous, and so filial, that he knew he had been right to stay.

The Virgin and her son often gazed at each other quite close to, and one couldn't tell which was the prouder of the other. "It seems to me that there should be universal rejoicing," thought the ox. "Never has there been seen a purer mother or a more beautiful child. But every now and then how grave they both look!"

The ox and the ass were preparing to return to the stable when the ox, after looking carefully about for fear of making some mistake, said, "Do look at that star moving across the sky. It's so beautiful it warms my heart."

"Leave your heart out of it; it has nothing to do with the great events we've been witnessing lately."

"You can say what you like, but in my opinion that star is coming in our direction. See how low it is in the sky. It looks as though it's making for our stable. And below it there are three personages covered with precious stones."

The beasts reached the threshold of the stable.

"Well, ox, what is going to happen, according to you?"

"You expect too much of me, ass. I'm content to see what *is* happening, and that's already a good deal."

"I have my own idea."

"Now then, make way," Joseph said, opening the door. "Don't you see you're blocking the entrance and preventing these personages from coming in?"

The beasts moved aside to let the Magi pass. There were three of them, one of whom, completely black, represented Africa. At first the ox kept a discreet but watchful eye on him. He wanted to be sure the Negro had none but good intentions toward the newborn. But when the black man, who must have been a little shortsighted, bent down to see Jesus close to, his face, polished and lustrous as a mirror, reflected the image of the child with so much deference, so great a self-forgetfulness, that the heart of the ox was pierced with exceptional sweetness because of it.

"It's somebody very distinguished," he thought. "The two others would never

have been able to do that." After a few moments he added, "He is indeed the best of the three." The ox had just surprised the white kings at the moment when they were very carefully stowing away in their luggage a wisp of straw, which they had just stolen from the manger. The black king had not wanted to take anything.

The kings slept side by side on an improvised bed lent by some neighbors. "How odd to keep your crown on for sleeping!" thought the ox. "A hard thing like that must be much more uncomfortable than horns. And it must be difficult to get to sleep with all those shining jewels on one's head."

They slept soberly, like statues stretched out on tombs. And their star shone above the manger.

Just before dawn all three got up at the same time, with identical movements. In a dream they had just seen the same angel, who advised them to leave at once

"I," said the sheep,
with curly horn,
"I gave Him my wool
for His blanket warm,
He wore my coat
on Christmas morn;
I," said the sheep,
with curly horn.

and not to go back to the jealous Herod to tell him that they had seen the Child Jesus.

They went out, leaving the star shining above the manger so that everyone should know that that was the place.

The ox prayed: "Celestial Child, please don't judge me by my dazed and obtuse air. May I not one day cease to look like a little lump of rock rolling along?

"As for these horns, I must explain that they are more an ornament than anything else; I'll even admit to you that I've never made use of them.

"Jesus, shed a little of your light on all these imperfections, these confusions that are in me. Teach me a little of your delicacy, you whose tiny feet and hands are attached with such minute care to your body. Can you tell me, little sir, why one day it was enough for me to turn my head to see the whole of you? How I thank you for having been allowed to kneel down before you, marvelous Child, and to live on familiar terms in this way with stars and angels! Sometimes I wonder if you may not have been misinformed, and if I am really the one who ought to be here. Perhaps you haven't noticed that I have a great scar on my back and that some of the hair has been rubbed off my coat on the sides, which is rather unpleasant. Even without going outside my own family, they might have chosen to come here my brother or my cousins who are much better looking than I. Wouldn't the lion or the eagle have been a more suitable choice?"

"Be quiet," said the ass. "Why do you keep sighing like that? Don't you see you're preventing him sleeping, with all those ruminations of yours?"

"He's right," said the ox to himself. "One ought to know when it's time to be silent, even if one is conscious of a happiness so great that one doesn't know where to put it."

But the ass was praying too! "Draught asses and pack asses, our path in life is going to be beautiful, and our foals will wait in cheerful pastures to see what happens next. Thanks to you, my little man, stones will remain in their proper places at the side of the road and we shan't have them falling on top of us. And another thing. Why should there still be hills and even mountains in our way? Wouldn't it suit everyone better to have flat country everywhere? And why does the ox, who is stronger than I, never carry anyone on his back? And why are my ears so long, and I've no hair on my tail, and my shoes are so small, and my chest is narrow, and my voice has the color of bad weather? But perhaps these things haven't yet been finally settled?"

During the nights which followed, it was the task now of one star and now of another to be on guard; and sometimes of whole constellations. In order to hide the secret of the sky, a cloud always occupied the place where the absent stars ought to have been, and it was marvelous to see the Infinitely Remote making themselves quite tiny so as to take up their positions over the crib, and keeping their excess of heat and light, and their immensity, for themselves alone, giving off only enough to warm and light the stable, and not to frighten the child. In those first nights of Christianity, the Virgin, Joseph, the Child, the ox, and the ass were extraordinarily themselves. During the daytime this likeness to themselves was less noticeable, being scattered about among the visitors; but after sunset it became miraculously concentrated and reliable.

Many animals approached the ox and the ass to ask if they could make the acquaintance of the Child Jesus. And one fine day a horse, known for his friendly disposition and his speed, was chosen by the ox, with Joseph's agreement, to summon the very next day all those who wanted to come.

The ass and the ox wondered whether they ought to let the wild beasts enter, and also the dromedaries, camels, and elephants, all of them animals whose humps and trunks and surplus of flesh and bone render them somewhat suspect.

There was the same doubt about such frightful insects as the scorpions, tarantulas, great trapdoor spiders, and vipers who, both male and female, secrete poison in their glands night and day, and even at dawn, when all things are pure.

The Virgin did not hesitate. "You can let them all come in. My child is as safe in his crib as he would be in the topmost heights of heaven."

"And one by one!" added Joseph, in an almost military tone. "I don't want to have two animals at a time passing through the door, or we shan't know where we are."

The poisonous animals were allowed in first, since everyone felt that one owed them this compensation. Particularly noticeable was the tact of the serpents, who avoided looking at the Virgin, gliding by as far away from her person as possible. And they departed with as much calmness and dignity as if they had been doves or watchdogs.

There were also some animals so small that it was difficult to know if they were there or still waiting outside. These atoms were allowed a whole hour in which to present themselves and make the tour of the crib. When the time was up, although Joseph felt from a slight pricking of his skin that they had not all gone, he ordered the next animals to appear.

The dogs could not help showing their surprise that they had not been allowed to live in the stable like the ox and the ass. Everyone stroked them by way of an answer, whereupon they retired full of visible gratitude.

When it was evident from his smell that the lion was approaching, in spite of everything the ox and the ass were not easy in their minds, and the less so because that smell passed right through the incense and myrrh and other perfumes which the three kings had liberally diffused, without even taking any notice of them.

The ox appreciated the generous motives which inspired the confidence of the Virgin and Joseph; but to put such a delicate flame as a child beside a beast whose strength might extinguish it with a single puff . . . !

The anxiety of the ox and the ass was the greater because, as they clearly saw, it was only fitting that they should be totally paralyzed before the lion. They

could no more think of attacking him than of thunder or lightning. And the ox, weakened by fasting, felt airy rather than pugnacious.

The lion entered with his mane, which only the wind of the desert had ever combed, and his melancholy eyes which said, "I am the lion, I can't help it, I am only the king of beasts." You could see that his chief concern was to take up as little room as possible in the stable, which was not easy, to breathe without upsetting anything around him, and to forget his retractile claws and the very powerful muscles that moved his jaws. He advanced with lowered lids, hiding his admirable teeth like a shameful disease, and with such a modest bearing that it was quite obvious he belonged to the family of lions who were one day to refuse to devour Saint Blandina. The Virgin took pity and tried to reassure him with a smile like those she kept for her child.

The lion gazed straight in front of him, as though to say in a tone still more desperate than a moment ago, "What have I done that I should be so big and strong? You know well that I've never eaten except when hunger and fresh air compelled me. And you know, too, that I had to consider the cubs. All of us have tried, more or less, to be herbivorous. But grass doesn't suit us; we can't digest it."

Then, in the midst of a great silence which embarrassed everyone, he bent his huge head, like an explosion of hair and fur, and laid it sadly on the hard earth, while the tuft at the end of his tail seemed as overcome as his head.

When it was the tiger's turn, he flattened himself out on the ground until, by sternly humbling himself, he became a veritable bedside mat at the foot of the crib. Then in a moment, with incredible exactitude and elasticity, he reconstituted himself and went out without a word.

The giraffe showed his feet for a moment in the embrasure of the door, and it was unanimously agreed that "that counted" as if he had walked all round the crib.

It was the same with the elephant; all he did was to kneel before the threshold and swing his trunk with a kind of censing movement which was greatly appreciated by all.

A tremendously woolly sheep clamored to be shorn on the spot. They thanked her but did not take her fleece.

The mother kangaroo was desperately eager to give Jesus one of her young, pleading that she really longed to make the present, that it was no sacrifice for her, and that she had other little kangaroos at home. But Joseph took a different view, and she had to take her child away.

The ostrich was more fortunate; she took advantage of a moment of inattention to lay her egg in a corner and quietly depart, leaving this souvenir which no one noticed till the next morning.

The ass discovered it. He had never seen anything so big or so hard in the way of an egg, and thought it was a miracle. Joseph did his best to undeceive him; he made an omelet of it.

The fish, not having been able to put in an appearance because of their wretched breathing when out of water, had delegated a sea gull to represent them.

The birds departed leaving their songs, the pigeons their loves, the monkeys their tricks, the cats their gaze, and the turtledoves their throaty sweetness.

The animals who have not yet been discovered would have liked to present themselves too, those who await a name in the bosom of the earth or the sea, in depths so great that for them it is always night, without stars or moon or change of seasons.

One could feel, beating in the air, the souls of those who had not been able to

"I"
I, said the dove,
from the rafters high,
"Cooed Him to sleep,
my mate and I,
We cooed Him to sleep,
my mate and I;
I," said the dove, from
the rafters high.

And every
beast, by some
good spell,
In the stable dark
was glad to tell,
Of the gift he gave
Immanuel,
The gift he gave
Immanuel.

AUTHOR UNKNOWN

come, or were late, and of others who, living at the end of the world, had nevertheless set out on insect feet so small that they could only have gone a yard in an hour, and whose life was so short that they could never hope to cover more than half a yard—and even that only with a good deal of luck.

There were some miracles: the tortoise hurried, the iguana slackened his pace, the hippopotamus was graceful in his genuflections, and the parrots kept silence.

A little before sunset something happened which upset everyone. Exhausted from having superintended the procession all day without a bite to eat, in an absentminded moment Joseph squashed a poisonous spider with his foot, forgetting that it had come to pay its respects to the Child. And the saint looked so upset that everyone felt distressed for quite a long time.

Certain animals who might have been expected to show more discretion lingered in the stable; the ox had to drive out the ferret, the squirrel, and the badger, who did not want to leave.

A few moths remained, taking advantage of the fact that they were the same color as the beams of the roof to spend the whole night above the crib. But the first sunbeam next day revealed them, and since Joseph did not wish to favor anyone he turned them out immediately.

Some flies, who were also asked to leave, conveyed by their reluctance to depart that they had always been there, and Joseph did not know what to say to them.

The supernatural apparitions among which the ox lived often took his breath away. Having got into the habit of holding it, as Eastern ascetics do, like them he became a visionary; and although much less at ease among great than among humble things, he experienced genuine ecstasies. But he was governed by a scruple which would not let him imagine angels or saints. He saw them only when they really were in the neighborhood.

"Poor me!" thought the ox, scared by these apparitions, which seemed to him suspect. "Poor me, who am only a beast of burden, or maybe even the devil. Why have I got horns like him, when I've never done evil? And what if I were nothing but a sorcerer?"

Joseph did not fail to notice the anxieties of the ox, who was growing visibly thinner.

"Go and eat out of doors!" he cried. "You stay here glued to us all day, soon you'll be nothing but skin and bones."

The ass and the ox went out.

"It's true you're thin," said the ass. "Your bones have become so sharp that you'll have horns sticking out all over your body."

"Don't talk to me of horns!"

And the ox said to himself, "He's quite right, of course, one must live. Go on, then, eat that lovely tuft of green! And what about that other one? What's the matter with you, are you wondering if it's poisonous? No, I'm not hungry. All the same, how beautiful that child is! And those splendid figures who come and go, breathing through their ever-beating wings, all those celestial great ones who find their way into our simple stable without ever getting dirty. Come now, eat, ox, don't trouble your head with all that. And another thing, you mustn't always wake up when happiness tugs at your ears in the middle of the night. And don't

stay so long on one knee near the crib that it hurts you. Your hide is all worn away at the knee joint; a bit more and the flies will be at it."

One night it was the turn of Taurus, the constellation of the bull, to stand guard above the manger, against a stretch of black sky. The red eye of Aldebaran, blazing and magnificent, shone quite close, and the taurine flanks and horns were adorned with huge precious stones. The ox was proud to see the Child so well guarded. Everyone was sleeping peacefully, the ass with his ears trustingly lowered. But the ox, although fortified by the supernatural presence of that constellation which was both a relation and a friend, felt weak all over. He thought of his sacrifices for the Child, of his useless vigils, of the paltry protection he had offered.

"Has the constellation of the bull seen me?" he wondered. "Does that big starry eye, shining enough to frighten you, know that I'm here? Those stars are

The stable is
a Prince's courte,
The cribb His
chaire of State;
The beastes
are parcell of
His pompe,
The wodden dishe
His plate.

ROBERT SOUTHWELL

so high and so far off that one doesn't even know which way they're looking."

Suddenly Joseph, who had been tossing on his bed for the past few moments, got up, raising his arms to heaven. Though as a rule so restrained in words and gestures, he now wakened everyone, even the Child.

"I've seen the Lord in a dream. We must leave without delay. It's because of Herod, he wants to get hold of Jesus."

The Virgin took her son in her arms as though the king of the Jews were already at the door, with a butcher's knife in his hand.

The ass got to his feet.

"And what about him?" said Joseph to the Virgin, pointing to the ox.

"I'm afraid he's too weak to come with us."

The ox wanted to show that it wasn't so. He made a terrific effort to rise, but never had he felt himself so tethered to the ground. Desperate for help, he looked up at the constellation of the bull, on which alone he now relied for strength to leave. But the celestial bovine, still in profile to the ox, his eye red and blazing as ever, gave no sign.

"It's several days now since he ate anything," said the Virgin to Joseph.

"Oh, I know very well they're going to leave me here," thought the ox. "It was too good to last. Besides, I should only have been a bony, laggard apparition on the road. All my ribs are tired of my skin, and the only thing they want now is to lie down and rest under the open sky."

The ass went up to the ox and rubbed his muzzle against that of the ruminant, to let him know that the Virgin had just recommended him to a neighbor, and that he would lack nothing after their departure. But the ox, his lids half closed, seemed utterly crushed.

The Virgin stroked him and said, "But we're not going on a journey, of course we aren't. It was only to frighten you!"

"Why of course, we're coming back immediately," added Joseph. "One doesn't set out on a far journey in the middle of the night like this."

"It's a very beautiful night," went on the Virgin, "and we're going to take advantage of it to give the Child some air; he's a bit palish these last days."

"That's absolutely true," said the holy man.

It was a pious lie. The ox knew it and, not wanting to embarrass the travelers in their preparations, he pretended to fall into a deep sleep. That was his way of lying.

"He's fallen asleep," said the Virgin. "Let's put the straw of the crib quite near to him, so that he'll lack nothing when he wakes. And let's leave the flageolet within reach of his breath," she went on in a low voice. "He's very fond of playing it when he's alone."

They got ready to leave. The stable door creaked. "I ought to have oiled it," thought Joseph, who was afraid of wakening the ox. But the ox went on pretending to be asleep. They closed the door carefully.

While the ass of the manger was gradually turning into the ass of the flight into Egypt, the ox remained with his eyes fixed on that straw where a short while before the Infant Jesus lay. Well he knew that he would never touch it, any more than he would touch the flageolet.

The constellation of the bull regained the zenith with a bound, and with a single toss of his horns settled back in the sky in the place which he would never leave again.

When the neighbor came in a little after dawn, the ox had ceased to ruminate.

Translated by Enid McLeod

HEAVEN CANNOT
HOLD HIM

In the bleak midwinter
　　Frosty wind made moan,
Earth stood hard as iron,
　　Water like a stone;
Snow had fallen, snow on snow,
　　Snow on snow,
In the bleak midwinter
　　Long ago.

Our God, Heaven cannot hold Him
　　Nor earth sustain;
Heaven and earth shall flee away
　　When He comes to reign:
In the bleak midwinter
　　A stable-place sufficed
The Lord God Almighty
　　Jesus Christ.

Enough for Him, whom cherubim
   Worship night and day,
A breastful of milk
   And a mangerful of hay;
Enough for Him, whom angels
   Fall down before,
The ox and ass and camel
   Which adore.

Angels and archangels
   May have gathered there,
Cherubim and seraphim
   Thronged the air;
But only His mother
   In her maiden bliss
Worshipped the Beloved
   With a kiss.

What can I give Him,
   Poor as I am?
If I were a shepherd
   I would bring a lamb,
If I were a Wise Man
   I would do my part, —
Yet what I can I give Him,
   Give my heart.

Christina Rossetti

WHY THE CHIMES RANG
by Raymond MacDonald Alden

THERE WAS ONCE, in a faraway country where few people have ever traveled, a wonderful church. It stood on a high hill in the midst of a great city; and every Sunday, as well as on sacred days like Christmas, thousands of people climbed the hill to its great archways, looking like lines of ants all moving in the same direction.

When you came to the building itself, you found stone columns and dark passages, and a grand entrance leading to the main room of the church. This room was so long that one standing at the doorway could scarcely see to the other end, where the choir stood by the marble altar. In the farthest corner was the organ; and this organ was so loud that, sometimes when it played, the people for miles around would close their shutters and prepare for a great thunderstorm. Altogether, no such church as this was ever seen before, especially when it was lighted up for some festival, and crowded with people, young and old. But the strangest thing about the whole building was the wonderful chime of bells.

At one corner of the church was a great gray tower, with ivy growing over it as far up as one could see. I say as far as one could see, because the tower was quite great enough to fit the great church, and it rose so far into the sky that it was only in very fair weather that anyone claimed to be able to see the top. Even then one could not be certain that it was in sight. Up, and up, and up climbed the stones and the ivy; and, as the men who built the church had been dead for hundreds of years, everyone had forgotten how high the tower was supposed to be.

Now all the people knew that at the top of the tower was a chime of Christmas bells. They had hung there ever since the church had been built, and were the most beautiful bells in the world. Some thought it was because a great musician had cast them and arranged them in their place; others said it was because of the great height, which reached up where the air was clearest and purest; however that might be, no one who had ever heard the chimes denied that they were the sweetest in the world. Some described them as sounding like angels far up in the sky; others, as sounding like strange winds singing through the trees.

Sing sweet
as the flute,
Sing clear
as the horn,
Sing joy of
the Children
Come Christmas
the morn!
Little Christ Jesus
Our Brother
is born.

ELEANOR FARJEON

But the fact was that no one had heard them for years and years. There was an old man living not far from the church, who said that his mother had spoken of hearing them when she was a little girl, and he was the only one who was sure of as much as that. They were Christmas chimes, you see, and were not meant to be played by men or on common days. It was the custom on Christmas Eve for all the people to bring to the church their offerings to the Christ child; and when the greatest and best offering was laid on the altar, there used to come sounding through the music of the choir the Christmas chimes far up in the tower. Some said that the wind rang them, and others that they were so high that the angels could set them swinging. But for many long years they had never been heard. It was said that people had been growing less careful of their gifts for the Christ child, and that no offering was brought, great enough to deserve the music of the chimes.

Every Christmas Eve the rich people still crowded to the altar, each one trying to bring some better gift than any other, without giving anything that he wanted for himself, and the church was crowded with those who thought that perhaps the wonderful bells might be heard again. But although the service was splendid, and the offerings plenty, only the roar of the wind could be heard, far up in the stone tower.

Now, a number of miles from the city, in a little country village, where nothing could be seen of the great church but glimpses of the tower when the weather was fine, lived a boy named Pedro, and his little brother. They knew very little about the Christmas chimes, but they had heard of the service in the church on Christmas Eve, and had a secret plan, which they had often talked over when by themselves, to go to see the beautiful celebration.

"Nobody can guess, Little Brother," Pedro would say, "all the fine things there are to see and hear; and I have even heard it said that the Christ child sometimes comes down to bless the service. What if we could see Him?"

The day before Christmas was bitterly cold, with a few lonely snowflakes flying in the air, and a hard white crust on the ground. Sure enough, Pedro and Little Brother were able to slip quietly away early in the afternoon; and although the walking was hard in the frosty air, before nightfall they had trudged so far, hand in hand, that they saw the lights of the big city just ahead of them. Indeed, they were about to enter one of the great gates in the wall that surrounded it, when they saw something dark on the snow near their path, and stepped aside to look at it.

It was a poor woman, who had fallen just outside the city, too sick and tired to get in where she might have found shelter. The soft snow made of a drift a sort of pillow for her, and she would soon be so sound asleep, in the wintry air, that no one could ever waken her again.

All this Pedro saw in a moment, and he knelt down beside her and tried to rouse her, even tugging at her arm a little, as though he would have tried to carry her away. He turned her face toward him, so that he could rub some of the snow on it, and when he had looked at her silently a moment he stood up again, and said:

"It's no use, Little Brother. You will have to go on alone."

"Alone?" cried Little Brother. "And you not see the Christmas festival?"

"No," said Pedro, and he could not keep back a bit of a choking sound in his throat. "See this poor woman. Her face looks like the Madonna in the chapel window, and she will freeze to death if nobody cares for her. Everyone has gone to the church now, but when you come back you can bring someone to help her. I will rub her to keep her from freezing, and perhaps get her to eat the bun that is left in my pocket."

"But I cannot bear to leave you, and go on alone," said Little Brother.

"Both of us need not miss the service," said Pedro, "and it had better be I than you. You can easily find your way to the church; and you must see and hear everything twice, Little Brother—once for you and once for me. I am sure the Christ child must know how I should love to come with you and worship Him; and oh! if you get a chance, Little Brother, to slip up to the altar without getting in anyone's way, take this little silver piece of mine, and lay it down for my offering, when no one is looking. Do not forget where you have left me, and forgive me for not going with you."

In this way he hurried Little Brother off to the city, and winked hard to keep back the tears, as he heard the crunching footsteps sounding farther and farther away in the twilight. It was pretty hard to lose the music and splendor of the Christmas celebration that he had been planning for so long, and spend the time instead in that lonely place in the snow.

The great church was a wonderful place that night. Everyone said that it had never looked so bright and beautiful before. When the organ played and the thousands of people sang, the walls shook with the sound, and little Pedro, away outside the city wall, felt the earth tremble around him.

At the close of the service came the procession with the offerings to be laid on the altar. Rich men and great men marched proudly up to lay down their gifts to the Christ child. Some brought wonderful jewels, some baskets of gold so heavy that they could scarcely carry them down the aisle. A great writer laid down a book that he had been making for years and years. And last of all walked the king of the country, hoping with all the rest to win for himself the chime of the Christmas bells. There went a great murmur through the church, as the people saw the king take from his head the royal crown, all set with precious stones, and lay it gleaming on the altar, as his offering to the Holy

Child. "Surely," everyone said, "we shall hear the bells now, for nothing like this has ever happened before."

But still only the cold old wind was heard in the tower, and the people shook their heads; and some of them said, as they had before, that they never really believed the story of the chimes, and doubted if they ever rang at all.

The procession was over, and the choir began the closing hymn. Suddenly the organist stopped playing as though he had been shot, and everyone looked at the old minister, who was standing by the altar, holding up his hand for silence. Not a sound could be heard from anyone in the church, but as all the people strained their ears to listen, there came softly, but distinctly, swinging through the air, the sound of the chimes in the tower. So far away, and yet so clear the music seemed—so much sweeter were the notes than anything that had been heard before, rising and falling away up there in the sky, that the people in the church sat for a moment as still as though something held each of them by the shoulders. Then they all stood up together and stared straight at the altar, to see what great gift had awakened the long-silent bells.

But all that the nearest of them saw was the childish figure of Little Brother, who had crept softly down the aisle when no one was looking, and had laid Pedro's little piece of silver on the altar.

CHRISTMAS IN MAINE
by Robert P. Tristram Coffin

IF YOU WANT to have a Christmas like the one we had on Paradise Farm when I was a boy, you will have to hunt up a saltwater farm on the Maine coast, with bays on both sides of it, and a road that goes around all sorts of bays, up over Misery Hill and down, and through the fir trees so close together that they brush you and your horse on both cheeks. That is the only kind of place a Christmas like that grows. You must have a clear December night, with blue Maine stars snapping like sapphires with the cold, and the big moon flooding full over Misery, and lighting up the snowy spruce boughs like crushed diamonds. You ought to be wrapped in a buffalo robe to your nose and be sitting in a family pung, and have your breath trailing along with you as you slide over the dry, whistling snow. You will have to sing the songs we sang, "God Rest You Merry, Gentlemen" and "Joy to the World," and you will be able to see your songs around you in the air like blue smoke. That's the only way to come to a Paradise Christmas.

And you really should cross over at least one broad bay on the ice, and feel the tide rifts bounce you as the runners slide over them. And if the whole bay booms out, every now and then, and the sound echoes around the wooded islands for miles, you will be having the sort of ride we loved to take from town the night before Christmas.

I won't insist on your having a father like ours to drive you home to your Christmas. One with a wide mustache full of icicles, and eyes like the stars of the morning. That would be impossible, anyway, for there has been only one of him in the world. But it is too bad, just the same. For you won't have the stories we had by the fireplace. You won't hear about Kitty Wells who died beautifully in song just as the sun came over the tops of the eastern mountains and just after her lover had named the wedding day, and you will not hear how Kitty's departure put an end to his mastering the banjo:

> But death came in my cabin door
> And took from me my joy, my pride,
> And when they said she was no more,
> I laid my banjo down and cried.

But you will be able to have the rooms of the farmhouse banked with emerald jewels clustered on bayberry boughs, clumps of everlasting roses with gold spots in the middle of them, and rose hips stuck in pine boughs. And there will be caraway seeds in every crust and cookie in the place.

An aunt should be on hand, an aunt who believes in yarrow tea and the Bible as the two things needed to keep children well. She will read the Nativity story aloud to the family, hurrying over the really exciting parts that happened at the stable, and bearing down hard on what the angels had to say and the more edifying points that might be supposed to improve small boys who like to lie too long abed in the mornings. She will put a moral even into Christmas greens, and she will serve well as a counterirritant to the overeating of mince pies.

The Christmas tree will be there, and it will have a top so high that it will have to be bent over and run along the ceiling of the sitting room. It will be the best fir tree of the Paradise forests, picked from ten thousand almost perfect ones, and every bough on it will be like old-fashioned fans wide open. You will have brought it home that very morning, on the sled, from Dragonfly Spring.

Dragonfly Spring was frozen solid to the bottom, and you could look down into it and see the rainbows where you dented it with your copper-toed boots, see whole ferns caught motionless in the crystal deeps, and a frog, too, down

There are no bells
in all the world
so sweet as sleigh
bells over snow.
The horses arch
their necks to hear
that pretty music
as they go.

If it is dark, you
cannot see
the horses curvetting
and prancing,
but you would know
to hear the bells
that those who
shook them
must be dancing.

ELIZABETH COATSWORTH

99

there, with hands just like a baby's on him. Your small sister—the one with hair like new honey laid open in the middle of a honeycomb—had cried out, "Let's dig him up and take him home and warm his feet!"

Your dog, Snoozer, who is a curious and intricate combination of many merry pugs and many mournful hound dogs, was snuffling all the time, hot on the featherstitching the mice had made from bush to bush while you were felling the Christmas tree. A red squirrel was taking a white-pine cone apart on a hemlock bough, and telling Snoozer what he thought of him and all other dogs.

There will be a lot of aunts in the house besides the Biblical one. Aunts of every complexion and cut. Christmas is the one time that even the most dubious of aunts take on value. One of them can make up wreaths, another can make rock candy, and still another can steer your twelve-seater bobsled—and turn it over, bottom up, with you all in just the right place for a fine spill.

There will be uncles, too, to hold one end of the molasses taffy you will pull sooner or later, yanking it out till it flashes and turns into cornsilk that almost floats in the air, tossing your end of it back and probably lassoing your uncle around his neck as you do it, and pulling out a new rope of solid honey. The uncles will rig up schooners no bigger than your thumb, with shrouds like cobwebs; they will mend the bobsled, tie up cut fingers, and sew on buttons after you shin up to the cupola in the barn; and—if you get on the good side of them—they will saw you up so much birchwood that you won't have to lay hand to a bucksaw till after New Year's.

There will be cousins by the cartload. He-ones and she-ones. The size you can sit on, and the size that can sit on you. Enough for two armies, on Little Round Top and on Big, up in the haymow. You will play Gettysburg there till your heads are full of hay chaff that will keep six aunts busy cleaning it out. And then you will come into the house and down a whole crock of molasses cookies which somebody was foolish enough to leave the cover off.

Every holiday that came along, in my father's house, was the gathering of an Anglo-Saxon clan. My father was built for lots of people round him. But Christmas was a whole assembly of the West Saxons! There were men with wide mustaches and men with smooth places on top of their heads, women wide and narrow. Hired men were there, too. They were special guests and had to be handled with kid gloves, as New England hired men must. They had to have the best of everything, and you could not find fault with them, as you could with uncles, if they smacked you for upsetting their coffee into their laps. Babies were underfoot in full cry. The older children hunted in packs. The table had to be pieced out with flour barrels and breadboards and ironing boards. It was a house's length from the head of the table, where your father sat and manufactured the roast up into slivers, to your mother dishing out the pork gravy.

Whole geese disappeared on the way down. The Christmas cake, which had been left sweetly to itself for a month to age into a miracle, was a narrow isthmus when it got to Mother. But Mother always said that Christmas, to her, was watching other people eat. She was the kind of mother who claimed that the neck and the back of the chicken were the tastiest parts.

The prize goose, whom you had brought up by hand and called Oliver Cromwell, Old Ironsides, or some such distinguished title, was duly carved. And Father found his wishbone snow-white and you all applauded, for that meant lots of snow and two more months of coasting on your sleds. There were mince pies by the legion. And if Uncle Tom were there, a whole raccoon baked just for him and girt around with browned sweet potatoes. Of course, there will be an apple pudding at such a season. Steamed in a lard bucket, and cut open with a string. A sauce of oranges and lemons to make an ocean around each steaming volcano of suet and russet apples as it falls crumbling from the loop of twine.

The secret of the best Christmases is everybody doing the same things all at the same time. You will all fall to and string cranberries and popcorn for the tree, and the bright lines each of you has a hold on will radiate from the tree like ribbons on a maypole. Everybody will have needles and thread in the mouth, you will all get in each other's way, but that is the art of doing Christmas right. You will all bundle up together for a ride in the afternoon. You had better take the horse sled, as the pung will not begin to hold you. Even then a dozen or so of assorted uncles and aunts and cousins will have to come trooping after through the deep snow and wait for their turn on the straw in the sled. And the hullabaloo will send the rabbits flying away through the woods, showing their bobbing scuts.

Everybody will hang presents on the tree at once, when the sun has dipped down into the spruces in the west and you are back home in the sitting room. There will be no nonsense of tiptoeing up and edging a package on when nobody is looking. Everybody knows who is giving him what. There is no mystery about it. There will be so many hands at work on the tree at once that the whole thing will probably go over two or three times, and it will be well to make it fast with a hawser or so.

And then you will turn right around and take the presents off again, the minute you have got them all on and have lighted the candles up. There will be no waiting, with small children sitting around with aching hearts. The real candles will be a problem in all that mass of spills. Boughs will take fire here and there. But there will be plenty of uncles around to crush out the small bonfires in their big brown hands. All the same, it would be well to have an uncle Thomas who can take up a live coal in his thumb and finger, and light his pipe from it, cool as a cucumber. Better turn the extinguishing of the tree over to him.

There will be boughten presents, to be sure—a turtle of cardboard in a glassed,

H
eap on
more wood! the wind
is chill; but
let it whistle
as it will
We'll keep
our Christmas
merry still.

SIR WALTER SCOTT

dainty box, hung on springs and swimming for dear life with all four feet, and popguns with their barrels ringed and streaked with red and yellow lines. Somebody will probably get one of those Swiss music boxes that will eke out a ghostly "Last Rose of Summer" if tenderly cranked. There should be those little bottles of transparent candies with real syrup in them, which I used to live for through the years. And there must be a German doll for every last girl, with mountains of yellow hair and cheeks looking as if life were a continuous blowing of bubbles. Boughten things are all right.

But if it is going to be our kind of Christmas, most of the presents will be homemade. Socks knit by the aunt who swears only by useful gifts. You have seen those socks growing up from their white toes for the last two weeks. Wristers, always red. A box of Aunt Louise's candied orange peel that she will never let on to anybody how she makes. Your father will have made a sled for every mother's son and daughter of you, with a bluebird, or robin redbreast, painted on each one and your name underneath. You will never have another present to match that, though you grow up and become Midases. Popcorn balls, big as muskmelons, will be common ware. They will be dripping with molasses, and will stick your wristers and socks and other treasures together.

But the pith of the party is not reached until the whole nation of you sits down in rocking chairs, or lies down on their bellies in front of the six-foot gulf of the fireplace. The presents are all stowed, heaped and tucked away, stuck fast with cornballs. The last lamps are out. The fireplace dances on the ceiling. All the babies will be hushed and put away. All the younger fry will be more than half asleep. The toasted cheese and smoked herring will go round.

Then you had best find a fair substitute for my father. Give him the best chair in the house—and the way to find *that* is to push the cat out of it—and let him tear! He will tell you about such people as the brilliant young ladies of Philadelphia who had a piano too big to fit their house, so they put it on the porch and played on it through the open window. Then he will work his way to the caliph of Bagdad who had a daughter so homely that she had to wear a sack on her head when her suitors came awooing, and how she fell down a well and made herself a great fortune, and won the handsomest husband that ever wore a turban.

The firelight will get into your father's eyes and on his hair. He will move on from Bagdad to Big Bethel, and tell you all how the Yankee campfires looked like the high Milky Way itself all night long before the battle; how the dew silvered every sleeping soldier's face and the stacked rifles as the dawn came up with the new day and death. And you will hug your knees and hear the wind outside going its rounds among the snowy pines, and you will listen on till the story you are hearing becomes a part of the old winds of the world and the motion of the bright stars. And probably it will take two uncles at least to carry you to bed.

102

A LETTER FROM SANTA CLAUS

by Mark Twain

Clara, Samuel and Susie Clemens, 1877

Palace of St. Nicholas
In the Moon
Christmas Morning

MY DEAR SUSIE CLEMENS:

I have received and read all the letters which you and your little sister have written me by the hand of your mother and your nurses; I have also read those which you little people have written me with your own hands—for although you did not use any characters that are in grown peoples' alphabet, you used the characters that all children in all lands on earth and in the twinkling stars use; and as all my subjects in the moon are children and use no character but that, you will easily understand that I can read your and your baby sister's jagged and fantastic marks without any trouble at all. But I had trouble with those letters which you dictated through your mother and the nurses, for I am a foreigner and cannot read English writing well. You will find that I made no mistakes about the things which you and the baby ordered in your own letters—I went down your chimney at midnight when you were asleep and delivered them all myself—and kissed both of you, too, because you are good children, well trained, nice mannered, and about the most obedient little people I ever saw. But in the letter which you dictated there were some words which I could not make out for certain, and one or two small orders which I could not fill because we ran out of stock. Our last lot of kitchen furniture for dolls has just gone to a very poor little child in the North Star away up in the cold country above the Big Dipper. Your mama can show you that star and you will say: "Little Snow Flake," (for that is the child's name) "I'm glad you got that furniture, for you need it more than I." That is, you must *write* that, with your own hand, and Snow Flake will write you an answer. If you only spoke it she wouldn't hear you. Make your letter light and thin, for the distance is great and the postage very heavy.

There was a word or two in your mama's letter which I couldn't be certain of. I took it to be "a trunk full of doll's clothes." Is that it? I will call at your kitchen door about nine o'clock this morning to inquire. But I must not see anybody and I must not speak to anybody but you. When the kitchen doorbell rings, George must be blindfolded and sent to open the door. Then he must go

103

back to the dining room or the china closet and take the cook with him. You must tell George he must walk on tiptoe and not speak—otherwise he will die someday. Then you must go up to the nursery and stand on a chair or the nurse's bed and put your ear to the speaking tube that leads down to the kitchen and when I whistle through it you must speak in the tube and say, "Welcome, Santa Claus!" Then I will ask whether it was a trunk you ordered or not. If you say it was, I shall ask you what *color* you want the trunk to be. Your mama will help you to name a nice color and then you must tell me every single thing in detail which you want the trunk to contain. Then when I say "Good-by and a merry Christmas to my little Susie Clemens," you must say "Good-by, good old Santa Claus, I thank you very much and please tell that little Snow Flake I will look at her star tonight and she must look down here—I will be right in the west bay window; and every fine night I will look at her star and say, 'I know somebody up there and *like* her, too.'" Then you must go down into the library and make George close all the doors that open into the main hall, and everybody must keep still for a little while. I will go to the moon and get those things and in a few minutes I will come down the chimney that belongs to the fireplace that is in the hall—if it is a trunk you want—because I couldn't get such a thing as a trunk down the nursery chimney, you know.

People may talk if they want, until they hear my footsteps in the hall. Then you tell them to keep quiet a little while till I go back up the chimney. Maybe you will not hear my footsteps at all—so you may go now and then and peep through the dining-room doors, and by and by you will see that thing which you want, right under the piano in the drawing room—for I shall put it there. If I should leave any snow in the hall, you must tell George to sweep it into the fireplace, for I haven't time to do such things. George must not use a broom, but a rag—else he will die someday. You must watch George and not let him run into danger. If my boot should leave a stain on the marble, George must not holystone it away. Leave it there always in memory of my visit; and whenever you look at it or show it to anybody you must let it remind you to be a good little girl. Whenever you are naughty and somebody points to that mark which your good old Santa Claus's boot made on the marble, what will you say, little sweetheart?

Good-by for a few minutes, till I come down to the world and ring the kitchen doorbell.

Your loving SANTA CLAUS
Whom people sometimes call "The Man in the Moon"

104

'Twas the night before Christmas, when all through
    the house
Not a creature was stirring, not even a mouse;
The stockings were hung by the chimney with care,
In hopes that St. Nicholas soon would be there;
The children were nestled all snug in their beds,
While visions of sugar-plums danced in their heads;
And Mamma in her 'kerchief, and I in my cap,
Had just settled our brains for a long winter's nap;
When out on the lawn there arose such a clatter,
I sprang from the bed to see what what was the matter.
Away to the window I flew like a flash,
Tore open the shutters and threw up the sash.
The moon, on the breast of the new-fallen snow,
Gave the lustre of mid-day to objects below,
When, what to my wondering eyes should appear,
But a miniature sleigh, and eight tiny rein-deer,
With a little old driver, so lively and quick,
I knew in a moment it must be St. Nick.

More rapid than eagles his coursers they came,

And he whistled, and shouted, and called them by name;

"Now, Dasher! now, Dancer! now, Prancer and Vixen!

On, Comet! on, Cupid! on, Donder and Blitzen!

To the top of the porch! to the top of the wall!

Now dash away! dash away! dash away all!"

As dry leaves that before the wild hurricane fly,

When they meet with an obstacle, mount to the sky;

So up to the house-top the coursers they flew,

With the sleigh full of Toys, and St. Nicholas too.

And then, in a twinkling, I heard on the roof

The prancing and pawing of each little hoof —

As I drew in my head, and was turning around,

Down the chimney St. Nicholas came with a bound.

He was dressed all in fur, from his head to his foot,

And his clothes were all tarnished with ashes and soot;

A bundle of Toys he had flung on his back,

And he look'd like a pedlar just opening his pack.

His eyes — how they twinkled! his dimples how merry!

His cheeks were like roses, his nose like a cherry!

His droll little mouth was drawn up like a bow,

And the beard of his chin was as white as the snow;

The stump of a pipe he held tight in his teeth,

And the smoke it encircled his head like a wreath;

He had a broad face and a little round belly

That shook, when he laughed, like a bowl full of jelly.

He was chubby and plump, a right jolly old elf,

And I laughed, when I saw him, in spite of myself;

A wink of his eye and a twist of his head,

Soon gave me to know I had nothing to dread;

He spoke not a word, but went straight to his work,
And fill'd all the stockings; then turned with a jerk,
And laying his finger aside of his nose,
And giving a nod, up the chimney he rose;
He sprang to his sleigh, to his team gave a whistle,
And away they all flew like the down of a thistle.
But I heard him exclaim, ere he drove out of sight,
"Happy Christmas to all, and to all a good night."

Clement C. Moore,
1862, March 13th originally written
many years ago.

MY FIRST CHRISTMAS TREE
by Hamlin Garland

I WILL BEGIN by saying that we never had a Christmas tree in our house in the Wisconsin coulee; indeed, my father never saw one in a family circle till he saw that which I set up for my own children last year. But we celebrated Christmas in those days, always, and I cannot remember a time when we did not all hang up our stockings for "Sandy Claws" to fill. As I look back upon those days it seems as if the snows were always deep, the night skies crystal clear, and the stars especially lustrous with frosty sparkles of blue and yellow fire—and probably this was so, for we lived in a northern land where winter was usually stern and always long.

I recall one Christmas when "Sandy" brought me a sled, and a horse that stood on rollers—a wonderful tin horse which I very shortly split in two in order to see what his insides were. Father traded a cord of wood for the sled, and the horse cost twenty cents—but they made the day wonderful.

Another notable Christmas Day, as I stood in our front yard, midleg-deep in snow, a neighbor drove by closely muffled in furs, while behind his seat his son, a lad of twelve or fifteen, stood beside a barrel of apples, and as he passed he hurled a glorious big red one at me. It missed me, but bored a deep, round hole in the soft snow. I thrill yet with the remembered joy of burrowing for that delicious bomb. Nothing will ever smell quite as good as that Winesap or Northern Spy or whatever it was. It was a wayward impulse on the part of the boy in the sleigh, but it warms my heart after more than forty years.

We had no chimney in our home, but the stocking-hanging was a ceremony nevertheless. My parents, and especially my mother, entered into it with the best of humor. They always put up their own stockings or permitted us to do it for them—and they always laughed next morning when they found potatoes or ears of corn in them. I can see now that my mother's laugh had a tear in it, for she loved pretty things and seldom got any during the years that we lived in the coulee.

When I was ten years old we moved to Mitchell County, an Iowa prairie land, and there we prospered in such wise that our stockings always held toys of some sort, and even my mother's stocking occasionally sagged with a simple piece of jewelry or a new comb or brush. But the thought of a family tree remained the luxury of millionaire city dwellers; indeed it was not till my fifteenth or sixteenth year that our Sunday school rose to the extravagance of a tree, and it is of this wondrous festival that I write.

The land about us was only partly cultivated at this time, and our district schoolhouse, a bare little box, was set bleakly on the prairie; but the Burr Oak schoolhouse was not only larger, but it stood beneath great oaks as well and possessed the charm of a forest background through which a stream ran silently. It was our chief social center. There of a Sunday a regular preacher held "Divine service" with Sunday school as a sequence. At night—usually on Friday nights—the young people met in "ly-ceums," as we called them, to debate great questions or to "speak pieces" and read essays; and here it was that I saw my first Christmas tree.

I walked to that tree across four miles of moonlit snow. Snow? No, it was a floor of diamonds, a magical world, so beautiful that my heart still aches with the wonder of it and with the regret that it has all gone—gone with the keen eyes and the bounding pulses of the boy.

Our home at this time was a small frame house on the prairie almost directly west of the Burr Oak grove, and as it was too cold to take the horses out my brother and I, with our tall boots, our visored caps and our long woolen mufflers, started forth afoot defiant of the cold. We left the gate on the trot, bound for a sight of the glittering unknown. The snow was deep and we moved side by side in the grooves made by the hoofs of the horses, setting our feet in the shine left by the broad shoes of the wood sleighs whose going had smoothed the way for us. Our breaths rose like smoke in the still air. It must have been ten below zero, but that did not trouble us in those days, and at last we came in sight of the lights, in sound of the singing, the laughter, the bells of the feast.

It was a poor little building without tower or bell and its low walls had but three windows on a side, and yet it seemed very imposing to me that night as I crossed the threshold and faced the strange people who packed it to the door. I say "strange people," for though I had seen most of them many times they all seemed somehow alien to me that night. I was an irregular attendant at Sunday school and did not expect a present, therefore I stood against the wall

At Christmas
play and make
good cheer,
For Christmas
comes but
once a year.

THOMAS TUSSER

and gazed with open-eyed marveling at the shining pine which stood where the pulpit was wont to be. I was made to feel the more embarrassed by reason of the remark of a boy who accused me of having forgotten to comb my hair.

This was not true, but the cap I wore always matted my hair down over my brow, and then, when I lifted it off, invariably disarranged it completely. Nevertheless I felt guilty—and hot. I don't suppose my hair was artistically barbered that night—I rather guess Mother had used the shears—and I can believe that I looked the half-wild colt that I was; but there was no call for that youth to direct attention to my unavoidable shagginess.

I don't think the tree had many candles, and I don't remember that it glittered with golden apples. But it was loaded with presents, and the girls coming and going clothed in bright garments made me forget my own looks—I think they made me forget to remove my overcoat, which was a sodden thing of poor cut and worse quality. I think I must have stood agape for nearly two hours listening to the songs, noting every motion of Adoniram Burtch and Asa Walker as they directed the ceremonies and prepared the way for the great event—that is to say, for the coming of Santa Claus himself.

A furious jingling of bells, a loud voice outside, the lifting of a window, the nearer clash of bells, and the dear old saint appeared (in the person of Stephen Bartle) clothed in a red robe, a belt of sleigh bells, and a long white beard. The children cried out, "Oh!" The girls tittered and shrieked with excitement, and the boys laughed and clapped their hands. Then "Sandy" made a little speech about being glad to see us all, but as he had many other places to visit, and as there were a great many presents to distribute, he guessed he'd have to ask some of the many pretty girls to help him. So he called upon Betty Burtch and Hattie Knapp—and I for one admired his taste, for they were the most popular maids of the school.

They came up blushing, and a little bewildered by the blaze of publicity thus blown upon them. But their native dignity asserted itself, and the distribution of the presents began. I have a notion now that the fruit upon the tree was mostly bags of popcorn and "corny copias" of candy, but as my brother and I stood there that night and saw everybody, even the rowdiest boy, getting something we felt aggrieved and rebellious. We forgot that we had come from afar—we only knew that we were being left out.

But suddenly, in the midst of our gloom, my brother's name was called, and a lovely girl with a gentle smile handed him a bag of popcorn. My heart glowed with gratitude. Somebody had thought of us; and when she came to me, saying sweetly, "Here's something for you," I had not words to thank her. This happened nearly forty years ago, but her smile, her outstretched hand, her sympathetic eyes are vividly before me as I write. She was sorry for the shock-headed boy who stood against the wall, and her pity made the little box of candy a casket of pearls. The fact that I swallowed the jewels on the road home does not take from the reality of my adoration.

At last I had to take my final glimpse of that wondrous tree, and I well remember the walk home. My brother and I traveled in wordless companionship. The moon was sinking toward the west, and the snow crust gleamed with a million fairy lamps. The sentinel watchdogs barked from lonely farmhouses, and the wolves answered from the ridges. Now and then sleighs passed us with lovers sitting two and two, and the bells on their horses had the remote music of romance to us whose boots drummed like clogs of wood upon the icy road.

Our house was dark as we approached and entered it, but how deliciously warm it seemed after the pitiless wind! I confess we made straight for the cupboard for a mince pie, a doughnut and a bowl of milk!

As I write this there stands in my library a thick-branched, beautifully tapering fir tree covered with the gold and purple apples of Hesperides, together with crystal ice points, green and red and yellow candles, clusters of gilded grapes, wreaths of metallic frost, and glittering angels swinging in ecstasy; but I doubt if my children will ever know the keen pleasure (that is almost pain) which came to my brother and to me in those Christmas days when an orange was not a breakfast fruit, but a casket of incense and of spice, a message from the sunlands of the South.

That was our compensation—we brought to our Christmastime a keen appetite and empty hands. And the lesson of it all is, if we are seeking a lesson, that it is better to give to those who want than to those for whom "we ought to do something because they did something for us last year."

CHRISTMAS BELLS

I heard the bells on Christmas Day
Their old, familiar carols play,
   And wild and sweet
   The words repeat
Of peace on earth, good-will to men!

CHRISTMAS, 1863.

And thought how, as the day had come,
The belfries of all Christendom
　　Had rolled along
　　The unbroken song
Of peace on earth, good-will to men!

Till, ringing, swinging on its way,
The world revolved from night to day,
　　A voice, a chime,
　　A chant sublime
Of peace on earth, good-will to men!

Then from each black, accursèd mouth
The cannon thundered in the South,
　　And with the sound
　　The carols drowned
Of peace on earth, good-will to men!

It was as if an earthquake rent
The hearth-stones of a continent,
　　And made forlorn
　　The households born
Of peace on earth, good-will to men!

And in despair I bowed my head;
"There is no peace on earth," I said;
　　"For hate is strong,
　　And mocks the song
Of peace on earth, good-will to men!"

Then pealed the bells more loud and deep:
"God is not dead; nor doth He sleep!
　　The Wrong shall fail,
　　The Right prevail,
With peace on earth, good-will to men!"

Henry Wadsworth Longfellow

THE GIFT OF THE MAGI
by O. Henry

ONE DOLLAR AND EIGHTY-SEVEN CENTS. That was all. And sixty cents of it was in pennies. Pennies saved one and two at a time by bulldozing the grocer and the vegetable man and the butcher until one's cheeks burned with the silent imputation of parsimony that such close dealing implied. Three times Della counted it. One dollar and eighty-seven cents. And the next day would be Christmas.

There was clearly nothing to do but flop down on the shabby little couch and howl. So Della did it. Which instigates the moral reflection that life is made up of sobs, sniffles, and smiles, with sniffles predominating.

While the mistress of the home is gradually subsiding from the first stage to the second, take a look at the home. A furnished flat at eight dollars per week. It did not exactly beggar description, but it certainly had that word on the lookout for the mendicancy squad.

In the vestibule below was a letter box into which no letter would go, and an electric button from which no mortal finger could coax a ring. Also appertaining thereunto was a card bearing the name "Mr. James Dillingham Young."

The "Dillingham" had been flung to the breeze during a former period of prosperity when its possessor was being paid thirty dollars per week. Now, when the income was shrunk to twenty dollars, the letters of "Dillingham" looked blurred, as though they were thinking seriously of contracting to a modest and unassuming "D." But whenever Mr. James Dillingham Young came home and reached his flat above he was called "Jim" and greatly hugged by Mrs. James Dillingham Young, already introduced to you as Della. Which is all very good.

Della finished her cry and attended to her cheeks with the powder rag. She stood by the window and looked out dully at a gray cat walking a gray fence in

a gray backyard. Tomorrow would be Christmas Day and she had only one dollar and eighty-seven cents with which to buy Jim a present. She had been saving every penny she could for months, with this result. Twenty dollars a week doesn't go far. Expenses had been greater than she had calculated. They always are. Only one dollar and eighty-seven cents to buy a present for Jim. Her Jim. Many a happy hour she had spent planning for something nice for him. Something fine and rare and sterling—something just a little bit near to being worthy of the honor of being owned by Jim.

There was a pier glass between the windows of the room. Perhaps you have seen a pier glass in an eight-dollar flat. A very thin and very agile person may, by observing his reflection in a rapid sequence of longitudinal strips, obtain a fairly accurate conception of his looks. Della, being slender, had mastered the art.

Suddenly she whirled from the window and stood before the glass. Her eyes were shining brilliantly, but her face had lost its color within twenty seconds. Rapidly she pulled down her hair and let it fall to its full length.

Now, there were two possessions of the James Dillingham Youngs in which they both took a mighty pride. One was Jim's gold watch that had been his father's and his grandfather's. The other was Della's hair. Had the Queen of Sheba lived in the flat across the air shaft, Della would have let her hair hang out the window someday to dry just to depreciate her Majesty's jewels and gifts. Had King Solomon been the janitor, with all his treasures piled up in the basement, Jim would have pulled out his watch every time he passed, just to see him pluck at his beard from envy.

So now Della's beautiful hair fell about her, rippling and shining like a cascade of brown waters. It reached below her knee and made itself almost a garment for her. And then she did it up again nervously and quickly. Once she faltered for a minute and stood still while a tear or two splashed on the worn red carpet.

On went her old brown jacket; on went her old brown hat. With a whirl of skirts and with the brilliant sparkle still in her eyes, she fluttered out the door and down the stairs to the street.

Where she stopped the sign read: Mme. Sofronie. Hair Goods of All Kinds. One flight up Della ran, and collected herself, panting. Madame, large, too white, chilly, hardly looked the "Sofronie."

"Will you buy my hair?" asked Della.

"I buy hair," said Madame. "Take yer hat off and let's have a sight at the looks of it."

Down rippled the brown cascade.

"Twenty dollars," said Madame, lifting the mass with a practiced hand.

"Give it to me quick," said Della.

Oh, and the next two hours tripped by on rosy wings. Forget the hashed metaphor. She was ransacking the stores for Jim's present.

She found it at last. It surely had been made for Jim and no one else. There was no other like it in any of the stores, and she had turned all of them inside out. It was a platinum fob chain, simple and chaste in design, properly proclaiming its value by substance alone and not by meretricious ornamentation—as all good things should do. It was even worthy of The Watch. As soon as she saw it she knew that it must be Jim's. It was like him. Quietness and value—the description applied to both. Twenty-one dollars they took from her for it, and she hurried home with the eighty-seven cents. With that chain on his watch Jim might be properly anxious about the time in any company. Grand as the watch was, he sometimes looked at it on the sly on account of the old leather strap that he used in place of a chain.

When Della reached home her intoxication gave way a little to prudence and reason. She got out her curling irons and lighted the gas and went to work repairing the ravages made by generosity added to love. Which is always a tremendous task, dear friends—a mammoth task.

Within forty minutes her head was covered with tiny close-lying curls that made her look wonderfully like a truant schoolboy. She looked at her reflection in the mirror long, carefully, and critically.

"If Jim doesn't kill me," she said to herself, "before he takes a second look at me, he'll say I look like a Coney Island chorus girl. But what could I do—oh! what could I do with a dollar and eighty-seven cents?"

At seven o'clock the coffee was made and the frying pan was on the back of the stove, hot and ready to cook the chops.

Jim was never late. Della doubled the fob chain in her hand and sat on the corner of the table near the door that he always entered. Then she heard his step on the stair away down on the first flight, and she turned white for just a moment. She had a habit of saying little silent prayers about the simplest everyday things, and now she whispered: "Please, God, make him think I am still pretty."

The door opened and Jim stepped in and closed it. He looked thin and very serious. Poor fellow, he was only twenty-two—and to be burdened with a family! He needed a new overcoat and he was without gloves.

Jim stepped inside the door, as immovable as a setter at the scent of quail. His eyes were fixed upon Della, and there was an expression in them that she could not read, and it terrified her. It was not anger, nor surprise, nor disapproval, nor horror, nor any of the sentiments that she had been prepared for. He simply stared at her fixedly with that peculiar expression on his face.

Della wriggled off the table and went for him.

115

May you
have the gladness
of Christmas
Which is hope;
The spirit
of Christmas
Which is peace;
The heart
of Christmas
Which is love.

ADA V. HENDRICKS

116

"Jim, darling," she cried, "don't look at me that way. I had my hair cut off and sold it because I couldn't have lived through Christmas without giving you a present. It'll grow out again—you won't mind, will you? I just had to do it. My hair grows awfully fast. Say 'Merry Christmas!' Jim, and let's be happy. You don't know what a nice—what a beautiful, nice gift I've got for you."

"You've cut off your hair?" asked Jim laboriously, as if he had not arrived at that patent fact yet even after the hardest mental labor.

"Cut it off and sold it," said Della. "Don't you like me just as well anyhow? I'm me without my hair, ain't I?"

Jim looked about the room curiously.

"You say your hair is gone?" he said, with an air almost of idiocy.

"You needn't look for it," said Della. "It's sold, I tell you—sold and gone, too. It's Christmas Eve, boy. Be good to me, for it went for you. Maybe the hairs of my head were numbered," she went on with a sudden serious sweetness, "but nobody could ever count my love for you. Shall I put the chops on, Jim?"

Out of his trance Jim seemed quickly to wake. He enfolded his Della. For ten seconds let us regard with discreet scrutiny some inconsequential object in the other direction. Eight dollars a week or a million a year—what is the difference? A mathematician or a wit would give you the wrong answer. The magi brought valuable gifts, but that was not among them. This dark assertion will be illuminated later on.

Jim drew a package from his overcoat pocket and threw it upon the table.

"Don't make any mistake, Dell," he said, "about me. I don't think there's anything in the way of a haircut or a shave or a shampoo that could make me like my girl any less. But if you'll unwrap that package you may see why you had me going awhile at first."

White fingers and nimble tore at the string and paper. And then an ecstatic scream of joy; and then, alas! a quick feminine change to hysterical tears and wails, necessitating the immediate employment of all the comforting powers of the lord of the flat.

For there lay The Combs—the set of combs, side and back, that Della had worshipped for long in a Broadway window. Beautiful combs, pure tortoise-shell, with jeweled rims—just the shade to wear in the beautiful vanished hair. They were expensive combs, she knew, and her heart had simply craved and yearned over them without the least hope of possession. And now they were hers, but the tresses that should have adorned the coveted adornments were gone.

But she hugged them to her bosom, and at length she was able to look up with dim eyes and a smile and say, "My hair grows so fast, Jim!"

And then Della leaped up like a little singed cat and cried, "Oh, oh!"

Jim had not yet seen his beautiful present. She held it out to him eagerly upon her open palm. The dull precious metal seemed to flash with a reflection of her bright and ardent spirit.

"Isn't it a dandy, Jim? I hunted all over town to find it. You'll have to look at the time a hundred times a day now. Give me your watch. I want to see how it looks on it."

Instead of obeying, Jim tumbled down on the couch and put his hands under the back of his head and smiled.

"Dell," said he, "let's put our Christmas presents away and keep 'em awhile. They're too nice to use just at present. I sold the watch to get the money to buy your combs. And now suppose you put the chops on."

The magi, as you know, were wise men—wonderfully wise men—who brought gifts to the Babe in the manger. They invented the art of giving Christmas presents. Being wise, their gifts were no doubt wise ones, possibly bearing the privilege of exchange in case of duplication. And here I have lamely related to you the uneventful chronicle of two foolish children in a flat who most unwisely sacrificed for each other the greatest treasures of their house. But in a last word to the wise of these days let it be said that of all who give gifts these two were the wisest. Of all who give and receive gifts, such as they are wisest. Everywhere they are wisest. They are the magi.

I HEARD
A BIRD SING

I heard a bird sing
    In the dark of December
A magical thing
    And sweet to remember.

"We are nearer to Spring
    Than we were in September,"
I heard a bird sing
    In the dark of December.

Oliver Herford

THE CHRISTMAS OF
THE PHONOGRAPH RECORDS
by Mari Sandoz

IT SEEMS TO ME that I remember it all quite clearly. The night was very cold, footsteps squeaking in the frozen snow that had lain on for over two weeks, the roads in our region practically unbroken. But now the holidays were coming and wagons had pushed out on the long miles to the railroad, with men enough to scoop a trail for each other through the deeper drifts.

My small brother and I had been asleep in our attic bed long enough to frost the cover of the feather tick at our faces when there was a shouting in the road before the house, running steps, and then the sound of the broom handle thumping against the ceiling below us, and Father booming out, "Get up! The phonograph is here!"

The phonograph! I stepped out on the coyote skin at our bed, jerked on my woolen stockings and my shoes, buttoning my dress as I slipped down the outside stairs in the fading moon. Lamplight was pouring from the open door in a cloud of freezing mist over the back end of a loaded wagon, with three neighbors easing great boxes off, Father limping back and forth shouting, "Don't break me my records!" his breath white around his dark beard.

Inside the house Mother was poking sticks of wood into the firebox of the cookstove, her eyes shining, her concern about the extravagance of a talking machine when we needed overshoes for our chilblains apparently forgotten. The three largest boxes were edged through the doorway and filled much of the kitchen–living-room floor. The neighbors stomped their felt boots at the stove and held their hands over the hot lids while Father ripped at the boxes with his crowbar. First there was the machine, varnished oak, with a shining cylinder for the records, and then the horn, a great black, gilt-ribbed morning glory, and the crazy-angled rod arm and chain to hold it in place.

By now a wagon full of young people from the Dutch community on Mirage Flats turned into our yard. At a school program they had heard about the Edison phonograph going out to Old Jules Sandoz. They trooped in at our door, piled their wraps in the lean-to, and settled along the benches to wait.

Young Jule and James, the brothers next to me in age, were up too, and watching Father throw excelsior aside, exposing a tight packing of round paper containers, with more layers under these, and still more below. Father opened one, and while I read out the instructions in my German-accented fifth-grade country-school English, he slipped the brown wax cylinder on the machine, cranked the handle carefully, and set the needle down. Everybody waited, leaning forward. There was a rhythmic frying in the silence, and then a whispering of sound, soft and very, very far away.

It brought a murmur of disappointment and an escaping laugh, but gradually the whispers loudened into the sextet from *Lucia*, into what still seems to me the most beautiful singing in the world. We all clustered around, the visitors, fourteen, fifteen by now, and Mother too, caught while pouring hot chocolate into cups, her long-handled pan still tilted in the air. Looking back I realize something of the meaning of the light in her face: the hunger for music she must have felt, coming from Switzerland, the country of music, to a western Nebraska government claim. True, we sang old country songs in the evenings, she leading, teaching us all she knew, but plainly it had not been enough.

By now almost everybody pushed up to the boxes to see what there was to play, or called out some title hopefully. My job was to run the machine and play the two-minute records set before me. There were violin pieces for Father, among them "Alpine Violets" and "Listen to the Mocking Bird"; "Any Rags," "Red Wing," and "I'm Trying so Hard to Forget You" for the young people; "Rabbit Hash" for my brothers, their own selection from the catalogue; and Schubert's "Serenade" and *"Die Kapelle"* for Mother.

With the trail broken to the main bridge of the region, just below our house, and this Christmas Eve, there was considerable travel on the road, people passing most of the night. The lighted windows, the music, the gathering of teams and saddle horses in the yard, and the sub-zero weather tolled them in to the weathered little frame house. "You better set more yeast. We will have to bake again tomorrow," Mother told me as she cut into a *zopf*, one of the braids of coffee cake baked in tins as large as the circle of both her arms. This was the last of five planned to carry us into the middle of holiday week.

By now the phonograph had been moved to the top of the washstand in our parents' bedroom, people sitting on the two double beds, on the round-topped trunk, and on benches carried in, some squatting on their heels along the wall. The little round boxes stood everywhere, on the dresser and on the board laid from there to the washstand and on the windowsills, with more brought in to be played and Father still shouting, "Don't break me my records!"

When the Edison Military Band started a gay, blaring galop, Mother looked in at the bedroom door, pleased. Then she noticed all the records spread out there, and in the kitchen-living room behind her, and began to realize their number.

"Three hundred!" she exclaimed. "Looks to me like more than three thousand!"

119

Father scratched under his bearded chin, laughing slyly. "I added to the order," he admitted.

He didn't say how many, nor that there were other brands besides the Edison here, including several hundred foreign recordings obtained through a Swiss friend in New York, at a stiff price.

Mother looked at him, her blue eyes tragic, as she could make them. "You paid nothing on the mortgage! All the twenty-one-hundred-dollar inheritance wasted on a talking machine!"

No, Father denied, puffing at his corncob pipe. Not all. But Mother knew

him well. "You did not buy the overshoes for the children. You forgot everything except the phonograph!"

"The overshoes are coming. I got them cheaper on time."

"More debts!" she accused bitterly, but before she could add to this, one of the young Swiss grabbed her and whirled her back into the kitchen in the galop from the Edison band. He raced Mother from door to stove and back again, so her blue calico skirts flew out and the anger died from her face. Her eyes began to shine in an excitement I had never seen in them, and I realize now, looking back, all the fun our mother missed in her working life, even in her childhood in the old country, and during the much harder years later.

That galop started the dancing. The table was pushed against the wall, boxes piled on top of it, the big ones dragged into the lean-to. Waltzes, two-steps, quadrilles, and schottisches were sorted out and set in a row ready for me to play while one of the men shaved a candle over the kitchen floor. There was room for only one set of square dancers, but our neighbor, Charley Sears, called the turns with enthusiasm. The young women were outnumbered by the men, as is common in new communities. They waltzed, two-stepped, formed a double line for a Bohemian polka, or schottisched around the room, one couple close behind the other. Once Charley Sears grabbed my hand and drew me out to try a quadrille, towering over me as he swung me on the corner and guided me through the allemande left. My heart pounded in shyness and my homemade shoes compounded my awkwardness. Later someone else dragged me out into a two-step, saying, "Like this: one, two; one, two. Just let yourself go."

That night even Old Jules had to try a round polka, even with his foot crippled in a long-ago well accident. When he took his pipe out of his mouth, dropped it lighted into his pocket, and whirled Mother around several times, we knew that this was a special occasion. Before this we had never seen him even put an arm around her.

After the boys had heard their selection again, they fell asleep on the floor and were carried to their bed in the lean-to. Suddenly I remembered little Fritzlie alone in the attic, perhaps half frozen. I hurried up the slippery, frosted steps. He was crying, huddled under the feather tick, cold and afraid. I brought the boy down, heavy hulk that he was, and laid him in with his brothers. By then the last people started to talk of leaving, but the moon had clouded over, the night-dark roads winding and treacherous through the drifts. Still, those who had been to town must get home with the Christmas supplies and such presents as they could manage for their children when they awoke in the morning.

Toward dawn Father dug out "Sempach," a song of a heroic Swiss battle, in which one of Mother's ancestors fell. Hiding her pleasure at these records, Mother hurried away to the cellar under the house for two big hams, one to boil while the Canada goose roasted for the Christmas dinner. From the second ham she sliced great red rounds for the frying pan, and I mixed up a triple batch of baking-powder biscuits and set on the two-gallon coffeepot. When the sun glistened on the frosted snow, the last of the horses huddled together in our yard were on the road. By then some freighters forced to camp out by an upset wagon came whipping their teams up the icy pitch from the Niobrara River and stopped in. Father was slumped in his chair, letting his pipe fall into his beard, but he looked up and recognized the men as from a ranch accused of driving out bona fide settlers. Instead of rising to order them off the place, he merely said "How!" in the Plains greeting, and dropped back into his doze. Whenever the music stopped noticeably, he lifted his shaggy head, complaining, "Can't you keep the machine going?"

Soon my three brothers were up again and calling for their favorites as they

Come, sing
a hale Heigh-ho
For the Christmas
long ago!–
When the old log-
cabin homed us
From the night
of blinding snow,
Where the rarest
joy held reign,
And the chimney
roared amain,
With the firelight
like a beacon
Through the frosty
window-pane.

JAMES WHITCOMB RILEY

settled to plates of ham with red gravy and biscuits, Fritzlie from the top of two catalogues piled on a chair shouting too, just to be heard. None of them missed the presents that we never expected on Christmas; besides, what could be finer than the phonograph?

While Mother fed our few cattle and the hogs, I worked at the big stack of dishes with one of the freighters to wipe them. Afterward I got away to the attic and slept a little, the music from below faint through my floating of dreams. Suddenly I awoke, remembering what day this was and that young Jule and I had hoped Father might take us into the canyons up the river and help us drag home a little pine tree. Christmas had become a time for a tree, even without presents. I dressed and hurried down.

Father was asleep, and there were new people in the bedroom and in the kitchen too, talking about the wonder of the music rolling steadily from the big horn. In our Swiss way we had prepared for the usual visitors during the holidays, with family friends on Christmas and surely some of the European home-seekers Father had settled on free land, as well as passersby just dropping in to get warm and perhaps be offered a cup of coffee or chocolate or a glass of Father's homemade wine if particularly privileged. Early in the forenoon the Syrian peddler we called Solomon drew up in the yard with his high four-horse wagon. He liked to strike our place for Christmas because there might be customers around and, besides, there was no display of religion to make him uncomfortable in his Mohammedanism, Father said.

So far as I know, Solomon was the first to express what others must have thought. "Excuse it please, Mrs. Sandoz," he said, in the polite way of peddlers, "but it seem to uneducated man like me the new music is for fine palace—"

Father heard him. "Nothing's too good for my family and my neighbors," he roared out.

"The children have the frozen feet—" the man said quietly.

"Frozen feet heal! What you put in the mind lasts!"

The peddler looked down into his coffee cup and said no more.

It was true that we had always been money poor, but there was plenty of meat and game, plenty of everything that the garden, the young orchard, the field, and the open country could provide, and for all of which there was no available market. Our bread, dark and heavy, was from our hard macaroni wheat ground at a local water mill. The hams, sausage, and bacon were from our own smokehouse, the cellar full of our own potatoes, barrels of pickles and sauerkraut, and hundreds of jars of canned fruit and vegetables, crocks of jams and jellies, wild and tame, including buffalo berry, that wonderful, tart, golden-red jelly from the silvery bush that seems to retreat before close settlement much like the buffalo and the whooping crane. Most of the root crops were in a long pit outside, and the attic was strung with little sacks of herbs and poppy seed, bigger ones of dried green beans, sweet corn, chokecherries, sand cherries, and wild plums. Piled along the low sides of the attic were bushel bags of popcorn, peas, beans, lentils, and flour.

Sugar, coffee, and chocolate were practically all we bought for the table, with perhaps a barrel of blackstrap molasses for cookies and brown cake, all laid in while the fall roads were still open.

When the new batch of coffee cake was done and the fresh bread, and the goose in the oven, we took turns getting scrubbed at the heater in the lean-to, and put on our best clothes, mostly made-over from some adult's but well-sewn. Finally we spread Mother's two old-country linen cloths over the table lengthened out by boards laid on salt barrels for twenty-two places. While Mother passed the platters, I fed the phonograph with records that Mrs. Surber and her three musical daughters had selected, soothing music: Bach, Mozart, Brahms, and the "Moonlight Sonata," along with an a cappella *"Stille Nacht."* For lightness, Mrs. Surber had added "The Last Rose of Summer," to please Elsa, the young soprano soon to be a professional singer in Cleveland, while the young people wanted "Monkey Land" by Collins and Harlan.

There was stuffed Canada goose with the buffalo-berry jelly; ham boiled in a big kettle in the lean-to; watercress salad; chow-chow and pickles; dried green beans cooked with bacon, turnips, mashed potatoes and gravy, with coffee from the start to the pie, pumpkin and gooseberry. At the dishpan set on the high water bench, where I had to stand on a little box for comfort, the dishes were washed as fast as they came off the table, with a relay of wipers. There were also waiting young men and boys to draw water from the bucket well, to chop stovewood and carry it in.

There were people at the table for hours. The later uninvited guests got sausage and sauerkraut, squash, potatoes, and fresh bread, with canned plums and cookies for dessert. Still later there was a big roaster full of beans and side meat brought in by a lady homesteader, and some mince pies made with wild plums to lend tartness instead of apples, which cost money.

All this time there was the steady stream of music from the bedroom. One record set before me to put on was "Don't Get Married Any More, Ma," selected for a visiting Chicago widow looking for her fourth husband, or perhaps her fifth. Mother rolled her eyes up at this bad taste, but Father and the other old-timers laughed over their pipes.

We finally got Mother off to bed in the attic for her first nap since the records came. Downstairs the floor was cleared and the Surber girls showed their dancing-school elegance in the waltzes. There was a stream of young people later

in the afternoon, many from the skating party at the bridge. Father, red-eyed like the rest of us, limped among them, soaking up their praise, their new respect. By this time my brothers and I had given up having a tree. Then a big boy from up the river rode into the yard dragging a pine behind his horse. It was a shapely tree, and small enough to fit on a box in the window, out of the way. The youth was the son of Father's worst enemy, the man who had sworn in court that Jules Sandoz shot at him, and got our father thirty days in jail, although everybody, including the judge, knew that Jules Sandoz was a crack shot and what he fired at made no further appearances.

As the son came in with the tree, I saw Father look toward his Winchester on the wall, but he was not the man to quarrel with an enemy's children. Then he was told that the boy's father himself was in the yard. Now Jules Sandoz paled above his bearding, paled so the dancers stopped, the room silent under the suddenly foolish noise of the big-horned machine. Helpless, I watched Father jump toward the rifle. Then he turned, looked to the man's gaunt-faced young son. "Tell your old man to come in. We got some good Austrian music."

So the man came in, and sat hunched over near the door. Father said his "How!" to the man, and paid no attention when Mrs. Surber pushed me forward to make the proper thanks for the tree that we were starting to trim as usual. We played "The Blue Danube" for the man, and passed him the coffee and *küchli*. He tasted the thin flaky frycakes. "Your mother is a good cook," he told me. "A fine woman."

When he left with the skaters, all of Father's friends began to talk at once, fast, relieved. "You could have shot him down, on your own place, and not got a day in the pen for it," one said.

Old Jules nodded. "I got no use for his whole outfit, but the music is for everybody."

As I recall now, perhaps half a dozen of us, all children, worked at the tree, looping my strings of red rose hips and popcorn around it, hanging the people and animal cookies with chokecherry eyes, distributing the few Christmas-tree balls and the tinsel and candleholders that the Surbers had given us several years before. I brought out the boxes of candles I had made by dipping string in melted tallow, and we lit the candles, and with my schoolmates I ran out into the cold of the road to look. The tree showed fine through the glass.

Then I had to go to bed, although the room below me was still alive with dancing.

Holiday week was much like Christmas, the house full of visitors as the news of the fine music spread. People appeared from fifty, sixty miles away, for there was no other such collection of records in all of western Nebraska, and none with such an open door. There was something for everybody: Irishmen, Scots, Swedes, Danes, Poles, Czechs, as well as the Germans and the rest. But the greatest variety in tastes was among the Americans, from "Everybody Works But Father," "The Arkansas Traveler," and "Finkelstein at the Seashore" to love songs and the sentimental "Always in the Way"; from home and native-region pieces to the patriotic and religious. They had strong dislikes, too. One settler, a GAR veteran, burst into tears and fled from the house at the first notes of "Tenting Tonight." Perhaps it was the memories it awakened. Many Americans were as interested in classical music as any European, and it wasn't always

a matter of cultivated taste. One illiterate little woman cried with joy at Rubinstein's "Melody in F."

"I has heard me talkin' and singin' before," she said apologetically as she wiped her eyes, "but I wasn't knowin' there could be something sweet as that come from a horn."

Finally it was New Year, the day when the Sandoz relatives gathered, perhaps twenty of them immigrants brought in by the land locator, Jules. This year they were only a sort of eddy in the regular stream of outsiders. Instead of nostalgic jokes and talk of the family and the old country, there were the records to hear, and the melodies of the old violin lessons that the brothers had taken, and the guitar and mandolin of their one sister. Jules had to endure a certain amount of joking over the way he spent most of his inheritance. One brother was building a cement-block home in place of his soddy with his, and a green-

At Christmas
be merry,
and thankful
withal,
And feast thy
poor neighbors,
the great
with the small.

THOMAS TUSSER

house. The sister was to have a fine large barn instead of a new home because her husband believed that next year Halley's comet would bring the end of the world. The youngest of the brothers had put his money into wildcat oil stock and planned to become very wealthy.

They complimented Mother on the excellence of her chocolate and her golden fruitcake. Then they were gone, hot bricks at their feet, and calling back their adieus from the freezing night. It was a good thing they left early, Mother told me. She had used up the last of the chocolate, the last cake of the twenty-five-pound caddies. We had baked up two sacks of flour, forty-nine pounds each, in addition to all that went into the Christmas preparations before the phonograph came. Three-quarters of a hundred-pound bag of coffee had been roasted, ground, and used during the week, and all the winter's sausage and ham. The floor of the kitchen-living room, old and worn anyway, was much thinner for the week of dancing. New Year's night a man who had been there every day, all week, tilted back on one of the kitchen chairs and went clear through the floor.

"Oh, the fools!" Father shouted at us all. "Had to wear out my floor dancing!"

But plainly he was pleased. It was a fine story to tell for years, all the story of the phonograph records. He was particularly gratified by the praise of those who knew something about music, people like the Surbers and a visitor from a Czech community, a relative of Dvorak, the great composer. The man wrote an item for the papers, saying, "This Jules Sandoz has not only settled a good community of homeseekers, but is enriching their cultural life with the greatest music of the world."

"Probably wants to borrow money from you," Mother said. "He has come to the wrong door."

Gradually the records for special occasions and people were stored in the lean-to. For those used regularly, Father and a neighbor made a lot of flat boxes to fit under the beds, always handy, and a cabinet for the corner at the bedroom door. The best recordings were put into this cabinet, with a door that didn't stay closed. One warmish day when I was left alone with the smaller children, the water pail needed refilling. I ran out to draw a bucket from the well. It was a hard and heavy pull for a growing girl and I hated it, always afraid that I wouldn't last, and would have to let the rope slip and break the windlass.

Somehow, in my uneasy hurry, I left the door ajar. The wind blew it back and when I had the bucket started up the sixty-five-foot well, our big old sow, loose in the yard, pushed her way into the house. Horrified, I shouted to Fritzlie to get out of her way, but I had to keep pulling and puffing until the bucket was at the top. Then I ran in. Fritzlie was up on a chair, safe, but the sow had knocked down the record cabinet and scattered the cylinders over the floor. Standing among them as in corn, she was chomping down the wax records that had rolled out of the boxes, eating some, box and all. Furiously I thrashed her out with the broom, amidst squealings and shouts. Then I tried to save what I could. The sow had broken at least thirty or thirty-five of the best records and eaten all or part of twenty more. *"La Paloma"* was gone, and *"Träumerei"* and "Spring Song"; "Evening Star" too, and half of the "Moonlight Sonata."

I got the worst whipping of my life for my carelessness, but the loss of the records hurt more, and much, much longer.

VELVET SHOES

Let us walk in the white snow
  In a soundless space;
With footsteps quiet and slow,
  At a tranquil pace,
  Under veils of white lace.

I shall go shod in silk,
  And you in wool,
White as a white cow's milk,
  More beautiful
  Than the breast of a gull.

We shall walk through the still town
  In a windless peace;
We shall step upon white down,
  Upon silver fleece,
  Upon softer than these.

We shall walk in velvet shoes:
  Wherever we go
Silence will fall like dews
  On white silence below.
  We shall walk in the snow.

Elinor Wylie

127

THE FIR TREE

by Hans Christian Andersen

O<small>UT IN THE FOREST</small> stood a pretty little Fir Tree. It had a good place; it could have sunlight, air there was in plenty, and all around grew many larger comrades—pines as well as firs. But the little Fir Tree wished ardently to become greater. It did not care for the warm sun and the fresh air; it took no notice of the peasant children, who went about talking together, when they had come out to look for strawberries and raspberries. Often they came with a whole potful, or had strung berries on a straw; then they would sit down by the little Fir Tree and say, "How pretty and small that one is!" and the Fir Tree did not like to hear that at all.

Next year he had grown a great joint, and the following year he was longer still, for in fir trees one can always tell by the number of rings they have how many years they have been growing.

"Oh, if I were only as great a tree as the others!" sighed the little Fir. "Then I would spread my branches far around and look out from my crown into the wide world. The birds would then build nests in my boughs, and when the wind blew I could nod just as grandly as the others yonder."

He took no pleasure in the sunshine, in the birds, and in the red clouds that went sailing over him morning and evening.

When it was winter, the snow lay all around, white and sparkling, a hare would often come jumping along, and spring right over the little Fir Tree. Oh! This made him so angry. But two winters went by, and when the third came the little Tree had grown so tall that the hare was obliged to run around it.

Oh! To grow, to grow, and become old; that's the only fine thing in the world, thought the Tree.

In the autumn woodcutters always came and felled a few of the largest trees; that was done this year, too, and the little Fir Tree, that was now quite well grown, shuddered with fear, for the great stately trees fell to the ground with a crash, and their branches were cut off, so that the trees looked quite naked, long, and slender—they could hardly be recognized. But then they were laid upon wagons, and horses dragged them away out of the wood. Where were they going? What destiny awaited them?

In the spring when the Swallows and the Stork came, the Tree asked them, "Do you know where they were taken? Did you not meet them?"

The Swallows knew nothing about it, but the Stork looked thoughtful, nodded his head, and said, "Yes, I think so. I met many new ships when I flew out of Egypt; on the ships were stately masts; I fancy these were the trees. They smelled like fir. I can assure you they're stately—very stately."

"Oh, that I were only big enough to go over the sea! What kind of thing is this sea, and how does it look?"

"It would take too long to explain all that," said the Stork, and he went away.

"Rejoice in thy youth," said the Sunbeams; "rejoice in thy fresh growth, and in the young life that is within thee."

And the Wind kissed the Tree, and the Dew wept tears upon it; but the Fir Tree did not understand about that.

When Christmastime approached, quite young trees were felled, sometimes trees which were neither so old nor so large as this Fir Tree, that never rested, but always wanted to go away. These young trees, which were always the most beautiful, kept all their branches; they were put upon wagons, and horses dragged them away out of the wood.

"Where are they all going?" asked the Fir Tree. "They are not greater than I—indeed, one of them was much smaller. Why do they keep all their branches? Whither are they taken?"

"We know that! We know that!" chirped the Sparrows. "Yonder in the town we looked in at the windows. We know where they go. Oh! They are dressed up in the greatest pomp and splendor that can be imagined. We have looked in at the windows, and have perceived that they are planted in the middle of a warm room, and adorned with the most beautiful things—gilt apples, honey cakes, playthings, and many hundreds of candles."

"And then?" asked the Fir Tree, and trembled through all its branches. "And then? What happens then?"

"Why, we have not seen anything more. But it is incomparable."

"Perhaps I may be destined to tread this glorious path one day!" cried the Fir Tree rejoicingly. "That is even better than traveling across the sea. How painfully I long for it! If it were only Christmas now! Now I am great and

O Christmas tree, O Christmas tree, With happiness we greet you.

129

grown up, like the rest who were led away last year. Oh, if I were only on the carriage! If I were only in the warm room, among all the pomp and splendor! And then? Yes, then something even better will come, something far more charming, or else why should they adorn me so? There must be something grander, something greater still to come; but what? Oh! I'm suffering. I'm longing! I don't know myself what is the matter with me!"

"Rejoice in us," said the Air and Sunshine. "Rejoice in thy fresh youth here in the woodland."

But the Fir Tree did not rejoice at all, but it grew and grew; winter and

summer it stood there, green, dark green. The people who saw it said, "That's a handsome tree!" and at Christmastime it was felled before any of the others. The axe cut deep into its marrow, and the Tree fell to the ground with a sigh; it felt a pain, a sensation of faintness, and could not think at all of happiness, for it was sad at parting from its home, from the place where it had grown up; it knew that it should never again see the dear old companions, the little bushes and flowers all around—perhaps not even the birds. The parting was not at all agreeable.

The Tree only came to itself when it was unloaded in a yard, with other trees, and heard a man say, "This one is famous; we want only this one!"

Now two servants came in gay liveries and carried the Fir Tree into a large, beautiful salon. All around the walls hung pictures, and by the great stove stood large Chinese vases with lions on the covers; there were rocking chairs, silken sofas, great tables covered with picture books, and toys worth a hundred times a hundred dollars, at least the children said so. And the Fir Tree was put into a great tub filled with sand; but no one could see that it was a tub, for it was hung round with green cloth, and stood on a large, many-colored carpet. Oh, how the Tree trembled! What was to happen now? The servants, and the young ladies also, decked it out. On one branch they hung little nets, cut out of colored paper; every net was filled with sweetmeats; golden apples and wal-nuts hung down, as if they grew there, and more than a hundred little candles, red, white, and blue, were fastened to the different boughs. Dolls that looked exactly like real people—the Tree had never seen such before—swung among the foliage, and high on the summit of the Tree was fixed a tinsel star. It was splendid, particularly splendid.

"This evening," said all, "this evening it will shine."

Oh, thought the Tree, that it were evening already! Oh, that the lights may soon be lit up! When may that be done? Will the Sparrows fly against the panes? Shall I grow fast here, and stand adorned in summer and winter?

Yes, he did not guess badly. But he had a complete backache from mere long-ing, and backache is just as bad for a tree as a headache for a person.

At last the candles were lighted. What a brilliance, what a splendor! The Tree trembled so in all its branches that one of the candles set fire to a green twig, and it was scorched.

"Heaven preserve us!" cried the young ladies; and they hastily put the fire out.

Now the Tree might not even tremble. Oh, that was terrible! It was so afraid of setting fire to some of its ornaments, and it was quite bewildered with all the brilliance. And now the folding doors were thrown wide open, and a number of children rushed in as if they would have overturned the whole Tree; the older people followed more deliberately. The little ones stood quite silent, but only for a minute; then they shouted till the room rang; they danced glee-fully round the Tree, and one present after another was plucked from it.

What are they about? thought the Tree. What's going to be done?

And the candles burned down to the twigs, and as they burned down they were extinguished, and then the children received permission to plunder the Tree. Oh! They rushed in upon it, so that every branch cracked again: if it had not been fastened by the top and by the golden star to the ceiling, it would have fallen down.

The children danced about with their pretty toys. No one looked at the Tree except one old man, who came up and peeped among the branches, but only to see if a fig or an apple had not been forgotten.

"A story! A story!" shouted the children; and they drew a little fat man

When
decked with
candles
once a year,
You fill
our hearts
with Yuletide
cheer.
O Christmas
tree,
O Christmas
tree,
With happiness
we
greet you.

131

toward the Tree; and he sat down just beneath it—"for then we shall be in the greenwood," said he, "and the Tree may have the advantage of listening to my tale. But I can only tell one. Will you hear the story of Ivede-Avede, or of Klumpey-Dumpey, who fell downstairs, and still was raised up to honor and married the princess?"

"Ivede-Avede!" cried some. "Klumpey-Dumpey!" cried others, and there was a great crying and shouting. Only the Fir Tree was quite silent, and thought, Shall I not be in it? Shall I have nothing to do in it? But he had been in the evening's amusement, and had done what was required of him.

And the fat man told about Klumpey-Dumpey, who fell downstairs and yet was raised to honor and married a princess. And the children clapped their hands and cried, "Tell another! Tell another!" and they wanted to hear about Ivede-Avede; but they only got the story of Klumpey-Dumpey. The Fir Tree stood quite silent and thoughtful; never had the birds in the wood told such a story as that. Klumpey-Dumpey fell downstairs, and yet came to honor and married a princess!

Yes, so it happens in the world! thought the Fir Tree, and believed it must be true, because that was such a nice man who told it.

Well, who can know? Perhaps I shall fall downstairs, too, and marry a princess! And it looked forward with pleasure to being adorned again, the next evening, with candles and toys, gold and fruit. Tomorrow I shall not tremble, it thought. I shall rejoice in all my splendor. Tomorrow I shall hear the story of Klumpey-Dumpey again, and perhaps that of Ivede-Avede, too.

And the Tree stood all night, quiet and thoughtful.

In the morning the servants and the chambermaid came in.

Now my splendor will begin afresh, thought the Tree. But they dragged him out of the room and upstairs to the garret, and here they put him in a dark corner where no daylight shone. What's the meaning of this? thought the Tree. What am I to do here? What is to happen?

And he leaned against the wall, and thought, and thought. And he had time enough, for days and nights went by, and nobody came up; and when at length someone came, it was only to put some great boxes in a corner. Now the Tree stood quite hidden away, and the supposition is that it was quite forgotten.

Now it's winter outside, thought the Tree. The earth is hard and covered with snow, and people cannot plant me; therefore I suppose I'm to be sheltered here until spring comes. How considerate that is! How good people are! If it were only not so dark here, and so terribly solitary! Not even a little hare? That was pretty out there in the wood, when the snow lay thick and the hare sprang past; yes, even when he jumped over me; but then I did not like it. It is terribly lonely up here!

"Piep! Piep!" said a little Mouse, and crept forward, and then came another little one. They smelled at the Fir Tree and then slipped among the branches.

"It's horribly cold," said the two little Mice, "or else it would be comfortable here. Don't you think so, old Fir Tree?"

"I'm not old at all," said the Fir Tree. "There are many much older than I."

"Where do you come from?" asked the Mice. "And what do you know?" They were dreadfully inquisitive. "Tell us about the most beautiful spot on earth. Have you been there? Have you been in the storeroom, where cheeses lie on the shelves, and hams hang from the ceiling, where one dances on tallow candles, and goes in thin and comes out fat?"

"I don't know that," replied the Tree; "but I know the wood, where the sun shines and the birds sing."

And then it told all about its youth.

And the little Mice had never heard anything of the kind; and they listened and said, "What a number of things you have seen! How happy you must have been!"

"I?" replied the Fir Tree; and it thought about what it had told. "Yes, those were really quite happy times." But then he told of the Christmas Eve, when he had been hung with sweatmeats and candles.

"Oh!" said the little Mice. "How happy you have been, you old Fir Tree."

"I'm not old at all," said the Tree. "I only came out of the wood this winter. I'm only rather backward in my growth."

O Christmas tree, O Christmas tree, How lovely are your branches.

133

In summer

sun,

in winter

snow,

A dress of

green

you always

show.

O Christmas

tree,

O Christmas

tree,

How lovely

are

your branches.

OLD CAROL

"What splendid stories you can tell!" said the little Mice.

And the next night they came with four other little Mice, to hear what the Tree had to relate; and the more it said, the more clearly did it remember everything, and thought, Those were quite merry days! But they may come again. Klumpey-Dumpey fell downstairs, and yet he married a princess. Perhaps I shall marry a princess, too! And the Fir Tree thought of a pretty little Birch Tree that grew out in the forest; for the Fir Tree, that Birch was a real princess.

"Who's Klumpey-Dumpey?" asked the little Mice.

And then the Fir Tree told the whole story. It could remember every single word; and the little Mice were ready to leap to the very top of the Tree with pleasure. Next night a great many more Mice came, and on Sunday two Rats even appeared; but these thought the story was not pretty, and the little Mice were sorry for that, for now they also did not like it so much as before.

"Do you know only one story?" asked the Rats.

"Only that one," replied the Tree. "I heard that on the happiest evening of my life; I did not think then how happy I was."

"That's a very miserable story. Don't you know any about bacon and tallow candles—a storeroom story?"

"No," said the Tree.

"Then we'd rather not hear you," said the Rats. And they went back to their own people.

The little Mice at last stayed away also; and then the Tree sighed and said, "It was very nice when they sat round me, the merry little Mice, and listened when I spoke to them. Now that's past, too. But I shall remember to be pleased when they take me out."

But when did that happen? Why, it was one morning that people came and rummaged in the garret; the boxes were put away, and the Tree brought out; they certainly threw him rather roughly on the floor, but a servant dragged him away at once to the stairs, where the daylight shone.

Now life is beginning again! thought the Tree.

It felt the fresh air and the first sunbeam, and now it was out in the court-yard. Everything passed so quickly that the Tree quite forgot to look at itself, there was so much to look at all round. The courtyard was close to a garden, and here everything was blooming; the roses hung fresh over the paling, the linden trees were in blossom, and the Swallows cried, "Quinze-wit! Quinze-wit! My husband's come!" But it was not the Fir Tree that they meant.

"Now I shall live!" said the Tree rejoicingly, and spread its branches far out; but, alas! They were all withered and yellow; and it lay in the corner among nettles and weeds. The tinsel star, still upon it, shone in the bright sunshine.

In the courtyard a couple of the merry children were playing who had danced round the tree at Christmastime and had rejoiced over it. One of the youngest ran up and tore off the golden star.

"Look what is sticking to the ugly old Fir Tree!" said the child, and he trod upon the branches till they cracked again under his boots.

And the Tree looked at all the blooming flowers and the splendor of the garden, and then looked at itself, and wished it had remained in the dark corner of the garret; it thought of its fresh youth in the wood, of the merry Christmas Eve, and of the little Mice which had listened so pleasantly to the story of Klumpey-Dumpey.

"Past! Past!" said the old Tree. "Had I but rejoiced when I could have done so! Past! Past!"

And the servant came and chopped the Tree into little pieces; a whole bundle lay there; it blazed brightly under the great brewing copper, and it sighed deeply, and each sigh was like a little shot; and the children who were at play there ran up and seated themselves at the fire, looked into it, and cried, "Puff! Puff!" But at each explosion, which was a deep sigh, the Tree thought of a summer day in the woods, or of a winter night there, when the stars beamed; he thought of Christmas Eve and of Klumpey-Dumpey, the only story he had ever heard or knew how to tell; and then the Tree was burned.

The boys played in the garden, and the youngest had on his breast a golden star, which the Tree had worn on its happiest evening. Now that was past, and the Tree's life was past, and the story is past, too: past! past! And that's the way with all stories.

LANDING OF THE PILGRIMS AT PLYMOUTH DEC.1620.

Munday, the 25 Day, we went on shore, some to fell tymber, some to saw, some to riue, and some to carry, so that no man rested all that day, but towards night, some, as they were at worke, heard a noyse of some Indians, which caused vs all to goe to our Muskets, but we heard no further; so we came aboord againe, and left some twentie to keepe the court of gard; that night we had a sore storme of winde and raine· Munday the 25 being Christmas day, we began to drinke water aboord, but at night, the Master caused vs to have some Beere, and so on board we had diverse times now and then some Beere, but on shore none at all·

One y day called Christmas·day, y Gov'r caled them out to worke (as was used), but y most of this new company excused themselves, and said it went against their consciences to worke on y day· So y Gov'r tould them that if they made it a mater of conscience, he would spare them till they were better informed· So he led away y rest, and left them: but when they came home at noone from their worke, he found them in y streete at play, openly; some pitching y barr, and some at stoole ball, and such like sports· So he went to them and tooke away their implements, and told them it was against his conscience that they should play, and others worke· If they made y keeping of it matter of devotion, let them kepe their houses, but there should be no gameing or revelling in y streets· Since which time nothing hath been attempted that way, at least, openly·

Artist's rendering of extracts from *Mourt's Relation* or *Journal of the Plantation at Plymouth*, attributed to Governor William Bradford and Edward Winslow (above), and from *History of Plymouth Plantation* by William Bradford (below).

TO SPRINGVALE FOR CHRISTMAS
by Zona Gale

WHEN President Arthur Tilton of Briarcliff College, who usually used a two-cent stamp, said, "Get me Chicago, please," his secretary was impressed, looked for vast educational problems to be in the making, and heard instead:

"Ed? Well, Ed, you and Rick and Grace and I are going out to Springvale for Christmas. . . . Yes, well, I've got a family too, you recall. But Mother was seventy last fall and— Do you realize that it's eleven years since we all spent Christmas with her? Grace has been every year. She's going this year. And so are we! And take her the best Christmas she ever had, too. Ed, Mother was *seventy* last fall. . . ."

At dinner, he asked his wife what would be a suitable gift, a very special gift, for a woman of seventy. And she said: "Oh, your mother. Well, dear, I should think the material for a good wool dress would be right. I'll select it for you, if you like. . . ." He said that he would see, and he did not reopen the subject.

In town on December twenty-fourth he timed his arrival to allow him an hour in a shop. There he bought a silver-gray silk of a fineness and a lightness which pleased him and at a price which made him comfortably guilty. And at the shop, Ed, who was Edward McKillop Tilton, head of a law firm, picked him up.

"Where's your present?" Arthur demanded.

Edward drew a case from his pocket and showed him a tiny gold wristwatch of decent manufacture and explained: "I expect you'll think I'm a fool, but you know that Mother has told time for fifty years by the kitchen clock, or else the shield of the black marble parlor angel who never goes—you get the idea?—and so I bought her this."

At the station was Grace, and the boy who bore her bag bore also a parcel of great dimensions.

"Mother already has a feather bed," Arthur reminded her.

"They won't let you take an automobile into the coach," Edward warned her.

"It's a rug for the parlor," Grace told them. "You know it *is* a parlor—one of the few left in the Mississippi Valley. And Mother has had that ingrain down since before we left home. . . ."

Grace's eyes were misted. Why would women always do that? This was no occasion for sentiment. This was a merry Christmas.

"Very nice. And Ricky'd better look sharp," said Edward dryly.

Ricky never did look sharp. About trains he was conspicuously ignorant. He had no occupation. Some said that he "wrote," but no one had ever seen anything that he had written. He lived in town—no one knew how—never accepted a cent from his brothers and was beloved of everyone, most of all of his mother.

"Ricky won't bring anything, of course," they said.

But when the train pulled out without him, observably, a porter came staggering through the cars carrying two great suitcases and following a perturbed man of forty-something who said, "Oh, here you are!" as if it were they who were missing, and squeezed himself and his suitcases among brothers and sister and rug. "I had only a minute to spare," he said regretfully. "If I'd had two, I could have snatched some flowers. I flung 'em my card and told 'em to send 'em."

"Why are you taking so many lugs?" they wanted to know.

Ricky focused on the suitcases. "Just necessities," he said. "Just the presents. I didn't have room to get in anything else."

"Presents! What?"

"Well," said Ricky, "I'm taking books. I know Mother doesn't care much for books, but the bookstore's the only place I can get trusted."

They turned over his books: fiction, travels, biography, a new illustrated edition of the Bible—they were willing to admire his selection. And Grace said confusedly but appreciatively: "You know, the parlor bookcase has never had a thing in it excepting a green curtain *over* it!"

And they were all borne forward, well pleased.

Springvale has eight hundred inhabitants. As they drove through the principal street at six o'clock on that evening of December twenty-fourth, all that they expected to see abroad was the popcorn wagon and a cat or two. Instead they counted seven automobiles and estimated thirty souls, and no one paid the slightest attention to them as strangers. Springvale was becoming metropolitan. There was a new church on one corner and a store building bore the sign Public Library. Even the little hotel had a rubber plant in the window and a strip of cretonne overhead.

The three men believed themselves to be a surprise. But, mindful of the panic to be occasioned by four appetites precipitated into a Springvale ménage, Grace had told. Therefore the parlor was lighted and heated, there was in the air of the passage an odor of brown gravy which, no butler's pantry ever having inhibited, seemed a permanent savory. By the happiest chance, Mrs. Tilton had not heard their arrival nor—the parlor angel being in her customary eclipse and the kitchen grandfather's clock wrong—had she begun to look for them. They slipped in, they followed Grace down the hall, they entered upon her in her gray gingham apron worn over her best blue serge, and they saw her first in profile, frosting a lemon pie. With some assistance from her, they all took her in their arms at once.

"Aren't you surprised?" cried Edward in amazement.

"I haven't got over being surprised," she said placidly, "since I first heard you were coming!"

She gazed at them tenderly, with flour on her chin, and then said: "There's something you won't like. We're going to have the family dinner tonight."

Their clamor that they would entirely like that did not change her look.

"Our church couldn't pay the minister this winter," she said, "on account of the new church building. So the minister and his wife are boarding around with the congregation. Tomorrow's their day to come here for a week. It's a hard life and I didn't have the heart to change 'em."

Her family covered their regret as best they could and entered upon her little feast. At the head of her table, with her four "children" about her, and Father's armchair left vacant, they perceived that she was not quite the figure they had been thinking her. In this interval they had grown to think of her as a pathetic figure. Not because their father had died, not because she insisted on Springvale as a residence, not because of her eyes. Just pathetic. Mothers of grown children, they might have given themselves the suggestion, were always pathetic. But here was Mother, a definite person, with poise and with ideas, who might be proud of her offspring, but who, in her heart, never forgot that they *were* her offspring and that she was the parent stock.

"I wouldn't eat two pieces of that pie," she said to President Tilton; "it's pretty rich." And he answered humbly: "Very well, Mother." And she took with composure Ricky's light chant:

> *"Now, you must remember, wherever you are,*
> *That you are the jam, but your mother's the jar."*

"Certainly, my children," she said. "And I'm about to tell you when you may have your Christmas presents. Not tonight. Christmas Eve is no proper time for presents. It's stealing a day outright! And you miss the fun of looking forward all night long. The only proper time for the presents is after breakfast on Christmas morning, *after* the dishes are washed. The minister and his wife may get here any time from nine on. That means we've got to get to bed early!"

President Arthur Tilton lay in his bed looking at the muslin curtain on which the streetlamp threw the shadow of a bare elm which he remembered. He thought: She's a pioneer spirit. She's the kind who used to go ahead anyway, even if they had missed the emigrant party, and who used to cross the plains

Everywhere, everywhere, Christmas tonight! Christmas in lands of the fir-tree and pine, Christmas in lands of the palm-tree and vine, Christmas where snow peaks stand solemn and white.

Christmas where
cornfields stand
sunny and bright. . . .
Christmas where
peace, like a dove
in its flight
Broods o'er
brave men in the
thick of the fight;
Everywhere,
everywhere,
Christmas tonight.

PHILLIPS BROOKS

alone. She's the backbone of the world. I wish I could megaphone that to the students at Briarcliff who think their mothers "try to boss" them!

"Don't leave your windows open too far," he heard from the hall. "The wind's changed."

In the light of a snowy morning the home parlor showed the cluttered commonplace of a room whose furniture and ornaments were not believed to be beautiful and most of them known not to be useful. Yet when—after the dishes were washed—these five came to the leather chair which bore the gifts, the moment was intensely satisfactory. This in spite of the sense of haste with which the parcels were attacked—lest the minister and his wife arrive in their midst.

"That's one reason," Mrs. Tilton said, "why I want to leave part of my Christmas for you until I take you to the train tonight. Do you care?"

"I'll leave a present I know about until then too," said Ricky. "May I?"

"Come on now, though," said President Arthur Tilton. "I want to see Mother get her dolls."

It was well that they were not of an age to look for exclamations of delight from Mother. To every gift her reaction was one of startled rebuke.

"Grace! How could you? All that money! Oh, it's beautiful! But the old one would have done me all my life. . . . Why, Edward! You extravagant boy! I never had a watch in my life. You ought not to have gone to all that expense. Arthur Tilton! A silk dress! What a firm piece of goods! I don't know what to say to you—you're all too good to me!"

At Ricky's books she stared and said: "My dear boy, you've been very reckless. Here are more books than I can ever read—now. Why, that's almost more than they've got to start the new library with. And you spent all that money on me!"

It dampened their complacence, but they understood her concealed delight and they forgave her an honest regret of their modest prodigality. For, when they opened her gifts for them, they felt the same reluctance to take the hours and hours of patient knitting for which these stood.

"Hush, and hurry," was her comment, "or the minister'll get us!"

The minister and his wife, however, were late. The second side of the turkey was ready and the mince pie hot when, toward noon, they came to the door— a faint little woman and a thin man with beautiful, exhausted eyes. They were both in some light glow of excitement and disregarded Mrs. Tilton's efforts to take their coats.

"No," said the minister's wife. "No. We do beg your pardon. But we find we have to go into the country this morning."

"It is absolutely necessary that we go into the country," said the minister earnestly. "This morning," he added impressively.

"Into the country! You're going to be here for dinner."

They were firm. They had to go into the country. They shook hands almost tenderly with these four guests. "We just heard about you in the post office," they said. "Merry Christmas—oh, merry Christmas! We'll be back about dark."

They left their two shabby suitcases on the hall floor and went away.

"All the clothes they've got between them would hardly fill these up," said Mrs. Tilton mournfully. "Why on earth do you suppose they'd turn their back on a dinner that smells so good and go off into the country at noon on Christmas Day? They wouldn't do that for another invitation. Likely somebody's sick," she ended, her puzzled look denying her tone of finality.

"Well, thank the Lord for the call to the country," said Ricky shamelessly. "It saved our day."

They had their Christmas dinner; they had their afternoon—safe and happy and uninterrupted. Five commonplace-looking folk in a commonplace-looking house, but the eye of love knew that this was not all. In the wide sea of their routine they had found and taken for their own this island day, unforgettable.

"I thought it was going to be a gay day," said Ricky at its close, "but it hasn't. It's been heavenly! Mother, shall we give them the rest of their presents now, you and I?"

"Not yet," she told them. "Ricky, I want to whisper to you."

She looked so guilty that they all laughed at her. Ricky was laughing when he came back from that brief privacy. He was still laughing mysteriously when his mother turned from a telephone call.

"What do you think?" she cried. "That was the woman that brought me my turkey. She knew the minister and his wife were to be with me today. She wants to know why they've been eating a lunch in a cutter out that way. Do you suppose . . ."

They all looked at one another doubtfully, then in abrupt conviction. "They went because they wanted us to have the day to ourselves!"

"Arthur," said Mrs. Tilton with immense determination, "let me whisper to you, too." And from that moment's privacy he also returned smiling, but a bit ruefully.

"Mother ought to be the president of a university," he said.

"Mother ought to be the head of a law firm," said Edward.

"Mother ought to write a book about herself," said Ricky.

"Mother's Mother," said Grace, "and that's enough. But you're all so mysterious, except me."

"Grace," said Mrs. Tilton, "you remind me that I want to whisper to you."

Their train left in the late afternoon. Through the white streets they walked to the station, the somber little woman, the buoyant, capable daughter, the

Candle, candle,
Burning bright
On our window
sill tonight,
Like the shining
Christmas star
Guiding shepherds
From afar,
Lead some weary
Traveler here,
That he may share
Our Christmas cheer.

ISABEL SHAW

three big sons. She drew them to seclusion down by the baggage room and gave them four envelopes.

"Here's the rest of my Christmas for you," she said. "I'd rather you'd open it on the train. Now, Ricky, what's yours?"

She was firm to their protests. The train was whistling when Ricky owned up that the rest of his Christmas present for his mother was a brand-new daughter, to be acquired as soon as his new book was off the press. "We're going to marry on the advance royalty," he said importantly, "and live on . . ." The rest was lost in the roar of the express.

"Edward!" shouted Mrs. Tilton. "Come here. I want to whisper. . . ."

She was obliged to shout it, whatever it was. But Edward heard, and nodded, and kissed her. There was time for her to slip something in Ricky's pocket and for the other good-bys, and then the train drew out. From the other platform they saw her brave, calm face against the background of the little town. A mother of "grown children" pathetic? She seemed to them at that moment the one supremely triumphant figure in life.

They opened their envelopes soberly and sat soberly over the contents. The note, scribbled to Grace, explained: Mother wanted to divide up now what she had had for them in her will. She would keep one house and live on the rent from the other one, and "here's all the rest." They laughed at her postscript:

"Don't argue. I ought to give the most—I'm the mother."

"And look at her," said Edward solemnly. "As soon as she heard about Ricky, there at the station, she whispered to me that she wanted to send Ricky's sweetheart the watch I'd just given her. Took it off her wrist then and there."

"That must be what she slipped in my pocket," said Ricky.

It was.

"She asked me," he said, "if I minded if she gave those books to the new Springvale Public Library."

"She asked me," said Grace, "if I cared if she gave the new rug to the new church that can't pay its minister."

President Arthur Tilton shouted with laughter. "When we heard where the minister and his wife ate their Christmas dinner," he said, "she whispered to ask me whether she might give the silk dress to her when they get back tonight."

All this they knew by the time the train reached the crossing where they could look back on Springvale. On the slope of the hill lay the little cemetery, and Ricky said, "And she told me that if my flowers got there before dark, she'd take them up to the cemetery for Christmas for Father. By night she won't have even a flower left to tell her we've been there."

"Not even the second side of the turkey," said Grace, "and yet I think . . ."

"So do I," her brothers said.

CHRISTMAS DAY AT SEA
by Joseph Conrad

IN ALL MY twenty years of wandering over the restless waters of the globe I can only remember one Christmas Day celebrated by a present given and received. It was, in my view, a proper live-sea transaction, no offering of Dead Sea fruit; and in its unexpectedness perhaps worth recording. Let me tell you first that it happened in the year 1879, long before there was any thought of wireless messages, and when an inspired person trying to prophesy broadcasting would have been regarded as a particularly offensive nuisance and probably sent to a rest-cure home. We used to call them madhouses then, in our rude, caveman way.

The daybreak of Christmas Day in the year 1879 was fine. The sun began to shine sometime about four o'clock over the somber expanse of the Southern Ocean in latitude 51; and shortly afterwards a sail was sighted ahead. The wind was light, but a heavy swell was running. Presently I wished a "Merry Christmas" to my captain. He looked sleepy, but amiable. I reported the distant sail to him and ventured the opinion that there was something wrong with her. He said, "Wrong?" in an incredulous tone. I pointed out that she had all her upper sails furled and that she was brought to the wind, which, in that region of the world, could not be accounted for on any other theory. He took the glasses from me, directed them towards her stripped masts waggling to and fro ridiculously in that heaving and austere wilderness of countless water hills, and returned them to me without a word. He only yawned. This marked display of callousness gave me a shock. In those days I was generally inexperienced and still a comparative stranger in that particular region of the world of waters.

The captain, as is a captain's way, disappeared from the deck; and after a time our carpenter came up the poop ladder carrying an empty small wooden keg, of the sort in which certain ship's provisions are packed. I said, surprised, "What do you mean by lugging this thing up here, Chips?"

"Captain's orders, sir," he explained shortly.

I did not like to question him further, and so we only exchanged Christmas greetings and he went away. The next person to speak to me was the steward. He came running up the companion stairs. "Have you any old newspapers in your room, sir?"

We had left Sydney, N.S.W., eighteen days before. There were several old Sydney *Heralds*, *Telegraphs*, *Bulletins* in my cabin, besides a few home papers received by the last mail. "Why do you ask, steward?" I inquired naturally.

"The captain would like to have them," he said.

And even then I did not understand the inwardness of these eccentricities. I was only lost in astonishment at them. It was eight o'clock before we had closed with that ship, which, under her short canvas and heading nowhere in particular, seemed to be loafing aimlessly on the very threshold of the gloomy home of storms. But long before that hour I learned from the number of boats she carried that this nonchalant ship was a whaler. She had hoisted the Stars and Stripes at her peak, and her signal flags had already told us that her name was *Alaska*—two years out from New York—east from Honolulu—two hundred and fifteen days on the cruising ground.

We passed, sailing slowly, within a hundred yards of her; and just as our steward started ringing the breakfast bell, the captain and I held aloft, in good view of the figures watching us over her stern, the keg, properly headed up and containing, besides an enormous bundle of newspapers, two boxes of figs in honor of the day. We flung it far out over the rail. Instantly our ship, sliding down the slope of a high swell, left it far behind in our wake. On board the *Alaska* a man in a fur cap flourished an arm; another, a much bewhiskered person, ran forward suddenly. I never saw anything so ready and so smart as the way that whaler, rolling desperately all the time, lowered one of her boats. The Southern Ocean went on tossing the two ships like a juggler his gilt balls, and the microscopic white speck of the boat seemed to come into the game instantly, as if shot out from a catapult on the enormous and lonely stage. That Yankee whaler lost not a moment in picking up her Christmas present from the English wool clipper.

Before we had increased the distance very much she dipped her ensign in thanks and asked to be reported "All well, with a catch of three fish." I suppose it paid them for two hundred and fifteen days of risk and toil, away from the sounds and sights of the inhabited world, like outcasts devoted, beyond the confines of mankind's life, to some enchanted and lonely penance.

DECEMBER

I like days
with a snow-white collar,
and nights when the moon
is a silver dollar,

hills are filled
h eiderdown stuffing
your breath makes smoke
an engine puffing.

e days
en feathers are snowing,
all the eaves
e petticoats showing,
the air is cold,
the wires are humming,
you feel all warm . . .

with Christmas coming!

Aileen Fisher

The Holly and the Ivy,
  When they are both full grown
Of all the trees are in the wood,
  The Holly bears the crown.

O the rising of the sun,
  And the running of the deer,
The playing of the merry organ,
  Sweet singing in the choir.

The Holly bears a blossom
  As white as any flower;
And Mary bore sweet Jesus Christ
  To be our sweet Saviour.

The Holly bears a berry
  As red as any blood;
And Mary bore sweet Jesus Christ
  To do poor sinners good.

The Holly bears a prickle
  As sharp as any thorn;
And Mary bore sweet Jesus Christ
  On Christmas in the morn.

The Holly bears a bark
  As bitter as any gall;
And Mary bore sweet Jesus Christ
  For to redeem us all.

The Holly and the Ivy
  Now both are full well grown:
Of all the trees are in the wood
  The Holly bears the crown.

Fifteenth-century English carol

A CHRISTMAS CAROL

by Charles Dickens

MARLEY'S GHOST

Marley was dead, to begin with. There is no doubt whatever about that. The register of his burial was signed by the clergyman, the clerk, the undertaker, and the chief mourner. Scrooge signed it. And Scrooge's name was good upon 'Change for anything he chose to put his hand to. Old Marley was as dead as a doornail.

Mind! I don't mean to say that I know what is particularly dead about a door-nail. I'd be inclined, myself, to regard a coffin nail as the deadest piece of iron-mongery in the trade. But the wisdom of our ancestors is in the simile. You will therefore permit me to repeat, emphatically, that Marley was as dead as a door-nail. This must be distinctly understood, or nothing wonderful can come of the story I am going to relate.

Scrooge knew he was dead? Of course he did. Scrooge and he were partners for I don't know how many years. Scrooge was his sole executor, his sole legatee, his sole friend and sole mourner. And even Scrooge was not so dread-fully cut up by the sad event but that he was an excellent man of business on the very day of the funeral, and solemnized it with an undoubted bargain.

Scrooge never painted out old Marley's name. There it stood, years after-wards, above the warehouse door: Scrooge and Marley. Sometimes people new to the business called Scrooge Scrooge, and sometimes Marley, but he answered to both names. It was all the same to him.

Oh! but he was a tightfisted hand at the grindstone, Scrooge! a squeezing, wrenching, grasping, scraping, covetous old sinner! Hard and sharp as flint, from which no steel had ever struck out generous fire; secret, and self-contained, and solitary as an oyster. The cold within him froze his old features, nipped his pointed nose, shriveled his cheek, stiffened his gait; made his eyes red, his thin lips blue; and spoke out in his grating voice. A frosty rime was on his head, and on his eyebrows, and his wiry chin. He carried his own low temperature with him; he iced his office in the dog days, and didn't thaw it one degree at Christmas.

151

Let every
pudding burst
with plums,
And every tree
bear dolls
and drums,
In the week
when Christmas
comes.

Nobody ever stopped him in the street to say, with gladsome looks, "My dear Scrooge, how are you?" No beggars implored him to bestow a trifle, no children asked him what it was o'clock, no man or woman ever inquired the way to such and such a place, of Scrooge. Even the blind men's dogs appeared to know him; and, when they saw him coming, would tug their owners into doorways, and then wag their tails as though they said, "No eye at all is better than an evil eye, dark master!"

But what did Scrooge care? He liked to edge his way along the crowded paths of life, warning all human sympathy to keep its distance.

Once upon a time—of all the good days in the year, on Christmas Eve—old Scrooge sat busy in his countinghouse. It was bleak, biting, foggy weather. He could hear the people in the court outside go wheezing up and down, beating their hands upon their breasts, and stamping their feet to warm them. The City clocks had only just gone three, but it was dark already. The fog came pouring in at every chink and keyhole, and was so dense without, that, although the court was of the narrowest, the houses opposite were mere phantoms.

Scrooge's door was open, that he might keep his eye upon his clerk, who in a dismal little cell, a sort of tank, was copying letters. Scrooge had a very small fire, but the clerk's fire was so much smaller that it looked like one coal. He couldn't replenish it, for Scrooge kept the coalbox in his own room; so he wore his white comforter, and tried to warm himself at the candle; in which effort, not being a man of strong imagination, he failed.

"A merry Christmas, uncle! God save you!" cried a cheerful voice. It was the voice of Scrooge's nephew, who came upon him so quickly that this was the first intimation he had of his approach.

"Bah!" said Scrooge. "Humbug!"

He had so heated himself with rapid walking in the fog and frost, this nephew of Scrooge's, that he was all in a glow; his face was ruddy and handsome; his eyes sparkled.

"Christmas a humbug, uncle!" said Scrooge's nephew. "You don't mean that, I am sure?"

"I do," said Scrooge. "Merry Christmas! What right have you to be merry? You're poor enough."

"Come, then," returned the nephew gaily. "What right have you to be dismal? You're rich enough."

Scrooge, having no better answer ready, said, "Bah!" again; and followed it up with "Humbug!"

"Don't be cross, uncle," said the nephew.

"What else can I be when I live in such a world of fools as this? Merry Christmas! Out upon merry Christmas! What's Christmastime to you but a time for paying bills without money; a time for finding yourself a year older, and not an hour richer? If I could work my will," said Scrooge indignantly, "every idiot who goes about with 'Merry Christmas' on his lips should be boiled with his own pudding, and buried with a stake of holly through his heart. He should!"

"Uncle!" pleaded the nephew.

"Nephew!" returned the uncle sternly, "keep Christmas in your own way, and let me keep it in mine."

"Keep it!" repeated Scrooge's nephew. "But you don't keep it."

"Let me leave it alone, then," said Scrooge. "Much good it has ever done you!"

"There are many good things from which I have not profited, I daresay," returned the nephew; "Christmas among them. But I am sure I have always thought of Christmas as a good time; a kind, forgiving, charitable, pleasant time; the only time I know of, in the long calendar of the year, when men seem by one consent to open their shut-up hearts freely. And therefore, though it has never put a scrap of gold in my pocket, I believe that it *has* done me good; and I say, God bless it!"

The clerk in the tank involuntarily applauded. Becoming immediately sensible of the impropriety, he poked the fire, and extinguished the last frail spark forever.

"Let me hear another sound from *you*," said Scrooge, "and you'll keep your Christmas by losing your situation! You're quite a powerful speaker, sir," he added, turning to his nephew. "I wonder you don't go into Parliament."

"Don't be angry, uncle," the nephew repeated. "Come! Dine with us tomorrow."

Scrooge said that he would see him— Yes, indeed he did. He said that he would see him in that extremity first.

"But why?" cried Scrooge's nephew. "Why?"

"Why did you get married?" said Scrooge.

"Because I fell in love."

"Because you fell in love!" growled Scrooge, as if that were the only one thing in the world more ridiculous than a merry Christmas. "Good afternoon!"

"I am sorry to find you so resolute. But I'll keep my Christmas humor to the last. A merry Christmas, uncle!"

"Good afternoon!" said Scrooge.

"And a happy New Year!"

"Good afternoon!" said Scrooge.

His nephew left the room without an angry word, notwithstanding. He stopped at the outer door to bestow the greetings of the season on the clerk, who, cold as he was, was warmer than Scrooge; for he returned them cordially.

Let every
hall have
boughs of
green,
With berries
glowing in
between,
In the week
when
Christmas
comes.

ELEANOR FARJEON

"There's another," muttered Scrooge: "my clerk, with fifteen shillings a week, and a wife and family, talking about a merry Christmas. I'll retire to Bedlam."

The clerk, in letting Scrooge's nephew out, had let two other people in. They were portly gentlemen, pleasant to behold, and now stood, with their hats off, in Scrooge's office.

"Scrooge and Marley's, I believe," said one of the gentlemen. "Have I the pleasure of addressing Mr. Scrooge, or Mr. Marley?"

"Mr. Marley has been dead these seven years," Scrooge replied. "He died seven years ago, this very night."

"We have no doubt his liberality is well represented by his surviving partner," said the gentleman, presenting his credentials.

It certainly was; for they had been two kindred spirits. At the ominous word "liberality," Scrooge frowned.

"At this festive season of the year, Mr. Scrooge," the gentleman continued, taking up a pen, "it is more than usually desirable that we should make some slight provision for the poor and destitute, who suffer greatly at the present time. Many thousands are in want of common comforts, sir."

"Are there no prisons?" asked Scrooge.

"Plenty of prisons," said the gentleman, laying down the pen.

"And the workhouses?" demanded Scrooge. "Are they still in operation?"

"They are. I wish I could say they were not."

"The Treadmill and the Poor Law are in full vigor, then?" said Scrooge.

"Both very busy, sir."

"I am very glad to hear it," said Scrooge.

"Since they scarcely furnish Christian cheer to the multitude," returned the gentleman, "a few of us are endeavoring to raise a fund to buy the Poor some meat and drink, and means of warmth. This is the time, of all others, when Want is keenly felt, and Abundance rejoices. What shall I put you down for?"

"Nothing!" said Scrooge. "I don't make merry myself at Christmas and I can't afford to make idle people merry. I help to support the establishments I have mentioned—they cost enough: and those who are badly off must go there."

"Many can't go there; and many would rather die."

"If they would rather die," said Scrooge, "they had better do it, and decrease the surplus population. Good afternoon, gentlemen!"

Seeing clearly that it would be useless to pursue their point, the gentlemen withdrew and Scrooge resumed his labors with an improved opinion of himself.

Meanwhile the fog and darkness thickened so that people ran about with flaring links, proffering their services to go before horses and carriages. The ancient tower of a church, whose gruff old bell was always peeping slyly down at Scrooge out of a Gothic window in the wall, became invisible, and struck the

154

hours and quarters in the clouds with tremulous vibrations. The cold became intense. At the corner of the court, some laborers, repairing the gas pipes, had lighted a fire in a brazier, round which a party of ragged men and boys were gathered: warming their hands and winking their eyes before the blaze in rapture. The brightness of the shops, where holly sprigs and berries crackled in the heat of the lamps, made pale faces ruddy as they passed. The Lord Mayor, in the Mansion House, gave orders to his fifty cooks and butlers to keep Christmas as a Lord Mayor's household should; and even the little tailor, whom he had fined five shillings on the previous Monday for being drunk and bloodthirsty in the streets, stirred up tomorrow's pudding in his garret, while his lean wife and the baby sallied out to buy the beef.

Foggier yet, and colder! Piercing, biting cold. The owner of one scant young nose, gnawed and mumbled by the hungry cold as bones are gnawed by dogs, stooped down at Scrooge's keyhole to regale him with a Christmas carol; but at the first sound of

> "God bless you merry gentleman!
> May nothing you dismay!"

Scrooge seized the ruler with such energy of action that the singer fled in terror, leaving the keyhole to the fog and frost.

At length the hour of shutting up arrived. With an ill will Scrooge dismounted from his stool, thereby admitting the fact to the clerk, who instantly snuffed his candle out, and put on his hat. "You'll want all day tomorrow, I suppose?" said Scrooge.

"If quite convenient, sir."

"It's not convenient, and it's not fair. If I was to stop your wages for it, you'd think yourself ill-used, I'll be bound?" The clerk smiled faintly. "And yet," said Scrooge, "you don't think *me* ill-used when I pay a day's wages for no work."

The clerk observed that it was only once a year.

"A poor excuse for picking a man's pocket every twenty-fifth of December!" said Scrooge, buttoning his greatcoat. "But I suppose you must have the whole day. Be here all the earlier next morning."

The clerk promised that he would; and Scrooge walked out with a growl. The office was closed in a twinkling, and the clerk, with the long ends of his white comforter dangling below his waist (for he boasted no greatcoat), went down a slide on Cornhill, at the end of a lane of boys, twenty times, in honor of its being Christmas Eve, and then ran home as hard as he could pelt.

Scrooge took his melancholy dinner in his usual melancholy tavern; and, having beguiled the rest of the evening with his banker's book, went home to

bed. He lived in chambers which had once belonged to his deceased partner. They were a gloomy suite of rooms, in an old and dreary building far inside a courtyard. Nobody lived in the house but Scrooge, the other rooms being let out as offices. The yard was so dark that even Scrooge, who knew its every stone, was fain to grope with his hands to find the threshold.

Now, it is a fact that there was nothing at all particular about the knocker on the door, except that it was very large. It is also a fact that Scrooge had little of what is called fancy about him. Let it also be borne in mind that he had not bestowed one thought on Marley since his last mention of his seven-years-dead partner that afternoon. And then let any man explain to me, if he can, how it happened that Scrooge, having his key in the door, saw in the knocker, without its undergoing any intermediate process of change—not a knocker, but Marley's face.

Marley's face. It was not in impenetrable shadow, as the other objects in the yard were, but had a dismal light about it. It was not angry, but looked at Scrooge as Marley used to look; with ghostly spectacles turned up on its ghostly forehead. The hair was curiously stirred, as if by hot air; and, though the eyes were wide open, they were perfectly motionless. That, and its livid color, made it horrible; but its horror seemed to be in spite of the face, and beyond its control, rather than a part of its own expression.

As Scrooge looked fixedly at this phenomenon, it was a knocker again.

To say that he was not startled, or that his blood was not conscious of a terrible sensation to which it had been a stranger from infancy, would be untrue. But he turned the key sturdily, walked in, and lighted his candle. He *did* pause a moment before he shut the door; and he *did* look cautiously behind it, as if he half expected to see Marley's pigtail sticking out into the hall. But there was nothing there except the screws and nuts that held the knocker on, so he said, "Pooh!" and closed it with a bang.

The sound resounded through the house like thunder. Every room above, every cask in the wine merchant's cellars below, appeared to have a separate peal of echoes of its own. Scrooge was not a man to be frightened by echoes. He fastened the door, and walked up the stairs: slowly, too: trimming his candle as he went.

It was dark; but Scrooge didn't care: darkness is cheap, and he liked it. But, before he shut his heavy door, he walked through his rooms to see that all was right. He had just enough recollection of the face to desire to do that.

Sitting room, bedroom, storage room. All as they should be. Nobody under the table, nobody under the sofa; a small fire in the grate; and a little saucepan of gruel (Scrooge had a cold in his head) upon the hob. Nobody under the bed; nobody in his dressing gown, which was hanging up in a suspicious attitude against the wall. Storage room as usual. Old fireguard, old shoes, two fish baskets, washing stand on three legs, and a poker.

Satisfied, he locked himself in; double-locked himself in, which was not his custom. Then he put on his dressing gown and slippers, and his nightcap, and sat down before the fire to take his gruel.

It was a very low fire indeed. He was obliged to brood over it before he could extract from it the least sensation of warmth. The fireplace had been built by some Dutch merchant long ago, and paved all round with quaint Dutch tiles, illustrating the Scriptures. There were hundreds of figures there to attract his thoughts; and yet that face of Marley, seven years dead, came like the ancient Prophet's rod, and swallowed up the whole. If each smooth tile had been a blank, there would have been a copy of old Marley's head on every one.

"Humbug!" said Scrooge; and walked across the room.

As he sat down again and threw his head back in the chair, his glance happened to rest upon a bell that hung in the room, and communicated, for some purpose now forgotten, with a chamber in the highest story of the building. It was with astonishment and dread that, as he looked, he saw this bell begin to swing. It swung so softly in the outset that it scarcely made a sound; but soon it rang out loudly, and so did every bell in the house.

This might have lasted half a minute, but it seemed an hour. The bells ceased, as they had begun, together. They were succeeded by a clanking noise deep down below, as if someone were dragging a heavy chain over the casks in the wine merchant's cellar.

Then the cellar door flew open with a booming sound, and Scrooge heard the noise louder, coming up the stairs, then coming straight towards his door.

"It's humbug still!" said Scrooge. "I won't believe it."

His color changed though, when, without a pause, it came on through the heavy door and passed into the room before his eyes. Upon its coming in, the dying flame leaped up, as though it cried, "I know him! Marley's Ghost!" and fell again.

The same face: the very same. Marley in his pigtail, waistcoat, tights, and boots; the tassels on the latter bristling, like his pigtail, and his coat skirts, and the hair upon his head. The chain he drew was clasped about his middle. It was long, and wound about him like a tail; and it was made (for Scrooge observed it closely) of cashboxes, ledgers and heavy purses wrought in steel. His body was transparent: so that Scrooge, looking through his waistcoat, could see the two buttons on his coat behind.

Though he saw the Phantom standing before him; though he felt the chilling influence of its death-cold eyes, and marked the very texture of the folded kerchief bound about its head and chin, Scrooge fought against his senses.

We ring
the bells
on Christmas Day
Oh, why?
Oh, why?
To echo what
the angels say
On high!
On high!

ELSIE WILLIAMS CHANDLER

157

The Yule candles used long ago in France and England were so huge that holes had to be chiseled in the stone floors to serve as holders. Christmas dinner lasted as long as the candles burned.

"How now!" he said, caustic and cold as ever. "What do you want with me?"

"Much!"—Marley's voice; no doubt about it.

"Who are you?"

"In life I was your partner, Jacob Marley."

"Can you—can you sit down?" asked Scrooge, looking doubtfully at the transparent Spirit.

"I can."

"Do it then."

The Ghost sat down on the opposite side of the fireplace. "You don't believe in me," it observed. "Why do you doubt your senses?"

"Because," said Scrooge, "a little thing affects them. A slight disorder of the stomach makes them cheats. You may be an undigested bit of beef, a blot of mustard, a crumb of cheese, a fragment of an underdone potato. There's more of gravy than of grave about you!"

Scrooge was not in the habit of cracking jokes, nor did he feel by any means waggish. The truth is that he was trying to distract his own attention, and keep down his terror; for the Specter's voice disturbed the very marrow in his bones. To sit staring at those fixed eyes in silence would play, he felt, the very deuce with him. There was something awful, too, in its being provided with an infernal atmosphere of its own. Scrooge could not feel it himself, but this was clearly the case; for, though the Ghost sat motionless, its hair, and skirts, and tassels were agitated as by hot vapor from an oven.

"You see this toothpick?" he said, to divert the vision's stony gaze. "I have but to swallow it to be haunted by legions of goblins, all of my own creation. Humbug, I tell you!"

At this the Spirit raised a frightful cry, and shook its chain with a dismal and appalling noise; and how much greater was Scrooge's horror when, the Phantom taking off the bandage round its head as if it were too warm to wear indoors, its lower jaw dropped down upon its breast!

Scrooge fell upon his knees, and clasped his hands. "Mercy!" he said. "Dreadful apparition, why do you trouble me?"

"Man of the worldly mind!" replied the Ghost, "do you believe in me or not?"

"I do," said Scrooge; "I must. But why do spirits walk the earth, and why do they come to me?"

"It is required of every man," the Ghost returned, "that the spirit within him should walk abroad among his fellowmen; and if that spirit goes not forth in life, it is condemned to do so after death. It is doomed to wander through the world—oh, woe is me!—and witness what it cannot share, but might have shared on earth and turned to happiness!" And again the Specter raised a cry, and shook its chain and wrung its shadowy hands.

"You are fettered," said Scrooge, trembling. "Tell me why?"

"I wear the chain I forged in life," replied the Ghost. "I made it link by link; I girded it on of my own free will; of my own free will I wore it. Is its pattern strange to *you*?" Scrooge trembled more and more. "Or would you know," pursued the Ghost, "the weight and length of the strong coil you bear yourself?"

Scrooge glanced about him on the floor, in the expectation of finding himself surrounded by some fifty or sixty fathoms of iron cable; but he could see nothing. "Jacob!" he implored. "Tell me more. Speak comfort to me, Jacob."

"I have none to give," the Ghost replied. "It comes from other regions, Ebenezer, and is conveyed by other ministers, to other kinds of men. Little more is permitted to me: I cannot rest, I cannot linger. In life my spirit never walked beyond our countinghouse—mark me! Now weary journeys lie before me!"

It was a habit with Scrooge, whenever he became thoughtful, to put his hands in his breeches pockets. He did so now, but without lifting up his eyes, or getting off his knees. "You must have got over a great quantity of ground, Jacob," he observed in a businesslike manner, though with humility and deference. "Seven years dead, and traveling all the time?"

The Ghost, on hearing this, set up another cry, and clanked its chain hideously. "No rest, no peace," it cried. "Incessant torture of remorse. Oh! captive, bound, and double-ironed, not to know that no space of regret can make amends for one life's opportunities misused! Yet such was I! Oh, such was I!"

"But you were always a good man of business, Jacob," faltered Scrooge, who now began to apply this to himself.

"Business!" cried the Ghost, wringing its hands again. "Mankind was my business; charity, mercy, benevolence were all my business. My trade was but a drop of water in the ocean of my business!" It held up its chain at arm's length and flung it heavily upon the ground again. "At this time of the rolling year I suffer most. Why did I walk through crowds of fellow beings with my eyes turned down, and never raise them to that blessed Star which led the Wise Men to a poor abode? Were there no poor homes to which its light would have conducted *me*?"

Scrooge was dismayed and began to quake exceedingly.

"Hear me!" cried the Ghost. "My time is nearly gone."

"I will. But don't be hard upon me, Jacob! Pray!"

"How it is that I appear before you now, I may not tell. I have sat invisible beside you many a day."

It was not an agreeable idea. Scrooge shivered, and wiped the perspiration from his brow.

"I am here," pursued the Ghost, "to warn you that you have yet a chance of escaping my fate. A chance of my procuring, Ebenezer."

"You were always a good friend," said Scrooge. "Thank'ee!"

"You will be haunted," resumed the Ghost, "by Three Spirits."

Scrooge's countenance fell almost as low as the Ghost's. "Is that the chance you mentioned, Jacob?" he faltered.

"It is."

"I—I think I'd rather not," said Scrooge.

"Without their visits, you cannot hope to shun the path I tread. Expect the first tomorrow when the bell tolls One."

"Couldn't I take 'em all at once, and have it over, Jacob?" hinted Scrooge.

"Expect the second on the next night at the same hour. The third, upon the next night when the last stroke of Twelve has ceased to vibrate. Look to see me no more; and, for your own sake, remember what has passed between us!"

The Specter took its wrapper from the table, and bound it round its head: Scrooge knew this by the smart sound its teeth made when the jaws were brought together by the bandage. He ventured to raise his eyes, and found his supernatural visitor standing before him, with its chain wound over and about its arm.

It now walked backward from him; and, at every step it took, the window raised itself a little, so that, when the Specter reached it, it was wide open. It beckoned Scrooge to approach. Then, when they were within two paces of each other, it held up its hand, warning him to come no nearer.

Scrooge stopped, not so much in obedience as in surprise and fear; for he became sensible of confused noises in the air; sounds of lamentation and regret; wailings inexpressibly sorrowful and self-accusatory.

The Specter joined in the mournful dirge, and floated out upon the bleak, dark night.

Scrooge looked out the window, desperate in his curiosity. The air was filled with phantoms, wandering in restless haste, and moaning as they went. Every one of them wore chains like Marley's Ghost; some few (they might be guilty governments) were linked together. Many had been known to Scrooge in their lives.

He had been quite familiar with one old ghost in a white waistcoat, with a monstrous iron safe attached to its ankle, who cried piteously at being unable to assist a wretched woman with an infant whom it saw below upon a doorstep. The misery with them all was, clearly, that they sought to interfere, for good, in human matters, and had lost the power forever.

Finally, the spirits and their voices faded together into mist.

Scrooge closed the window, and examined his door. It was double-locked, as he had locked it with his own hands, and the bolts were undisturbed. He tried to say "Humbug!" but stopped at the first syllable. And being, from the emotion he had undergone, much in need of repose, he went straight to bed without undressing, and fell asleep upon the instant.

THE FIRST SPIRIT

Wᴴᴇɴ Sᴄʀᴏᴏɢᴇ awoke it was so dark that, looking out of bed, he could scarcely distinguish the window from the walls of his chamber. The chimes of a neighboring church struck the four quarters, and he listened for the hour. To his astonishment the heavy bell went on from six to seven, from seven to eight, and regularly up to twelve. Twelve! It was past two when he went to bed. The clock was wrong. An icicle must have got into the works. Twelve!

"I can't have slept through a whole day and into another night," said Scrooge. "It isn't possible that anything has happened to the sun, and this is twelve at noon!"

He scrambled out of bed, and groped his way to the window; but all he could make out was that it was still very foggy, cold and quiet. He went to bed again, and thought and thought, but could make nothing of it. Marley's Ghost bothered him exceedingly and he could not resolve within himself that it was all a dream. Then he remembered that the Ghost had warned him of a visitation when the bell tolled One. He resolved to lie awake until the hour was past; but the quarter was so long that he was more than once convinced he must have sunk into a doze and missed the clock. At length it broke upon his listening ear.

"Ding, dong! Ding, dong! Ding, dong!"

"A quarter to," said Scrooge, counting.

"Ding, dong!"

"The hour itself," said Scrooge triumphantly, "and nothing else!"

He spoke before the hour bell sounded, which it now did with a deep, dull, hollow, melancholy Oɴᴇ. Light flashed up in the room upon the instant, and the curtains of his bed were drawn.

The curtains of his bed were drawn aside, I tell you, by a hand; and Scrooge, starting up, found himself face-to-face with the unearthly visitor who drew them: as close to it as I am now to you, and I am standing in the spirit at your elbow.

It was a strange figure—like an old man viewed through some supernatural medium which diminished him to a child's proportions. Its hair was white as if with age; and yet the face had not a wrinkle in it. It wore a white tunic, bound with a sparkling belt, and held a branch of holly in its hand. But the strangest thing was that from the crown of its head there sprang a clear jet of light, by which all this was visible; which was doubtless why it held, under its arm, a great extinguisher for a cap.

As Scrooge looked at it the figure fluctuated in its distinctness; being now a thing with one arm, now with one leg, now with twenty legs, now a pair of legs without a head, now a head without a body; and, in the very wonder of this, it would be itself again; distinct and clear as ever. "Are you the Spirit, sir, whose coming was foretold to me?" asked Scrooge.

"I am!" The voice was soft and low, as if at a distance.

"Who and what are you?" Scrooge demanded.

"I am the Ghost of Christmas Past. Your Past. Your welfare brings me here."

Scrooge expressed himself much obliged, but could not help thinking that a night of unbroken rest would have been more conducive to that end. The Spirit must have heard him thinking, for it said, "Your reclamation, then. Take heed!" It clasped him gently by the arm. "Rise! and walk with me!"

It would have been in vain for Scrooge to plead that the thermometer was below freezing; that he was clad in slippers, dressing gown, and nightcap; and that he had a cold. The grasp, though gentle, was not to be resisted. He rose; but, as the Spirit made towards the window, clasped its robe in supplication. "I am a mortal," he remonstrated, "and liable to fall."

"Bear but a touch of my hand *there*," said the Spirit, laying it upon his heart, "and you shall be upheld in more than this!"

As the words were spoken, they passed through the wall, and stood upon an open country road. The city had vanished and the darkness and mist with it; it was a clear, cold, winter day, with snow upon the ground. "Good Heaven!" said Scrooge as he looked about him. "I was bred in this place. I was a boy here!"

"You recollect the way?" inquired the Spirit.

"Remember it!" cried Scrooge. "I could walk it blindfold."

"Strange to have forgotten it for so many years!" observed the Ghost. "Let us go on."

They walked along the road, Scrooge recognizing every gate and tree, until a little market town appeared in the distance, with its church and winding river. Some shaggy ponies were trotting towards them with boys upon their backs, who called to other boys in country carts, driven by farmers. All were in great spirits, and shouted to each other, until the broad fields were so full of merry music that the crisp air laughed to hear it.

"These are but shadows of the things that have been," said the Ghost. "They have no consciousness of us."

The travelers came on; Scrooge knew them every one. Why was he rejoiced beyond all bounds to see them? Why did his heart leap up when he heard them

Holly hung on the door at Christmastime was once believed to repel evil spirits and protect the house from lightning.

give each other merry Christmas as they parted for their several homes? What was merry Christmas to Scrooge? What good had it ever done him?

"The school is not quite deserted," said the Ghost. "A solitary child, neglected by his friends, is left there still."

Scrooge said he knew it. And he sobbed.

They left the highroad by a well-remembered lane and soon approached a mansion of dull red brick, with a cupola on the roof, and a bell hanging in it. Its windows were broken, the gates decayed. Fowls clucked and strutted in the stables; the coach houses and sheds were overrun with grass. Entering the dreary hall, and glancing into the many rooms, they found them poorly furnished, cold, and vast. There was a chill in the place, which associated itself somehow with too much getting up by candlelight and not too much to eat.

They went, the Ghost and Scrooge, to a room at the back of the house. It was a long, bare, melancholy room, made barer still by lines of plain deal benches and desks. At one of these a lonely boy was reading near a feeble fire; and Scrooge sat down, and wept to see his poor forgotten self as he had used to be. Not an echo in the house, not a scuffle from the mice behind the paneling, not a drip from the half-thawed waterspout in the yard behind, not the idle swinging of a door, but fell upon him with softening influence, and gave a freer passage to his tears.

The Spirit pointed to his younger self, intent upon his reading. Suddenly a man in foreign garments, wonderfully real, stood outside the window, with an axe stuck in his belt, and leading by the bridle an ass laden with wood.

"Why, it's Ali Baba!" Scrooge exclaimed in ecstasy. "It's dear old Ali Baba! Yes, yes; one Christmastime, when yonder solitary child was left here all alone, he *did* come, for the first time, just like that. And there's the Parrot! Green body and yellow tail, with a thing like a lettuce growing out of the top of his head. 'Poor Robin Crusoe' he called him, when he came home again after sailing round the island. Where have you been, Robin? And there goes Friday, running for his life to the little creek! Halloa! Hoop! Halloo!" Then, with a rapidity of transition very foreign to his usual character, he muttered, "Poor boy!" in pity for his former self. He dried his eyes. "I wish—but it's too late now. There was a boy singing a Christmas carol at my door last night. I should like to have given him something."

The Ghost smiled. "Let us see another Christmas!"

Scrooge's former self grew larger at the words, and the room became darker and more dirty. Windows cracked; plaster fell out of the ceiling; and there he was, alone again, when all the other boys had gone home for the jolly holidays.

He was not reading now, but walking up and down despairingly. Scrooge glanced anxiously towards the door.

It opened; and a little girl, much younger than the boy, came darting in, and, putting her arms about his neck and kissing him, addressed him as her "dear, dear brother." "I have come to bring you home!" said the child, clapping her tiny hands. "To bring you home for ever and ever! Father is much kinder than he used to be. He spoke so gently to me one night that I was not afraid to ask once more if you might come home; and he said you should, and sent me in a coach to bring you. You're never to come back here. And we're to be together all the Christmas long, and have the merriest time in the world!"

"You are quite a woman, little Fan!" exclaimed the boy.

She laughed, and stood on tiptoe to embrace him. Then she began to drag him, in her childish eagerness, towards the door.

A terrible voice in the hall cried, "Bring down Master Scrooge's box, there!" and in the hall appeared the schoolmaster himself, who glared on Master Scrooge with ferocious condescension, and threw him into a dreadful state of mind by shaking hands with him. He then conveyed him and his sister into the veriest old well of a shivering best parlor that ever was seen, produced a decanter of curiously light wine, and a block of curiously heavy cake, and administered installments of those dainties to the young people. Master Scrooge's trunk being by this time tied on to the top of the chaise, the children bade the schoolmaster good-by and drove gaily down the garden sweep, the quick wheels dashing snow from the evergreens like spray.

"Always a delicate creature, whom a breath might have withered," said the Ghost. "But she had a large heart! She died a woman, and had, as I think, a child. Your nephew!"

Scrooge seemed uneasy and answered briefly, "Yes."

Although they had but that moment left the school behind them, they were now in the busy thoroughfares of a city, where shadowy carts and coaches battled for the way. It was plain enough from the shops that here too it was Christmastime; but it was evening, and the streets were lighted up. The Ghost stopped at a warehouse door, and asked Scrooge if he knew it.

"Know it!" said Scrooge. "I was apprenticed here!"

They went in. At sight of an old gentleman in a wig, sitting behind such a high desk that, if he had been two inches taller he must have knocked his head against the ceiling, Scrooge cried in great excitement—"Why, it's old Fezziwig! Bless his heart!"

Old Fezziwig laid down his pen and looked up at the clock, which pointed to seven. He rubbed his hands; adjusted his capacious waistcoat; laughed all over himself; and called out in a comfortable, rich, fat, jovial voice—"Yo ho, there! Ebenezer! Dick!" And Scrooge's former self, now a young man, came briskly in with his fellow 'prentice.

In old England sprays of holly were placed on the hives to wish the bees a Merry Christmas. And the bees were said to hum a carol in honor of the Christ Child.

The holly's up,
the house
is all bright,
The tree
is ready,
the candles
alight;
Rejoice and
be glad,
all children
tonight.

FROM AN OLD CAROL

"Dick Wilkins, to be sure!" said Scrooge to the Ghost. "Bless me, there he is. He was much attached to me, was Dick."

"Yo ho, my boys!" said Fezziwig. "No more work tonight. Christmas Eve, Dick, Ebenezer. Let's have the shutters up," he cried, clapping his hands, "before a man can say Jack Robinson!"

You wouldn't believe how those two fellows went at it! They charged into the street with the shutters—one, two, three—had 'em up in their places—four, five, six—barred 'em and pinned 'em—seven, eight, nine—and came back before you could have got to twelve, panting like racehorses.

"Hilli-ho!" cried old Fezziwig, skipping down from the high desk with wonderful agility. "Clear away, my lads, and let's have lots of room here! Hilli-ho, Dick! Chirrup, Ebenezer!"

There was nothing they couldn't have cleared away with old Fezziwig looking on. Every movable was packed off; the floor was swept and watered, lamps trimmed, fuel heaped on the fire; and the warehouse was as snug, and warm, and bright a ballroom as you would desire to see upon a winter's night.

In came a fiddler with a music book, and went up to the lofty desk, and made an orchestra of it, and tuned like fifty stomachaches. In came Mrs. Fezziwig, one vast substantial smile. In came the three Miss Fezziwigs, beaming and lovable. In came the six young followers whose hearts they broke. In came all the young men and women employed in the business. In came the housemaid, with her cousin the baker. In came the cook with her brother's particular friend the milkman. In came the boy from over the way, who was suspected of not having board enough from his master; trying to hide himself behind the girl from next door but one, who was proved to have had her ears pulled by her mistress. In they all came, one after another, any how and every how. Away they went, twenty couple at once; hands half round and back again the other way; down the middle and up again; old top couple always turning up in the wrong place; new top couple starting off as soon as they got there; all top couples at last, and not a bottom one to help them! When this result was brought about, old Fezziwig, clapping his hands to stop the dance, cried out, "Well done!" and the fiddler plunged his hot face into a pot of porter. But upon his reappearance, he instantly began again, as if the other fiddler had been carried home, exhausted, on a shutter, and he were a brand-new man resolved to beat him out of sight or perish.

So there were more dances, and there were forfeits, and there was cake, and negus, and a great piece of Cold Roast, and a great piece of Cold Boiled, mince pies, and plenty of beer. But the great effect of the evening came after the Roast and Boiled, when the fiddler (an artful dog! a man who knew his business!) struck up "Sir Roger de Coverley." Then old Fezziwig stood out to dance with

Then be ye glad,
good people,
This night
of all the year.
And light ye up
your candles,
For His star
it shineth clear.

FROM AN OLD CAROL

Mrs. Fezziwig. Top couple, too, with a good stiff piece of work cut out for them; four and twenty pair of partners; people who would dance, and had no notion of walking.

But if they had been four times as many, old Fezziwig would have been a match for them; and as to Mrs. Fezziwig, she was worthy to be his partner in every sense of the term. A positive light appeared to issue from Fezziwig's calves. They shone in every part of the dance like moons. And when old Fezziwig and Mrs. Fezziwig had gone all through the dance: advance and retire, hands to your partner, bow and curtsy, thread-the-needle, and back again to your place: Fezziwig "cut"—cut so deftly that he appeared to wink with his legs, and came upon his feet again without a stagger.

When the clock struck eleven, this domestic ball broke up. Mr. and Mrs. Fezziwig took their stations at the door, and, shaking hands with every person, wished him or her a merry Christmas. They then did the same to the two 'prentices; and the lads were left to their beds under the counter.

During the whole of this time Scrooge had acted like a man out of his wits. His heart and soul were in the scene with his former self. He remembered everything, enjoyed everything, and underwent the strangest agitation. It was not until now, when the bright faces of his former self and Dick were turned away, that he remembered the Ghost, and became conscious that it was looking full upon him, while the light upon its head burned very clear.

"A small matter," said the Ghost, "to make these silly folks so full of gratitude."

"Small," echoed Scrooge.

The Spirit signed to him to listen to the two apprentices pouring out their hearts in praise of Fezziwig. "He has spent but a few pounds of your mortal money. Is that so much that he deserves this praise?"

"It isn't that," said Scrooge, unconsciously speaking like his former self. "Spirit, he has the power to make our service light or burdensome. His power lies in words and looks; it is impossible to add and count 'em up. What then? The happiness he gives is quite as great as if it cost a fortune."

He felt the Spirit's glance, and stopped.

"What is the matter?" asked the Ghost.

"Nothing particular," said Scrooge. "I should like to be able to say a word or two to my clerk just now! That's all."

His former self turned down the lamps at this; and Scrooge and the Ghost again stood side by side in the open air.

"My time grows short," observed the Spirit. "Quick!"

Again Scrooge saw himself. He was older now, in the prime of life, and his face had already begun to wear the signs of avarice. There was a greedy, restless motion in the eye, which showed the passion that had taken root. He sat by the side of a fair young girl. In her eyes there were tears, which sparkled in the light of the Ghost of Christmas Past.

"To you, it matters little," she said softly. "Another idol has displaced me. If it can cheer and comfort you in time to come as I would have tried to do, I have no just cause to grieve."

"What Idol has displaced you?" he rejoined.

"A golden one."

"This is the evenhanded dealing of the world!" he said. "There is nothing on which it is so hard as poverty; and there is nothing it professes to condemn so severely as the pursuit of wealth!"

"You fear the world too much," she answered gently, "with its sordid reproach. I have seen your aspirations fall off one by one until only the master passion, Gain, engrosses you."

"If I have grown so much wiser, what then? I am not changed towards you." She shook her head. "Am I?"

"Our contract," she said, "was made when we were both poor, and content to be so, until we could improve our fortune by patient industry. When it was made you were another man."

"I was a boy," he said impatiently.

"Your own feeling tells you that you were not what you are," she returned mildly. "Can even I believe that you would now choose a dowerless girl—you who weigh everything by Gain? With a full heart I release you, for the love of him you once were." He was about to speak, but, with her head turned from him, she resumed: "The memory of what is past half makes me hope you will—have pain in this. A very brief time, and you will dismiss it as a dream from which it happened well that you awoke. May you be happy in the life you have chosen!"

She left him, and they parted.

"Spirit!" said Scrooge, "show me no more! Why do you torture me?"

"One shadow more!" exclaimed the Ghost.

"No more!" cried Scrooge. "I don't wish to see it."

But the relentless Ghost pinioned him in both his arms, and forced him to observe what happened next.

They were in another place; a room not large or handsome but full of comfort. Near the fire sat a beautiful girl, so like the last that Scrooge believed it was the same, until he saw *her*, now a comely matron, sitting opposite her daughter. The noise in this room was perfectly tumultuous, for there were more children there than Scrooge in his agitated state could count; and every child there was conducting itself like forty. They were uproarious beyond belief; but no one

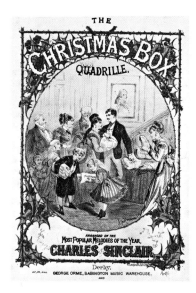

seemed to care; on the contrary, mother and daughter laughed heartily, and the latter, mingling in the sports, got pillaged by the young brigands ruthlessly.

A knocking at the door was heard, and a boisterous rush ensued to greet the father, laden with Christmas toys and presents. Then the shouting and the struggling, and the onslaught that was made on him! The scaling him, with chairs for ladders, to dive into his pockets, despoil him of parcels, hold on tight by his cravat and hug him round his neck in irrepressible affection! The shouts of wonder and delight with which each package was received! The terrible announcement that the baby had put a doll's frying pan into his mouth, and was suspected of having swallowed a fictitious turkey, glued on a wooden platter! The immense relief of finding this a false alarm! The joy, and gratitude, and ecstasy! They are all indescribable. It is enough that, by degrees, the children and their emotions got out of the parlor and, by one stair at a time, up to the top of the house, where they went to bed, and so subsided.

And now the master of the house, his daughter leaning fondly on him, sat down with her and her mother at his own fireside; and when Scrooge thought that such a creature, graceful and full of promise, might have called him father, and been a springtime in the haggard winter of his life, his sight grew dim indeed.

"Belle," said the husband, turning to his wife with a smile, "I saw an old friend of yours this afternoon. Guess who it was!"

"How can I? Tut, don't I know?" she added in the same breath, laughing as he laughed. "Mr. Scrooge."

"Mr. Scrooge it was. I passed his office window; and he had a candle inside. His partner lies at the point of death, I hear; and there he sat, quite alone in the world, I do believe."

"Spirit!" said Scrooge in a broken voice. "Remove me from this place. I cannot bear it." He turned upon the Ghost and, seeing it look upon him with a face in which in some strange way there were fragments of all the faces it had shown him, wrestled with it. "Take me back. Haunt me no longer!"

In the struggle, if that can be called a struggle in which the Ghost was undisturbed by any effort of its adversary, Scrooge observed that its light was burning high and bright; and dimly connecting that with its influence over him, he seized the extinguisher cap, and pressed it down upon its head.

The Spirit dropped beneath it, so that the extinguisher covered its whole form; but though Scrooge pressed down with all his force, he could not hide the light, which streamed from under it in an unbroken flood upon the ground. He was conscious of being exhausted and, further, of being in his own bedroom. He gave the cap a parting squeeze, in which his hand relaxed; and had barely time to reel to bed before he sank into a heavy sleep.

THE SECOND SPIRIT

A WAKING in the middle of a prodigiously tough snore, Scrooge had no occasion to be told that the bell was again upon the stroke of One. He felt that he was restored to consciousness in the nick of time to hold a conference with the second messenger dispatched to him through Jacob Marley. But finding that he turned uncomfortably cold when he began to wonder which of his bed curtains this new specter would draw back, he put every one aside with his own hands and, lying down again, established a sharp lookout all round the bed. For he wished to challenge the Spirit on the moment of its appearance, and not to be taken by surprise. He was ready for a good broad field of strange appearances, and nothing between a baby and a rhinoceros would have astonished him very much.

Now, being prepared for anything, he was by no means prepared for nothing; consequently, when the bell struck One, and no shape appeared, he was taken with a violent fit of trembling. A quarter of an hour went by, yet nothing came. All this time he lay upon his bed, the very core and center of a blaze of ruddy light, which streamed upon it when the clock proclaimed the hour; and which, being only light, was more alarming than a dozen ghosts, as he was powerless to make out what it meant. At last he began to think that the source of this ghostly light might be in the adjoining room, from whence it seemed to shine. He got up softly and shuffled in his slippers to the door; and the moment his hand was on the lock a voice bade him enter. He obeyed.

It was his own room. But it had undergone a transformation. The walls and ceiling were so hung with living green that it looked a perfect grove. The crisp leaves of holly, mistletoe, and ivy reflected back the light like so many mirrors; and such a mighty blaze went roaring up the chimney as that dull hearth had never known in Scrooge's time, or Marley's. Heaped up on the floor, to form a kind of throne, were turkeys, geese, game, great joints of meat, long wreaths of sausages, mince pies, plum puddings, barrels of oysters, red-hot chestnuts, cherry-cheeked apples, juicy oranges, and immense cakes. In easy state upon this couch there sat a jolly Giant, glorious to see, who bore a glowing torch, in shape like Plenty's horn, and held it high up, to shed its light on Scrooge as he came peeping round the door.

"Come in!" exclaimed the Ghost. "And know me better, man!"

Scrooge entered timidly and hung his head before this Spirit. He was not the dogged Scrooge he had been; though the Spirit's eyes were clear and kind, he

did not like to meet them. "I am the Ghost of Christmas Present," said the Spirit. "Look upon me!"

Scrooge reverently did so. It was clothed in one simple deep-green robe, bordered with fur; and on its head it wore a holly wreath, set here and there with shining icicles. Its dark-brown curls were long and free; free as its genial face, its open hand, its cheery voice, and its joyful air. Girded round its middle was an antique scabbard; but no sword was in it, and the ancient sheath was eaten up with rust. "You have never seen the like of me before!" exclaimed the Spirit.

"Never," Scrooge made answer to it.

The Ghost of Christmas Present rose.

"Spirit," said Scrooge submissively, "conduct me where you will. I went forth last night on compulsion, but I learned a lesson. Tonight, if you have aught to teach me, let me profit by it."

"Touch my robe!" Scrooge did as he was told, and held it fast.

The room, the fire, the night, all vanished instantly, and they stood in the city streets on Christmas morning, where (for the weather was severe) the people made a rough but pleasant kind of music, scraping the snow from the pavement and from the tops of their houses, whence it was mad delight to the boys to see it come plumping into the road below in little snowstorms.

The house fronts looked black, the windows blacker, contrasting with the white snow upon the roofs, and with the dirtier snow upon the streets, which had been plowed up in deep furrows by the heavy wheels of carts and wagons. The furrows were channels of yellow mud and icy water. The sky was gloomy, and the shortest streets were choked up with a dingy mist.

Yet the people on the housetops were full of glee; calling to one another, and now and then exchanging a snowball—laughing heartily if it went right, and not less heartily if it went wrong.

The poulterers' shops were still open, and the fruiterers' were radiant in their glory. There were great, potbellied baskets of chestnuts, shaped like the waistcoats of jolly old gentlemen, lolling at the doors and tumbling out into the street in their apoplectic opulence, and ruddy, brown-faced Spanish onions. There were blooming pyramids of pears and apples; and bunches of grapes, dangling from hooks so that people's mouths might water gratis as they passed; piles of nuts and apples, all beseeching to be carried home in paper bags and eaten after dinner.

And the grocers'! nearly closed, with perhaps two shutters down, but through those gaps such glimpses! It was not alone that the spices were so delicious, the candied fruits so caked with molten sugar; but the grocer and his people were so frank and fresh; and the customers were so hurried in the hopeful promise of the day that they tumbled up against each other at the door, clashing their wicker baskets wildly, left their purchases and came running back to fetch them, and committed hundreds of mistakes in the best humor possible.

But soon the steeples called good people all to church, and away they came, flocking through the streets in their best clothes and with their gayest faces. At the same time there emerged from lanes and nameless bystreets innumerable people, carrying their dinners to be cooked at bakers' shops. The sight of these poor revelers appeared to interest the Spirit very much, for he stood with Scrooge in a doorway, and, taking off the covers as their bearers passed, sprinkled incense on their dinners from his torch. It was a very uncommon kind of torch, for once or twice, when there were angry words between some dinner-carriers who had jostled each other, he shed a few drops on them from it, and their good humor was restored directly. It was a shame, they said, to quarrel on Christmas Day. And so it was! God love it, so it was!

"Is there a peculiar flavor in what you sprinkle from your torch?" asked Scrooge.

"There is. My own."

"Would it apply to any kind of dinner on this day?"

"To any kindly given. To a poor one most, because it needs it most."

They went on, invisible as before, into the suburbs. Notwithstanding his gigantic size, the Ghost could accommodate himself to any place with ease; and he stood beneath a low roof quite as gracefully as in any lofty hall. Perhaps it was the pleasure the good Spirit had in showing off this power of his, or else it was his sympathy with all poor men, that led him straight to Scrooge's clerk's; for there he went, and took Scrooge with him; and at the door the Spirit smiled, and stopped to bless Bob Cratchit's dwelling with the sprinklings of his torch. Think of that! Bob pocketed on Saturdays but fifteen shillings; and yet the Ghost of Christmas Present blessed his four-room house!

Then up rose Mrs. Cratchit, dressed but poorly in a twice-turned gown, but brave in ribbons, which are cheap, and make a goodly show for sixpence; and she laid the cloth, assisted by Belinda, second of her daughters, also brave in ribbons; while Master Peter Cratchit plunged a fork into the saucepan of potatoes and, getting the corners of his monstrous shirt collar (Bob's private property, conferred upon his son and heir in honor of the day) into his mouth, rejoiced to find himself so gallantly attired. And now two smaller Cratchits, boy and girl, came tearing in, screaming that at the baker's they had smelled the goose, and known it for their own; and, basking in luxurious thoughts of sage and onion, they danced about the table, and exalted Master Peter Cratchit to the skies, while he (although his collar nearly choked him) blew the fire until the potatoes, bubbling up, knocked loudly at the saucepan lid to be let out and peeled.

173

Now all our neighbors' chimneys smoke, And Christmas logs are burning; Their ovens with baked meats do choke, And all their spits are turning. Without the door let sorrow lie, And if for cold it hap to die, We'll bury it in Christmas pie, And evermore be merry!

GEORGE WITHER

"What has ever got your precious father, then?" said Mrs. Cratchit. "And your brother, Tiny Tim? And Martha warn't as late last Christmas Day by half an hour!"

"Here's Martha, mother!" said a girl, appearing as she spoke.

"Why, bless your heart alive, my dear, how late you are!" said Mrs. Cratchit, kissing her a dozen times, and taking off her shawl and bonnet for her.

"We'd a deal of work to finish up last night," replied the girl, "and had to clear away this morning, mother!"

"Well! never mind so long as you are come. Sit ye down before the fire, my dear, and have a warm, Lord bless ye!"

"No, no! There's father coming," cried the two young Cratchits, who were everywhere at once. "Hide, Martha, hide!"

So Martha hid herself, and in came little Bob, the father, with at least three feet of comforter hanging down before him, his threadbare clothes darned and brushed to look seasonable, and Tiny Tim upon his shoulder. Alas for Tiny Tim, he bore a little crutch, and had his limbs supported by an iron frame!

"Why, where's our Martha?" cried Bob Cratchit, looking round.

"Not coming," said Mrs. Cratchit.

"Not coming!" said Bob, with a sudden declension in his high spirits; for he had been Tim's blood horse all the way from church, and had come home rampant. "Not coming upon Christmas Day!"

Martha didn't like to see him disappointed, if only in joke; so she came out prematurely from behind the closet door and ran into his arms, while the two young Cratchits hustled Tiny Tim and bore him off to hear the pudding singing in the copper kettle.

"And how did little Tim behave?" asked Mrs. Cratchit when Bob had hugged his daughter to his heart's content.

"As good as gold," said Bob. "Somehow he gets thoughtful sitting by himself so much. He told me, coming home, that he hoped the people saw him in the church, because he was a cripple, and it might be pleasant to them to remember upon Christmas Day who made lame beggars walk and blind men see." Bob's voice was tremulous when he told them this, and trembled more when he said that Tiny Tim was growing strong and hearty.

His active little crutch was heard upon the floor, and back came Tiny Tim, escorted by his brother and sister to his stool beside the fire; and while Bob, turning up his cuffs, compounded some hot mixture with gin and lemons in a jug and put it on the hob to simmer, Master Peter and the two young Cratchits went to fetch the goose, with which they soon returned in high procession.

Such a bustle ensued that you might have thought a goose the rarest of all birds; and, in truth, it was something very like it in that house. Mrs. Cratchit

A man might
then behold
At Christmas,
in each hall,
Good fires to
curb the cold,
And meat for
great and small.

THOMAS HOOD

made the gravy hissing hot; Master Peter mashed the potatoes with incredible vigor; Miss Belinda sweetened up the applesauce; Martha dusted the hot plates; Bob took Tiny Tim beside him in a tiny corner at the table; the two young Cratchits set chairs for everybody, and crammed spoons into their mouths, lest they should shriek for goose before their turn came to be helped. At last the dishes were set on, and grace was said. It was succeeded by a breathless pause, as Mrs. Cratchit, looking slowly all along the carving knife, prepared to plunge it in the breast; but when she did, and when the long-expected gush of stuffing issued forth, one murmur of delight arose all round the board, and even Tiny Tim beat on the table with the handle of his knife and feebly cried Hurrah!

There never was such a goose. Bob said he didn't believe there ever was such a goose cooked. Its tenderness and flavor, size and cheapness, were the themes of universal admiration. Eked out by applesauce and mashed potatoes, it was a sufficient dinner for the whole family; indeed, as Mrs. Cratchit said with great delight (surveying one small atom of a bone upon the dish), they hadn't ate it all at last! Yet everyone had had enough, and the youngest Cratchits were steeped in sage and onion to the eyebrows!

Now Mrs. Cratchit left the room alone—too nervous to bear witnesses—to take the pudding up, and bring it in. Suppose it should not be done enough! Suppose it should break in turning out! Suppose somebody should have stolen it, while they were merry with the goose—a supposition at which the two young Cratchits became livid!

Hallo! A great deal of steam! The pudding was out of the copper. In half a minute Mrs. Cratchit entered—flushed, but smiling proudly—with the pudding, like a speckled cannonball, blazing in ignited brandy, with Christmas holly stuck into the top.

Oh, a wonderful pudding! Bob Cratchit said that he regarded it as the greatest success achieved by Mrs. Cratchit since their marriage. Mrs. Cratchit said that, now the weight was off her mind, she would confess she had her doubts about the quantity of flour. Everybody had something to say about it, but nobody said or thought it was at all a small pudding for so large a family. Any Cratchit would have blushed to hint at such a thing.

At last the dinner was done, the cloth cleared, the hearth swept, and the fire made up. The compound in the jug being tasted, and considered perfect, apples and oranges were put upon the table, and a shovelful of chestnuts on the fire. Then all the Cratchit family drew round the hearth in a half circle; and at Bob Cratchit's elbow stood the family display of glass: two tumblers and a custard cup without a handle. These held the hot stuff from the jug, however, as well as golden goblets would have done; and Bob served it out with beaming looks, while the chestnuts on the fire crackled noisily. Then Bob proposed:

"A merry Christmas to us all, my dears. God Bless us!"

Which all the family re-echoed.

"God bless us every one!" said Tiny Tim, the last of all.

He sat very close to his father's side, upon his little stool. Bob held his withered little hand in his, as if he wished to keep him by his side and dreaded that he might be taken from him.

"Spirit," cried Scrooge, "tell me if Tiny Tim will live."

"I see a vacant seat," replied the Ghost, "in the poor chimney corner, and a crutch without an owner, carefully preserved."

"No, no," said Scrooge. "Oh, say he will be spared!"

"If these shadows remain unaltered by the Future, the child will die. What then? If he be like to die, he had better do it, and decrease the surplus population."

Scrooge hung his head to hear his own words quoted by the Spirit, and was overcome with penitence and grief.

"Man," said the Ghost, "if man you be in heart, forbear that wicked cant until you have discovered what the surplus is, and where it is. Will you decide what men shall live, what men shall die? It may be that, in the sight of Heaven, you are more worthless and less fit to live than millions like this poor man's child!"

Scrooge bent before the rebuke, trembling. But he raised his eyes speedily on hearing his own name.

"Mr. Scrooge!" said Bob. "I'll give you Mr. Scrooge, the Founder of the Feast!"

"The Founder of the Feast, indeed!" cried Mrs. Cratchit, reddening. "I wish I had him here. I'd give him a piece of my mind to feast upon, and I hope he'd have a good appetite for it."

"My dear," said Bob, "the children! Christmas Day."

"It should be Christmas Day, I am sure," said she, "on which one drinks the health of such an odious, hard, unfeeling man. You know he is, Robert! Nobody knows it better than you, poor fellow!"

"My dear," was Bob's mild answer, "Christmas Day."

"I'll drink his health for your sake and the Day's," said Mrs. Cratchit, "not for his. A merry Christmas and a happy New Year to him! He'll be very merry and very happy, I have no doubt!"

The children drank the toast after her. It was the first of their proceedings which had no heartiness in it. Scrooge was the Ogre of the family. The mention of his name cast a dark shadow on the party, which was not dispelled for full five minutes.

After it had passed, they were ten times merrier than before, from mere relief.

The ceremonial Christmas drink in England was once lamb's wool: a mixture of hot ale, sugar, spices, eggs and roasted apples. Thick cream was sometimes added. It was served in a wassail bowl with pieces of toast floated on top. Hence, the origin of the drinking toast.

Bob Cratchit told them how he had a situation in his eye for Master Peter, which could bring in full five-and-sixpence weekly. The two young Cratchits laughed tremendously at the idea of Peter's being a man of business; and Peter himself looked thoughtfully at the fire, as if he were deliberating what investments he should favor when he came into the receipt of that bewildering income. Martha, who was apprenticed at a milliner's, then told them how she had seen a countess and a lord some days before, and how the lord "was much about as tall as Peter"; at which Peter pulled up his collar so high that you couldn't have seen his head if you had been there. All this time the chestnuts and the jug went round and round; and by-and-by they had a song, about a lost child in the snow, from Tiny Tim, who sang it very well indeed.

There was nothing of high mark in this. They were not a handsome family; they were not well-dressed; their shoes were far from being waterproof; their clothes were scanty. But they were happy, grateful, pleased with one another, and contented with the time; and when they faded, and looked happier yet in the bright sprinklings of the Spirit's torch at parting, Scrooge had his eye upon them, and especially on Tiny Tim, until the last.

By this time it was getting dark, and snowing heavily; and, as Scrooge and the Spirit went along the streets, the brightness of the roaring fires in the kitchens and parlors was wonderful. If you had judged from the numbers of people on their way to friendly gatherings, you might have thought that no one was at home to give them welcome when they got there, instead of every house expecting company. How the Ghost exulted! How it opened its palm, and poured its mirth on everything within its reach! The very lamplighter, dotting the dusky street with specks of light, laughed out loudly as the Spirit passed, though little kenned the lamplighter that he had any company but Christmas!

And now, without a word of warning, they stood upon a desert moor, where masses of rude stone were cast about, as though it were the burial place of giants. The setting sun had left a streak of fiery red, which glared upon the desolation for an instant, and, frowning lower yet, was lost in the thick gloom of night.

"What place is this?" asked Scrooge.

"A place where miners live, who labor in the bowels of the earth," returned the Spirit. "But they know me. See!"

A light shone from the window of a hut, and, swiftly passing through its wall of mud and stone, they found a cheerful company round the fire: an old, old man and woman, with their children and their children's children, all decked in holiday attire. The old man was singing them a Christmas song; and from time to time they all joined in the chorus.

Now the spirit bade Scrooge hold his robe, and, to Scrooge's horror, sped out to sea above the thundering water. Upon a dismal reef there stood a solitary lighthouse; but even here, two men who watched the light had made a fire that through the loophole in the thick stone wall shed out a ray of brightness on the awful sea. Joining their horny hands over the rough table at which they sat, they wished each other merry Christmas in their can of grog; and the elder of them, face scarred with weather as the figurehead of an old ship might be, struck up a sturdy song that was like a gale in itself.

It was a great surprise to Scrooge, as they moved on again through the lonely darkness, to hear, suddenly, a hearty laugh. It was a much greater surprise to recognize it as his own nephew's, and to find himself in a dry and gleaming room, with the Spirit smiling at that same nephew. "Ha, ha!" laughed Scrooge's nephew. "Ha, ha, ha!" If you should happen to know a man more blessed in a laugh than Scrooge's nephew, all I can say is, I should like to know him too.

It is an evenhanded adjustment of things that, while there is infection in disease and sorrow, there is nothing in the world so irresistibly contagious as laughter and good humor. When Scrooge's nephew laughed, Scrooge's niece, by marriage, laughed as heartily as he. And their assembled friends roared out lustily. "Ha, ha! Ha, ha, ha, ha!"

"He said that Christmas was a humbug, as I live!" cried Scrooge's nephew. "He believed it, too!"

"More shame for him, Fred!" said Scrooge's niece indignantly.

She was exceedingly pretty, with a dimpled, surprised-looking face; a ripe little mouth, that seemed made to be kissed—as no doubt it was; and the sunniest pair of eyes you ever saw. Altogether she was what you would call provoking; but satisfactory, too. Oh, perfectly satisfactory!

"He's a comical old fellow," said Scrooge's nephew; "that's the truth; and not so pleasant as he might be. But I am sorry for him."

"I'm sure he is very rich, Fred," hinted Scrooge's niece. "At least you always tell *me* so."

"What of that, my dear!" said Scrooge's nephew. "His wealth is of no use to him. He don't do any good with it. He don't make himself comfortable with it."

"I have no patience with him," observed Scrooge's niece. Scrooge's niece's sisters, and all the other ladies, expressed the same opinion.

"Oh, I have!" said Scrooge's nephew. "Who suffers by his ill whims? Himself always. Here he won't come and dine with us. What's the consequence? He don't lose much of a dinner."

"Indeed, I think he loses a very good dinner," interrupted Scrooge's niece. Everybody else said the same, and they must have been competent judges, because they had just had dinner; and were clustered round the fire, by lamplight.

"Well! I am glad to hear it," said Scrooge's nephew, "because I haven't any great faith in these young housekeepers. What do *you* say, Topper?"

The mistletoe
bough on
the festive throng
Looks down,
amid echoes
of mirthful song . . .
And who is she
that will not allow
A kiss claimed
under the
mistletoe bough?

ENGLISH BALLAD

Topper had clearly got his eye upon one of Scrooge's niece's sisters, for he answered that a bachelor was a wretched outcast who had no right to express an opinion on the subject. Whereat Scrooge's niece's sister—the plump one—blushed.

"Do go on, Fred," said Scrooge's niece. "He never finishes what he begins to say! He is such a ridiculous fellow!"

"I was only going to say," said Scrooge's nephew, "that the consequence of his not making merry with us is that he loses some pleasant moments which could do him no harm. I mean to give him the same chance every year, whether he likes it or not. He can't help thinking better of Christmas—I defy him—if he finds me going there year after year saying, 'Uncle Scrooge, how are you?' If it only put him in the vein to leave his poor clerk fifty pounds, *that's* something; and I think I shook him yesterday."

They laughed at the notion of his shaking Scrooge. He encouraged their merriment, and passed the bottle, joyously. After that, they had some singing. Then Scrooge's niece played upon the harp a simple little air which had been familiar to the child who fetched Scrooge from the boarding school. When this strain of music sounded, all the things that the Ghost of Christmas Past had shown him came upon Scrooge's mind; he thought that if he could have listened to this air often, years ago, he might have cultivated the kindnesses of life with his own hands, without resorting to Jacob Marley's Ghost.

After a while they played some games; for it is good to be children sometimes, and never better than at Christmas, when its mighty Founder was a child himself. There was first a game at blindman's buff. And I no more believe Topper was really blind than I believe he had eyes in his boots: the way he went after that plump sister was an outrage on human credulity. Knocking down the fire irons, tumbling over the chairs, bumping the piano, smothering himself in the curtains, wherever the plump sister went, there went he!

And when, at last, he got her into a corner whence there was no escape, then his conduct was monstrous. For his pretending not to know her; his pretending to assure himself of her identity by pressing a certain ring upon her finger, and a certain chain about her neck, was vile, outrageous! No doubt she told him her opinion of it when, another blind man being in office, they were so very confidential together behind the curtains.

Scrooge's niece was not one of the blindman's-buff party, but was made comfortable with a large chair and a footstool, in a snug corner where the Ghost and Scrooge were close behind her. But she joined in the game of How, When, and Where, and, to the secret joy of Scrooge's nephew, beat her sisters hollow. There might have been twenty people there, young and old, but they all played, and so did Scrooge; for, wholly forgetting that his voice made no sound in their ears, he came out with his guesses quite loud, and very often guessed right, too; for the sharpest needle was not sharper than Scrooge, blunt as he took it in his head to be.

The Ghost was greatly pleased to find him in this mood, and looked upon him with such favor that he begged like a boy to be allowed to stay until the guests departed.

"Here's a new game," said Scrooge. "One half hour, Spirit, only one!"

It was a game called Yes and No, where Scrooge's nephew had to think of something, and the rest must find out what, he only answering yes or no. They elicited from him that he was thinking of a savage animal, an animal that growled and grunted sometimes, and talked sometimes, and lived in London, and walked about the streets, and didn't live in a menagerie, and was never killed in a market, and was not a horse, or an ass, or a dog, or a cat, or a bear. At every fresh question the nephew burst into a fresh roar of laughter; and at last the plump sister cried out: "I have it, Fred! I know what it is!"

"What is it?" cried Fred.

"It's your uncle Scro-o-o-o-oge."

Which it certainly was. Admiration was the universal sentiment, though some objected that the reply to "Is it a bear?" ought to have been "Yes."

"He has given us plenty of merriment, I am sure," said Fred, "and it would be ungrateful not to drink his health. Here is a glass of mulled wine and I say, 'Uncle Scrooge!' A merry Christmas and a happy New Year to the old man, whatever he is!"

"Well! Uncle Scrooge!" they cried.

Uncle Scrooge had become so gay and light of heart that he would have pledged the unconscious company in return if the Ghost had given him time. But the whole scene now passed off in a breath, and he and the Spirit were again upon their travels.

Far they went, and many homes they visited, but always with a happy end. The Spirit stood beside sickbeds, and they were cheerful; on foreign lands, and they were close at home; by poverty, and it was rich. In hospital, and jail, in misery's every refuge, where vain man in his little brief authority had not made fast the door and barred the Spirit out, he left his blessing.

It was a long night, if it were only a night; but Scrooge had his doubts of this. It was strange that, while he remained unaltered, the Ghost grew clearly older. Scrooge spoke of this when he noticed that its hair was gray. "Are spirits' lives so short?" he asked.

"My life upon this globe is very brief," replied the Ghost. "It ends tonight."

"Tonight!" cried Scrooge.

"Tonight at midnight. Hark! The time is drawing near."

181

The chimes were ringing the three quarters past eleven.

"Forgive me," said Scrooge, looking intently at the Spirit's robe, "but I see something strange, and not belonging to yourself, protruding from your skirts. Is it a foot or a claw?"

"It might be a claw, for the flesh there is upon it," was the Spirit's sorrowful reply. "Look here!"

From the foldings of its robe it brought two children, frightful, hideous, miserable. They knelt down at its feet, and clung upon its garment. They were a boy and girl: ragged, scowling, wolfish, but abject, too, in their humility. Where youth should have filled their features out, a stale and shriveled hand had pinched and twisted them. Where angels might have sat enthroned, devils glared out menacing.

Scrooge started back, appalled. "Spirit! are they yours?"

"They are Man's," said the Spirit, looking down upon them. "And they cling to me, appealing from their fathers. This boy is Ignorance. This girl is Want. Beware them both."

"Have they no refuge or resource?" cried Scrooge.

"Are there no prisons?" said the Spirit, turning on him for the last time with his own words. "Are there no workhouses?"

The bell struck Twelve.

Scrooge looked about him for the Ghost, and saw it not. As the last stroke ceased to vibrate, he remembered the prediction of old Jacob Marley, and, lifting up his eyes, beheld a solemn Phantom, draped and hooded, coming like a mist along the ground towards him.

THE LAST OF THE SPIRITS

The phantom slowly, gravely, silently approached. When it came near him, Scrooge bent down upon his knee; for in the very air through which this Spirit moved it seemed to scatter gloom and mystery. Tall and stately, it was shrouded in a deep black garment, which left nothing of it visible save one outstretched hand.

"Are you the Ghost of Christmas Yet To Come?" said Scrooge.

The Spirit answered not, but pointed downward with its hand.

"You are about to show me shadows of the things that will happen in the time before us?" Scrooge pursued.

The Spirit seemed to incline its head. That was its only answer.

Although well used to ghostly company by this time, Scrooge feared the silent shape so much that his legs trembled beneath him when he prepared to follow it. The Spirit paused a moment, as if giving him time to recover. But Scrooge was all the worse for this. It thrilled him with a vague, uncertain horror to know that there were ghostly eyes intently fixed upon him, while he could see nothing but a spectral hand and one great heap of black.

"Ghost of the Future!" he exclaimed. "I fear you more than any specter I have seen. But as I hope to live to be another man from what I was, I am prepared to bear your company, and do it with a thankful heart. Will you not speak to me?"

It gave him no reply. The hand pointed before them.

"Lead on!" said Scrooge. "Lead on! The night is waning fast, and it is precious time to me, I know."

The Phantom moved away. Scrooge followed in the shadow of its dress, which bore him up, he thought, and carried him along.

They scarcely seemed to enter the City; but there they were in the heart of it, amongst the merchants, who hurried up and down, and chinked the money in their pockets, and conversed in groups, and looked at their watches, as Scrooge had seen them often.

The Spirit stopped beside one little knot of businessmen.

"No," said a fat man with a monstrous chin, "I don't know much about it. I only know he died last night."

"What was the matter with him?" asked another, taking some snuff. "I thought he'd never die."

"God knows," said the first, with a yawn.

"What has he done with his money?" asked a third.

"Left it to his company, perhaps," said the man with the chin. "He hasn't left it to *me*. That's all I know." This was received with a general laugh. "It's likely to be a very cheap funeral," the man went on; "for, upon my life, I don't know of anybody to go to it. Suppose we make up a party and volunteer?"

"I don't mind going if lunch is provided," observed one gentleman. "But I must be fed if I go."

Another laugh.

"Well," said the first speaker, "I never eat lunch. But I'll go if anybody else will. I'm not at all sure that I wasn't his most particular friend; we used to speak whenever we met. Bye, bye!"

Scrooge knew the men, and looked to the Spirit for an explanation.

The Phantom glided on. Its finger pointed to two persons.

Scrooge knew these men, also. They were men of business: wealthy, and of great importance. He had made a point—strictly in a business point of view—of standing well in their esteem.

"Well!" said one. "Old Scratch has got his own at last, hey?"

Freeze, freeze,
thou bitter sky,
Thou dost not
bite so nigh
As benefits forgot:
Though thou
the waters warp,
Thy sting is
not so sharp
As friend
remember'd not.

WILLIAM SHAKESPEARE

"So I am told," returned the second. "Cold, isn't it?"

"Seasonable for Christmastime. Are you a skater?"

"No. No. Something else to think of. Good morning!"

Not another word.

Scrooge was surprised that the Spirit should attach importance to conversations so trivial; but, sure that they must have some hidden purpose, he resolved to treasure up every word he heard; and especially to observe the shadow of himself when it appeared. For he had an expectation that the conduct of his future self would give him the clue he missed. He looked about for his own image, but another man stood in his accustomed corner. This gave him little surprise, however; for he had been revolving in his mind a change of life, and hoped he saw his newborn resolutions carried out in this.

Quiet and dark, beside him stood the Phantom; and when Scrooge roused himself from thought, he fancied that the Unseen Eyes were looking at him keenly. It made him shudder.

They left the busy scene, and went into an obscure part of the town, where Scrooge had never penetrated before, although he knew its bad repute. Alleys and archways disgorged their smell and filth upon the foul and narrow streets; the drunken, slipshod people, the wretched shops and houses, reeked with misery and crime.

Among them was a low-browed, beetling shop where refuse of all kinds was bought. Secrets that few would like to scrutinize were hidden there in mountains of rags and sepulchers of bones. Sitting among the wares he dealt in, by a charcoal stove, was a gray-haired rascal, nearly seventy years of age, who had screened himself from the cold by a frowzy curtain of miscellaneous tatters hung upon a line, and smoked his pipe in all the luxury of calm retirement.

A woman with a heavy bundle slunk into the shop. She had scarcely entered when another woman, similarly laden, came in too; and she was closely followed by a man in faded black. Startled at first by the sight of each other, they all three burst into a laugh.

"Charwoman first!" cried she who had entered first. "The laundress second; and here's the undertaker's man. If we haven't all three met here without meaning it!"

"You couldn't have met in a better place," said old Joe, removing his pipe from his mouth. "Come into the parlor. Stop till I shut the door of the shop. Ah! how it skreeks! There an't such a rusty bit of metal in the place as its own hinges, I believe; and I'm sure there's no such old bones here as mine. Ha! ha! We're all well matched. Come into the parlor."

The parlor was the space behind the screen of rags. The charwoman threw her bundle on the floor, and sat on a stool, looking with bold defiance at the other

184

O Christmas
is coming,
The geese are
getting fat,
Won't you please
put a penny
In a poor man's hat?
If you haven't
got a penny
A ha'penny will do.
If you haven't
got a ha' penny
Then God bless you!

AUTHOR UNKNOWN

two. She spoke again. "What odds then! What odds, Mrs. Dilber? Every person has a right to take care of themselves. *He* always did! And who's the worse for the loss of these things? Not a dead man, I suppose?"

"No, indeed," said Mrs. Dilber, laughing.

"If he'd been natural in his lifetime," pursued the woman, "he'd have had somebody to look after him, instead of lying gasping out his last there, alone by himself."

"It's a judgment on him," said Mrs. Dilber.

"I wish it was a little heavier one," replied the woman, looking at her bundle, "and it would have been if I could have laid my hands on anything else. Open that bundle, old Joe, and let me know the value of it."

But the gallantry of her friends would not allow of this; and the man in faded black produced *his* plunder first. It was not extensive: a seal or two, a pencil case, a pair of sleeve buttons, and a brooch of no great value. Old Joe chalked the sums he was disposed to give for each upon the wall, and added them into a total. "That's your account," said Joe. "And I wouldn't give another sixpence, if I was to be boiled for not doing it. Who's next?"

Mrs. Dilber was next. Sheets and towels, a little wearing apparel, two silver teaspoons, a pair of sugar tongs. Her account was stated on the wall in the same manner.

"I always give too much to ladies. It's a weakness of mine, and that's the way I ruin myself," said old Joe. "If you asked me for another penny, I'd repent of being so liberal, and knock off half a crown."

"And now undo *my* bundle, Joe," said the first woman.

Joe went down on his knees for the greater convenience of opening it, and, having unfastened a great many knots, dragged out a large heavy roll of some dark stuff. "Bed curtains?" said Joe.

"Ah!" returned the woman, laughing and leaning forward on her crossed arms. "Bed curtains!"

"You don't mean to say you took 'em down, rings and all, with him lying there?" said Joe. "His blankets, too?"

"Why not?" replied the woman. "He isn't likely to take cold without 'em, I daresay. Ah! that shirt is the best he had, and a fine one too. They'd have wasted it, if it hadn't been for me."

"What do you call wasting of it?" asked old Joe.

"Putting it on him to be buried in," replied the woman. "Somebody was fool enough to do it, but I took it off again."

Scrooge listened in horror which could hardly have been greater had they been demons marketing the corpse itself.

"Ha, ha!" laughed the charwoman when old Joe counted out their money.

"This is the end of it, you see! He frightened everyone away when he was alive, to profit us when he was dead!"

"Spirit!" said Scrooge, shuddering from head to foot. "I see, I see. The case of this unhappy man might be my own. My life tends that way now. Merciful Heaven, what is this?"

He recoiled in terror, for the scene had changed, and now he almost touched a bare, uncurtained bed on which, beneath a ragged sheet, there lay a something covered up. The room was dark, but a pale light fell upon the bed; and on it, plundered and bereft, unwatched, unwept, uncared for, was the body of this man. The Phantom's steady hand pointed to the head. The motion of a finger upon Scrooge's part would have raised the cover and disclosed the face; but he had no more power to withdraw the veil than to dismiss the Specter at his side. He thought, if this man could be raised up now, would he think of avarice and hard dealing? Here he lay with not a man, a woman, or a child to say: since he was kind to me in this or that, I will be kind to him. There was a sound of gnawing rats beneath the hearthstone. What *they* wanted in the room of death, Scrooge did not dare to think. "If there is any person in the town who feels emotion caused by this man's death," said Scrooge, quite agonized, "show that person to me, Spirit, I beseech you!"

The Phantom spread its robe before him like a wing; and, withdrawing it, revealed a room by daylight where a mother and her children were. She was expecting someone, and anxious; for she walked up and down the room, started at every sound, looked out from the window, glanced at the clock.

At length the long-expected knock was heard. She hurried to the door, and met her husband; a man whose face, though young, was careworn. There was a remarkable expression in it now, a kind of serious delight which, with shame, he struggled to repress.

"We are quite ruined?" she asked.

"No. There is hope yet, Caroline."

"If *he* relents," she said, "there is! Nothing is past hope, if such a miracle has happened."

"He is past relenting," said her husband. "He is dead."

She was a mild and patient creature, if her face spoke truth; but she was thankful in her soul to hear it, and she said so. She prayed forgiveness the next moment, and was sorry; but the first was the emotion of her heart.

He said, "What that half-drunken woman told me when I tried to see him and obtain a week's delay turns out to have been quite true. He was not only very ill, but dying then."

"To whom will our debt be transferred?"

"I don't know. But before that time we'll be ready with the money; and

even though we weren't, it would be bad fortune indeed to find another creditor so merciless. We may sleep tonight with light hearts, Caroline!"

Yes, their hearts were lighter. And the children's faces, clustered round to hear what they so little understood, were brighter for this man's death! The only emotion that the Ghost could show him, caused by the event, was one of pleasure.

"Let me see some tenderness connected with a death," said Scrooge; "or that dark chamber, Spirit, will be forever present to me."

Again, they entered poor Bob Cratchit's house, and found the mother and the children seated round the fire. Quiet. Very quiet. The mother and her daughters were engaged in sewing. The noisy little Cratchits were still as statues in one corner, and sat looking up at Peter, who had a book before him.

"And he took a child, and set him in the midst of them. . . ."

Why did the boy not go on reading? The mother laid her work upon the table, and put her hand up to her face. "The color hurts my eyes," she said. "I wouldn't show weak eyes to your father when he comes home for the world. It must be near his time."

"Past it rather," Peter answered, shutting up his book. "But he has walked a little slower than he used, these few last evenings."

They were quiet again. At last she said, in a steady voice that only faltered once: "I have known him walk with—I have known him walk with Tiny Tim upon his shoulder very fast indeed."

"And so have I," cried Peter. "Often."

"But he was very light to carry," she resumed, intent again upon her work, "and his father loved him so that it was no trouble. And there is your father at the door!"

She hurried out to meet him; and little Bob in his comforter—he had need of it, poor fellow—came in. His tea was ready for him on the hob, and they all tried who should help him to it most. Then the two young Cratchits got upon his knees, and laid, each child, a little cheek against his face, as if they said, "Don't mind it, father. Don't be grieved!"

Bob was very cheerful with them, looked at the work upon the table, and praised the industry and speed of Mrs. Cratchit and the girls. They would be done long before Sunday, he said.

"Sunday! You went today then, Robert?" said his wife.

"Yes, my dear. I wish you could have gone. It would have done you good to see how green a place it is. But you'll see it often. I promised him I would walk there on a Sunday. My little, little child!" cried Bob. "My little child!"

He broke down all at once. He couldn't help it. If he could have helped it, he and his child would have been farther apart, perhaps, than they were.

He went upstairs into the room above, which was lighted cheerfully, and hung with Christmas. There was a chair set close beside the child, and there were signs of someone having been there lately. Poor Bob sat down in it, and when he had composed himself a little, he kissed the boy's face and was reconciled to what had happened.

He went down again and they talked, the girls and mother working still. Bob told them of the kindness of Mr. Scrooge's nephew, who, meeting him in the street that day, and seeing that he looked a little—"just a little down, you know," said Bob, inquired what had happened to distress him. "On which," said Bob, "for he is the pleasantest-spoken gentleman you ever heard, I told him. 'I am heartily sorry for it, Mr. Cratchit,' he said, 'and heartily sorry for your good wife.' By the bye, how he ever knew *that* I don't know."

"Knew what, my dear?"

"Why, that you were a good wife," replied Bob.

"Everybody knows that," said Peter.

"Very well observed, my boy!" cried Bob. "I hope they do. 'If I can be of service to you in any way,' he said, giving me his card, 'pray come to me.' Now, it wasn't," cried Bob, "for the sake of anything he might be able to do for us, so much as for his kind way, that this was quite delightful. It really seemed as if he had known our Tiny Tim, and felt with us. I shouldn't be at all surprised—mark what I say!—if he got Peter a better situation."

"And then," cried one of the girls, "Peter will be keeping company with some-one, and setting up for himself."

"Get along with you!" retorted Peter, grinning.

"It's just as likely as not," said Bob, "one of these days, though there's plenty of time for that, my dear. But, however we part from one another, I am sure we shall none of us forget poor Tiny Tim, or this first parting that there was among us."

"Never, father!" cried they all.

"And I know, my dears," said Bob, "that when we recollect how patient and how mild he was, although he was a little, little child, we shall not quarrel easily among ourselves, and forget soon Tiny Tim in doing it."

"No, never, father!" they all cried again.

"I am very happy," said little Bob, "I am very happy!"

Mrs. Cratchit kissed him, his daughters kissed him, the two young Cratchits kissed him, and Peter and himself shook hands. Spirit of Tiny Tim, thy childish essence was from God!

"Specter," said Scrooge, "something informs me that our parting moment is at hand. I know it but I know not how. Tell me what man that was whom we saw lying dead?"

The Ghost of Christmas Yet To Come conveyed him, as before, into the resorts of businessmen, but went straight on, until they reached a churchyard. Here, then, the wretched man, whose name he had now to learn, lay underneath the ground. Walled in by houses; overrun by grass and weeds; choked up with too much burying. A worthy place!

The Spirit stood among the graves, and pointed down to One. He advanced towards it trembling.

"Before I draw nearer to that stone," said Scrooge, "answer me one question. Are these the shadows of the things that Will be, or are they shadows of the things that May be only?"

The Spirit was immovable as ever.

Scrooge crept towards it, trembling as he went; and, following the finger, read upon the stone of the neglected grave his own name, EBENEZER SCROOGE.

"Am I that man upon the bed?" he cried upon his knees.

The finger pointed from the grave to him, and back again.

"No, Spirit!" he cried, tight clutching at its robe, "hear me! I am not the man I was. Why show me this, if I am past all hope?"

For the first time the hand appeared to shake.

"Good Spirit," he pursued, as down he fell before it, "your nature intercedes for me, and pities me. Assure me that I yet may change these shadows you have shown me by an altered life?"

The kind hand trembled.

"I will honor Christmas in my heart, and try to keep it all the year. I will live in the Past, the Present, and the Future. The Spirits of all Three shall strive within me. I will not shut out the lessons that they teach. Oh, tell me I may sponge away the writing on this stone!"

In his agony, he caught the spectral hand. It sought to free itself, but he was strong in his entreaty, and detained it. The Spirit, stronger yet, repulsed him.

Holding up his hands in one last prayer to change his fate, he saw an alteration in the Phantom's hood and dress. It shrunk, collapsed, and dwindled down into a bedpost.

THE END OF IT

Yes! AND THE bedpost was his own. The bed was his own, the room was his own. Best and happiest of all, the Time before him was his own, to make amends in! "I will live in the Past, the Present, and the Future!" Scrooge repeated as he scrambled out of bed. "The Spirits of all Three shall strive within me. O Jacob

Marley! Heaven and Christmastime be praised for this! I say it on my knees, old Jacob; on my knees!" He was so fluttered and so glowing with his good intentions that his broken voice would scarcely answer to his call. He had been sobbing violently in his conflict with the Spirit, and his face was wet with tears. "They are not torn down," cried Scrooge, folding one of his bed curtains in his arms. "They are here—I am here—the shadows of the things that would have been may be dispelled. I know they will be!"

His hands were busy with his garments all this time: turning them inside out, putting them on upside down.

"I am as light as a feather!" cried Scrooge, laughing and crying in the same breath. "I am as happy as an angel, I am as merry as a schoolboy! I am as giddy as a drunken man. A merry Christmas to everybody! A happy New Year to all! Hallo here! Whoop! Hallo!"

He had frisked into the sitting room, and was now standing there, perfectly winded. "There's the saucepan that the gruel was in! There's the door by which the Ghost of Jacob Marley entered! There's the corner where the Ghost of Christmas Present sat! It's all right, it's all true, it all happened. Ha, ha, ha!"

Really, for a man who had been out of practice for so many years, it was a splendid laugh, a most illustrious laugh. The father of a long, long line of brilliant laughs!

"I don't know what day of the month it is," said Scrooge. "I don't know how long I have been among the Spirits. I don't know anything. Never mind. Hallo! Whoop! Hallo here!"

He was checked in his transports by the churches ringing out the lustiest peals he had ever heard. Clash, clang, hammer; ding, dong, bell! Bell, dong, ding; hammer, clang, clash! Oh, glorious!

Running to the window, he opened it, and put out his head. No fog, no mist; clear, stirring cold for the blood to dance to; golden sunlight; sweet fresh air; merry bells. Oh, glorious! Glorious! "What's today?" cried Scrooge, calling down to a boy in Sunday clothes.

"Eh?" returned the boy in wonder. "Why, CHRISTMAS DAY."

"It's Christmas Day!" said Scrooge to himself. "I haven't missed it. The Spirits have done it all in one night. They can do anything they like. Of course they can. Hallo, my fine fellow!"

"Hallo!" returned the boy.

"Do you know the poulterer's in the next street but one, at the corner?" Scrooge inquired.

"I should hope I did," replied the lad.

"An intelligent boy!" said Scrooge. "A remarkable boy! Do you know whether they've sold the prize turkey that was hanging up there?—the big one?"

Then let us sing amid our cheer, Old Christmas comes but once a year.

THOMAS MILLER

"What! the one as big as me?" returned the boy.

"What a delightful boy!" said Scrooge. "Yes, my buck! Go buy it, and tell 'em to bring it here, that I may tell them where to take it. Come back with the man, and I'll give you a shilling. Come back with him in less than five minutes, and I'll give you half a crown!"

The boy was off like a shot. "I'll send it to Bob Cratchit's," whispered Scrooge, rubbing his hands. "He shan't know who sends it. It's twice the size of Tiny Tim."

The hand in which he wrote the address was not steady; but write it he did, somehow, and went down to the street door to wait for the poulterer's man. As he stood there, the knocker caught his eye. "I shall love it as long as I live!" cried Scrooge. "What an honest expression it has! It's a wonderful knocker!— Here's the turkey. Hallo! How are you! Merry Christmas!"

It *was* a turkey! He never could have stood upon his legs, that bird. "Why, it's impossible to carry that to Camden Town," said Scrooge. "You must have a cab."

The chuckle with which he said this, and the chuckle with which he paid for the cab, and the chuckle with which he recompensed the boy, were only exceeded by the chuckle with which he sat down breathless in his chair again, and chuckled till he cried.

He dressed himself in his best, and at last got out into the streets. The people were by this time pouring forth, and Scrooge regarded everyone with a delighted smile. He looked so irresistibly pleasant that three or four good-humored fellows said, "A merry Christmas to you!" And Scrooge said often afterwards that, of all the sounds he had ever heard, those were the blithest in his ears.

He had not gone far when he saw the portly gentleman who had walked into his countinghouse the day before, and said, "Scrooge and Marley's, I believe?" It sent a pang across his heart to think how this old gentleman would look upon him when they met; but he knew what path lay straight before him, and he took it.

"My dear sir," said Scrooge, taking the old gentleman by both his hands, "how do you do? I hope you succeeded yesterday. It was very kind of you. A merry Christmas to you, sir!"

"Mr. Scrooge?"

"Yes," said Scrooge. "That is my name. Allow me to ask your pardon. And will you have the goodness—" here Scrooge whispered in his ear.

"Lord bless me!" cried the gentleman, as if his breath were taken away. "My dear Mr. Scrooge, are you serious?"

"If you please," said Scrooge. "Not a farthing less. A great many back payments are included in it, I assure you."

The legend tells that when Jesus was born the sun danced in the sky, the aged trees straightened themselves and put on leaves and sent forth the fragrance of blossoms. These are the symbols of what takes place in our hearts when the Christ Child is born anew each year.

B lessed by the
Christmas sunshine,
our natures, perhaps
long leafless, bring
forth new love, new
kindness, new mercy,
new compassion.

HELEN KELLER

"My dear sir," said the other, shaking hands with him, "I don't know what to say to such munifi—"

"Don't say anything, please," retorted Scrooge. "Come and see me. Will you come and see me?"

"I will!" cried the other. And it was clear he meant it.

Scrooge went to church, and walked about the streets, and watched the people hurrying to and fro, and patted children on the head, and looked down into kitchens, and found that everything could give him pleasure. In the afternoon he turned his steps towards his nephew's house. He passed the door a dozen times before he had the courage to knock. But he made a dash and did it.

"Is your master at home, my dear?" said Scrooge to the girl.

"Yes, sir. He's in the dining room, sir, along with mistress. I'll show you in, if you please."

"Thank'ee. He knows me," said Scrooge. "I'll go in, my dear."

He turned the doorknob gently, and sidled in. They were looking at the table (which was spread out in great array); for these young housekeepers are always nervous on such points, and like to see that everything is right.

"Fred!" said Scrooge.

Dear heart alive, how his niece by marriage started!

"Why, bless my soul!" cried Fred. "Who's that?"

"It's uncle Scrooge, come to dinner. Will you let me in?"

Let him in! It is a mercy Fred didn't shake his arm off. He was at home in five minutes. His niece looked just the same. So did Topper when *he* came. So did the plump sister when *she* came. So did everyone when *they* came. Wonderful party, wonderful games, wonderful unanimity, won-der-ful happiness!

But he was early at the office next morning. Oh, if he could only be there first, and catch Bob Cratchit coming late! That was the thing he had set his heart upon.

And he did it! The clock struck nine. No Bob. A quarter past. No Bob. He was full eighteen minutes and a half behind his time. Scrooge sat with his door wide open, that he might see him come into the tank.

His hat was off before he opened the door; his comforter too. He was on his stool in a jiffy, driving away with his pen, as if he were trying to overtake nine o'clock.

"Hallo!" growled Scrooge, in what he hoped was his accustomed voice. "What do you mean by coming at this hour?"

"I am very sorry, sir," said Bob. "I *am* behind my time."

"You are! Step this way, sir, if you please."

"It's only once a year, sir," pleaded Bob, appearing from the tank. "I was making rather merry yesterday, sir."

"I tell you what, my friend," said Scrooge. "I am not going to stand this sort of thing any longer. And therefore," he continued, leaping from his stool, and giving Bob such a dig in the waistcoat that he staggered—"I am about to raise your salary!"

Bob trembled. He had a momentary idea of knocking Scrooge down, holding him, and calling for help and a straitjacket.

"A merry Christmas, Bob!" said Scrooge, with an earnestness that could not be mistaken, as he clapped him on the back. "A merrier Christmas, Bob, my good fellow, than I have given you for many a year! I'll raise your salary, and assist your struggling family, and we will discuss your affairs this very afternoon, over a bowl of Christmas punch, Bob! Make up the fires and buy another coal scuttle before you dot another i, Bob Cratchit!"

Scrooge was better than his word. He did it all, and more; and to Tiny Tim, who did NOT die, he was a second father. He became as good a friend, as good a master, and as good a man as the good old City knew, or any other good old city or town in the good old world. Some people laughed to see the alteration in him, but he little heeded them; for he was wise enough to know that nothing ever happened on this globe for good at which some people did not laugh in the outset. His own heart laughed, and that was quite enough for him.

He had no further intercourse with Spirits; but it was said of him ever afterwards that he knew how to keep Christmas well, if any man alive possessed the knowledge. May that be truly said of us, and all of us! And so, as Tiny Tim observed, God Bless Us, Every One!

As fits the holy
Christmas birth,
Be this, good friends,
our carol still—
Be peace on earth,
be peace on earth,
To men of gentle will.

WILLIAM MAKEPEACE THACKERAY

One of the first Christmas cards,
designed for Sir Henry Cole by John C. Horsley in 1843.

195

WASSAIL SONG

Here we come a-wassailing
   Among the leaves so green,
Here we come a-wandering,
   So fair to be seen.

Love and joy come to you
And to you glad Christmas too;
And God bless you and send you
A happy New Year,
And God send you a happy New Year.

We are not daily beggars
   That beg from door to door,
But we are neighbors' children
   Whom you have seen before.

We have got a little purse
   Of stretching leather skin;
We want a little money
   To line it well within.

God bless the master of this house,
   Likewise the mistress too;
And all the little children
   That round the table go.

Good Master and good Mistress,
   While you sit by the fire,
Pray think of us poor children
   A-wandering in the mire.

               English carol

A CHRISTMAS MEMORY
by Truman Capote

Imagine a morning in late November. A coming of winter morning more than twenty years ago. Consider the kitchen of a spreading old house in a country town. A great black stove is its main feature; but there is also a big round table and a fireplace with two rocking chairs placed in front of it. Just today the fireplace commenced its seasonal roar.

A woman with shorn white hair is standing at the kitchen window. She is wearing tennis shoes and a shapeless gray sweater over a summery calico dress. She is small and sprightly, like a bantam hen; but, due to a long youthful illness, her shoulders are pitifully hunched. Her face is remarkable—not unlike Lincoln's, craggy like that, and tinted by sun and wind; but it is delicate too, finely boned, and her eyes are sherry-colored and timid. "Oh my," she exclaims, her breath smoking the windowpane, "it's fruitcake weather!"

The person to whom she is speaking is myself. I am seven; she is sixty-something. We are cousins, very distant ones, and we have lived together—well, as long as I can remember. Other people inhabit the house, relatives; and though they have power over us, and frequently make us cry, we are not, on the whole, too much aware of them. We are each other's best friend. She calls me Buddy, in memory of a boy who was formerly her best friend. The other Buddy died in the 1880s, when she was still a child. She is still a child.

"I knew it before I got out of bed," she says, turning away from the window with a purposeful excitement in her eyes. "The courthouse bell sounded so cold and clear. And there were no birds singing; they've gone to warmer country, yes indeed. Oh, Buddy, stop stuffing biscuit and fetch our buggy. Help me find my hat. We've thirty cakes to bake."

It's always the same: a morning arrives in November, and my friend, as though officially inaugurating the Christmas time of year that exhilarates her imagination and fuels the blaze of her heart, announces: "It's fruitcake weather! Fetch our buggy. Help me find my hat."

The hat is found, a straw cartwheel corsaged with velvet roses out-of-doors has faded: it once belonged to a more fashionable relative. Together, we guide our buggy, a dilapidated baby carriage, out to the garden and into a grove of pecan trees. The buggy is mine; that is, it was bought for me when I was born.

It is made of wicker, rather unraveled, and the wheels wobble like a drunkard's legs. But it is a faithful object; springtimes, we take it to the woods and fill it with flowers, herbs, wild fern for our porch pots; in the summer, we pile it with picnic paraphernalia and sugarcane fishing poles and roll it down to the edge of a creek; it has its winter uses, too: as a truck for hauling firewood from the yard to the kitchen, as a warm bed for Queenie, our tough little orange and white rat terrier who has survived distemper and two rattlesnake bites. Queenie is trotting beside it now.

Three hours later we are back in the kitchen hulling a heaping buggyload of windfall pecans. Our backs hurt from gathering them: how hard they were to

find (the main crop having been shaken off the trees and sold by the orchard's owners, who are not us) among the concealing leaves, the frosted, deceiving grass. Caarackle! A cheery crunch, scraps of miniature thunder sound as the shells collapse and the golden mound of sweet oily ivory meat mounts in the milk-glass bowl.

Queenie begs to taste, and now and again my friend sneaks her a mite, though insisting we deprive ourselves. "We mustn't, Buddy. If we start, we won't stop. And there's scarcely enough as there is. For thirty cakes." The kitchen is growing dark. Dusk turns the window into a mirror: our reflections mingle with the rising moon as we work by the fireside in the firelight. At last, when the moon is quite high, we toss the final hull into the fire and, with joined sighs, watch it catch flame. The buggy is empty, the bowl is brimful.

We eat our supper (cold biscuits, bacon, blackberry jam) and discuss to-morrow. Tomorrow the kind of work I like best begins: buying. Cherries and citron, ginger and vanilla and canned Hawaiian pineapple, rinds and raisins and walnuts and whiskey and oh, so much flour, butter, so many eggs, spices, flavorings: why, we'll need a pony to pull the buggy home.

But before these purchases can be made, there is the question of money. Neither of us has any. Except for skinflint sums persons in the house occasionally provide (a dime is considered very big money); or what we earn ourselves from various activities: holding rummage sales, selling buckets of handpicked blackberries, jars of homemade jam and apple jelly and peach preserves, rounding up flowers for funerals and weddings. Once we won seventy-ninth prize, five dollars, in a national football contest. Not that we know a fool thing about football. It's just that we enter any contest we hear about: at the moment our hopes are centered on the fifty-thousand-dollar Grand Prize being offered to name a new brand of coffee (we suggested "A.M."; and, after some hesitation, for my friend thought it perhaps sacrilegious, the slogan "A.M.! Amen!"). To tell the truth, our only *really* profitable enterprise was the Fun and Freak Museum we conducted in a backyard woodshed two summers ago. The Fun was a stereopticon with slide views of Washington and New York lent us by a relative who had been to those places (she was furious when she discovered why we'd borrowed it); the Freak was a three-legged biddy chicken hatched by one of our own hens. Everybody hereabouts wanted to see that biddy: we charged grown-ups a nickel, kids two cents. And took in a good twenty dollars before the museum shut down due to the decease of the main attraction.

But one way and another we do each year accumulate Christmas savings, a Fruitcake Fund. These moneys we keep hidden in an ancient bead purse under a loose board under the floor under a chamber pot under my friend's bed. The purse is seldom removed from this safe location except to make a deposit, or, as happens every Saturday, a withdrawal; for on Saturdays I am allowed ten cents to go to the picture show. My friend has never been to a picture show, nor does she intend to: "I'd rather hear you tell the story, Buddy. That way I can imagine it more. Besides, a person my age shouldn't squander their eyes. When the Lord comes, let me see Him clear." In addition to never having seen a movie, she has never: eaten in a restaurant, traveled more than five miles from home, received or sent a telegram, read anything except funny papers and the Bible, worn cosmetics, cursed, wished someone harm, told a lie on purpose, let a hungry dog go hungry. Here are a few things she has done, does do: killed with a hoe the biggest rattlesnake ever seen in this county (sixteen rattles), dip snuff (secretly), tame hummingbirds (just try it) till they balance on her finger, tell ghost stories (we both believe in ghosts), talk to herself, take walks in the rain, grow the prettiest japonicas in town, know the recipe for every sort of old-time Indian cure, including a magical wart remover.

Now, with supper finished, we retire to the room in a faraway part of the house

D on't wash and press a Christmas present before giving it, or you will wash out the good luck and press in the bad.

SUPERSTITION OF THE OLD SOUTH

199

Make a start on your year's work between Christmas and January fifth–a bit of ditching, a little plowing–to "show your intentions." But never fix your roof between Christmas and New Year's or the holes will come right back.

SUPERSTITION OF THE OLD SOUTH

where my friend sleeps in a scrap-quilt-covered iron bed painted rose pink, her favorite color. Silently, wallowing in the pleasures of conspiracy, we take the bead purse from its secret place and spill its contents on the scrap quilt. Dollar bills, tightly rolled and green as May buds. Somber fifty-cent pieces, heavy enough to weight a dead man's eyes. Lovely dimes, the liveliest coin, the one that really jingles. Nickels and quarters, worn smooth as creek pebbles. But mostly a hateful heap of bitter-odored pennies. Last summer others in the house contracted to pay us a penny for every twenty-five flies we killed. Oh, the carnage of August: the flies that flew to heaven! Yet it was not work in which we took pride. And, as we sit counting pennies, it is as though we were back tabulating dead flies. Neither of us has a head for figures; we count slowly, lose track, start again. According to her calculations, we have $12.73. According to mine, exactly $13. "I do hope you're wrong, Buddy. We can't mess around with thirteen. The cakes will fall. Or put somebody in the cemetery. Why, I wouldn't dream of getting out of bed on the thirteenth." This is true: she always spends thirteenths in bed. So, to be on the safe side, we subtract a penny and toss it out the window.

Of the ingredients that go into our fruitcakes, whiskey is the most expensive, as well as the hardest to obtain: state laws forbid its sale. But everybody knows you can buy a bottle from Mr. Haha Jones. And the next day, having completed our more prosaic shopping, we set out for Mr. Haha's business address, a "sinful" (to quote public opinion) fish-fry and dancing café down by the river. We've been there before, and on the same errand; but in previous years our dealings have been with Haha's wife, an iodine-dark Indian woman with brassy peroxided hair and a dead-tired disposition. Actually, we've never laid eyes on her husband, though we've heard that he's an Indian too. A giant with razor scars across his cheeks. They call him Haha because he's so gloomy, a man who never laughs. As we approach his café (a large log cabin festooned inside and out with chains of garish-gay naked light bulbs and standing by the river's muddy edge under the shade of river trees where moss drifts through the branches like gray mist) our steps slow down. Even Queenie stops prancing and sticks close by. People have been murdered in Haha's café. Cut to pieces. Hit on the head. There's a case coming up in court next month. Naturally these goings-on happen at night when the colored lights cast crazy patterns and the Victrola wails. In the daytime Haha's is shabby and deserted. I knock at the door, Queenie barks, my friend calls: "Mrs. Haha, ma'am? Anyone to home?"

Footsteps. The door opens. Our hearts overturn. It's Mr. Haha Jones himself! And he *is* a giant; he *does* have scars; he *doesn't* smile. No, he glowers at us through Satan-tilted eyes and demands to know: "What you want with Haha?"

For a moment we are too paralyzed to tell. Presently my friend half finds her voice, a whispery voice at best: "If you please, Mr. Haha, we'd like a quart of your finest whiskey."

His eyes tilt more. Would you believe it? Haha is smiling! Laughing, too. "Which one of you is a drinkin' man?"

"It's for making fruitcakes, Mr. Haha. Cooking."

This sobers him. He frowns. "That's no way to waste good whiskey." Nevertheless, he retreats into the shadowed café and seconds later appears carrying a bottle of daisy-yellow unlabeled liquor. He demonstrates its sparkle in the sunlight and says: "Two dollars."

We pay him with nickels and dimes and pennies. Suddenly, as he jangles

the coins in his hand like a fistful of dice, his face softens. "Tell you what," he proposes, pouring the money back into our bead purse, "just send me one of them fruitcakes instead."

"Well," my friend remarks on our way home, "there's a lovely man. We'll put an extra cup of raisins in *his* cake."

The black stove, stoked with coal and firewood, glows like a lighted pumpkin. Eggbeaters whirl, spoons spin round in bowls of butter and sugar, vanilla sweetens the air, ginger spices it; melting, nose-tingling odors saturate the kitchen, suffuse the house, drift out to the world on puffs of chimney smoke. In four days our work is done. Thirty-one cakes, dampened with whiskey, bask on windowsills and shelves.

Who are they for?

Friends. Not necessarily neighbor friends: indeed, the larger share is intended for persons we've met maybe once, perhaps not at all. People who've struck our fancy. Like President Roosevelt. Like the Reverend and Mrs. J. C.

Leave a loaf
of bread on
the table after
Christmas Eve
supper and
you will have
a full supply
until the next
Christmas.

SUPERSTITION OF THE
OLD SOUTH

Lucey, Baptist missionaries to Borneo who lectured here last winter. Or the little knife grinder who comes through town twice a year. Or Abner Packer, the driver of the six-o'clock bus from Mobile, who exchanges waves with us every day as he passes in a dust-cloud whoosh. Or the young Wistons, a California couple whose car one afternoon broke down outside the house and who spent a pleasant hour chatting with us on the porch (young Mr. Wiston snapped our picture, the only one we've ever had taken). Is it because my friend is shy with everyone *except* strangers that these strangers, and merest acquaintances, seem to us our truest friends? I think yes. Also, the scrapbooks we keep of thank-yous on White House stationery, time-to-time communications from California and Borneo, the knife grinder's penny postcards, make us feel connected to eventful worlds beyond the kitchen with its view of a sky that stops.

Now a nude December fig branch grates against the window. The kitchen is empty, the cakes are gone; yesterday we carted the last of them to the post office, where the cost of stamps turned our purse inside out. We're broke, but my friend insists on celebrating—with two inches of whiskey left in Haha's bottle. Queenie has a spoonful in a bowl of coffee (she likes her coffee chicory-flavored and strong). The rest we divide between a pair of jelly glasses. We're both quite awed at the prospect of drinking straight whiskey; the taste of it brings screwed-up expressions and sour shudders. But by and by we begin to sing, the two of us singing different songs simultaneously. I don't know the words to mine, just: *Come on along, come on along, to the darktown strutters' ball.* But I can dance: that's what I mean to be, a tap dancer in the movies. My dancing shadow rollicks on the walls; our voices rock the chinaware; we giggle: as if unseen hands were tickling us. Queenie rolls on her back, her paws plow the air, something like a grin stretches her black lips. Inside myself, I feel warm and sparky as those crumbling logs, carefree as the wind in the chimney. My friend waltzes round the stove, the hem of her poor calico skirt pinched between her fingers as though it were a party dress: *Show me the way to go home,* she sings, her tennis shoes squeaking on the floor.

Enter: two relatives. Very angry. Potent with eyes that scold, tongues that scald. Listen to what they have to say, the words tumbling together into a wrathful tune: "A child of seven! whiskey on his breath! are you out of your mind? road to ruination! remember Cousin Kate? Uncle Charlie? Uncle Charlie's brother-in-law? shame! scandal! humiliation! kneel, pray, beg the Lord!"

Queenie sneaks under the stove. My friend gazes at her shoes, her chin quivers, she lifts her skirt and blows her nose and runs to her room. Long after the town has gone to sleep and the house is silent except for the chimings of clocks and the sputter of fading fires, she is weeping into a pillow already as wet as a widow's handkerchief.

202

"Don't cry," I say, sitting at the bottom of her bed and shivering despite my flannel nightgown that smells of last winter's cough syrup, "don't cry," I beg, teasing her toes, tickling her feet, "you're too old for that."

"It's because," she hiccups, "I *am* too old. Old and funny."

"Not funny. Fun. More fun than anybody. Listen. If you don't stop crying you'll be so tired tomorrow we can't go cut a tree."

She straightens up. Queenie jumps on the bed (where Queenie is not allowed) to lick her cheeks. "I know where we'll find real pretty trees, Buddy. And holly, too. With berries big as your eyes. It's way off in the woods. Farther than we've ever been. Papa used to bring us Christmas trees from there: carry

them on his shoulder. That's fifty years ago. Well, now: I can't wait for morning."

Morning. Frozen rime lusters the grass; the sun, round as an orange and orange as hot-weather moons, balances on the horizon, burnishes the silvered winter woods. A wild turkey calls. A renegade hog grunts in the undergrowth. Soon, by the edge of knee-deep, rapid-running water, we have to abandon the buggy. Queenie wades the stream first, paddles across barking complaints at the swiftness of the current, the pneumonia-making coldness of it. We follow, holding our shoes and equipment (a hatchet, a burlap sack) above our heads. A mile more: of chastising thorns, burs and briers that catch at our clothes; of rusty pine needles brilliant with gaudy fungus and molted feathers. Here, there, a flash, a flutter, an ecstasy of shrillings remind us that not all the birds have flown south. Always, the path unwinds through lemony sun pools and pitch-black vine tunnels. Another creek to cross: a disturbed armada of speckled trout froths the water round us, and frogs the size of plates practice belly flops; beaver workmen are building a dam. On the farther shore, Queenie shakes

herself and trembles. My friend shivers, too: not with cold but enthusiasm. One of her hat's ragged roses sheds a petal as she lifts her head and inhales the pine-heavy air. "We're almost there; can you smell it, Buddy?" she says, as though we were approaching an ocean.

And, indeed, it is a kind of ocean. Scented acres of holiday trees, prickly-leafed holly. Red berries shiny as Chinese bells: black crows swoop upon them screaming. Having stuffed our burlap sacks with enough greenery and crimson to garland a dozen windows, we set about choosing a tree. "It should be," muses my friend, "twice as tall as a boy. So a boy can't steal the star." The one we pick is twice as tall as me. A brave handsome brute that survives thirty hatchet strokes before it keels with a creaking rending cry. Lugging it like a kill, we commence the long trek out. Every few yards we abandon the struggle, sit down and pant. But we have the strength of triumphant huntsmen; that and the tree's virile, icy perfume revive us, goad us on. Many compliments accompany our sunset return along the red clay road to town; but my friend is sly and noncommittal when passersby praise the treasure perched in our buggy: what a fine tree and where did it come from? "Yonderways," she murmurs vaguely. Once a car stops and the rich millowner's lazy wife leans out and whines: "Giveya two bits cash for that ol tree." Ordinarily my friend is afraid of saying no; but on this occasion she promptly shakes her head: "We wouldn't take a dollar." The millowner's wife persists. "A dollar, my foot! Fifty cents. That's my last offer. Goodness, woman, you can get another one." In answer, my friend gently reflects: "I doubt it. There's never two of anything."

Home: Queenie slumps by the fire and sleeps till tomorrow, snoring loud as a human.

A trunk in the attic contains: a shoe box of ermine tails (off the opera cape of a curious lady who once rented a room in the house), coils of frazzled tinsel gone gold with age, one silver star, a brief rope of dilapidated, undoubtedly dangerous candylike light bulbs. Excellent decorations, as far as they go, which isn't far enough: my friend wants our tree to blaze "like a Baptist window," droop with weighty snows of ornament. But we can't afford the made-in-Japan splendors at the five-and-dime.

So we do what we've always done: sit for days at the kitchen table with scissors and crayons and stacks of colored paper. I make sketches and my friend cuts them out: lots of cats, fish too (because they're easy to draw), some apples, some watermelons, a few winged angels devised from saved-up sheets of Hershey-bar tinfoil. We use safety pins to attach these creations to the tree; as a final touch, we sprinkle the branches with shredded cotton (picked in August for this

204

purpose). My friend, surveying the effect, clasps her hands together. "Now honest, Buddy. Doesn't it look good enough to eat?" Queenie tries to eat an angel.

After weaving and ribboning holly wreaths for all the front windows, our next project is the fashioning of family gifts. Tie-dyed scarves for the ladies, for the men a home-brewed lemon and licorice and aspirin syrup to be taken "at the first Symptoms of a Cold and after Hunting." But when it comes time for making each other's gift, my friend and I separate to work secretly. I would like to buy her a pearl-handled knife, a radio, a whole pound of chocolate-covered cherries (we tasted some once, and she always swears: "I could live on them, Buddy, Lord yes I could—and that's not taking His name in vain").

Instead, I am building her a kite. She would like to give me a bicycle (she's said so on several million occasions: "If only I could, Buddy. It's bad enough in life to do without something *you* want; but confound it, what gets my goat is not being able to give somebody something you want *them* to have. Only one of these days I will, Buddy. Locate you a bike. Don't ask how. Steal it, maybe"). Instead, I'm fairly certain that she is building me a kite—the same as last year, and the year before: the year before that we exchanged slingshots. All of which is fine by me. For we are champion kite fliers who study the wind like sailors; my friend, more accomplished than I, can get a kite aloft when there isn't enough breeze to carry clouds.

Christmas Eve afternoon we scrape together a nickel and go to the butcher's to buy Queenie's traditional gift, a good gnawable beef bone. The bone, wrapped in funny paper, is placed high in the tree near the silver star. Queenie knows it's there. She squats at the foot of the tree staring up in a trance of greed: when bedtime arrives she refuses to budge. Her excitement is equaled by my own. I

If you let a
fire go out
on Christmas
morning,
spirits will
come to you
then and
later in the
season.

SUPERSTITION OF THE
OLD SOUTH

kick the covers and turn my pillow as though it were a scorching summer's night. Somewhere a rooster crows: falsely, for the sun is still on the other side of the world.

"Buddy, are you awake?" It is my friend, calling from her room, which is next to mine; and an instant later she is sitting on my bed holding a candle. "Well, I can't sleep a hoot," she declares. "My mind's jumping like a jackrabbit. Buddy, do you think Mrs. Roosevelt will serve our cake at dinner?" We huddle in the bed, and she squeezes my hand I-love-you. "Seems like your hand used to be so much smaller. I guess I hate to see you grow up. When you're grown up, will we still be friends?" I say always. "But I feel so bad, Buddy. I wanted so bad to give you a bike. I tried to sell my cameo Papa gave me. Buddy"—she hesitates, as though embarrassed—"I made you another kite." Then I confess that I made her one, too; and we laugh.

The candle burns too short to hold. Out it goes, exposing the starlight, the stars spinning at the window like a visible caroling that slowly, slowly daybreak silences. Possibly we doze; but the beginnings of dawn splash us like cold water: we're up, wide-eyed and wandering while we wait for others to waken. Quite deliberately my friend drops a kettle on the kitchen floor. I tap-dance in front of closed doors. One by one the household emerges, looking as though they'd like to kill us both; but it's Christmas, so they can't. First, a gorgeous breakfast: just everything you can imagine—from flapjacks and fried squirrel to hominy grits and honey-in-the-comb. Which puts everyone in a good humor except my friend and me. Frankly, we're so impatient to get at the presents we can't eat a mouthful.

Well, I'm disappointed. Who wouldn't be? With socks, a Sunday-school shirt, some handkerchiefs, a hand-me-down sweater and a year's subscription to a religious magazine for children. *The Little Shepherd*. It makes me boil. It really does.

My friend has a better haul. A sack of satsumas, that's her best present. She is proudest, however, of a white wool shawl knitted by her married sister. But she *says* her favorite gift is the kite I built her. And it *is* very beautiful; though not as beautiful as the one she made me, which is blue and scattered with gold and green Good Conduct stars; moreover, my name is painted on it, "Buddy."

"Buddy, the wind is blowing."

The wind is blowing, and nothing will do till we've run to a pasture below the house where Queenie has scooted to bury her bone (and where, a winter hence, Queenie will be buried, too). There, plunging through the healthy waist-high grass, we unreel our kites, feel them twitching at the string like sky fish as they swim into the wind.

Satisfied, sun-warmed, we sprawl in the grass and peel satsumas and watch our kites cavort. Soon I forget the socks and hand-me-down sweater. I'm as happy as if we'd already won the fifty-thousand-dollar Grand Prize in that coffee-naming contest.

"My, how foolish I am!" my friend cries, suddenly alert, like a woman remembering too late she has biscuits in the oven. "You know what I've always thought?" she asks in a tone of discovery, and not smiling at me but a point beyond. "I've always thought a body would have to be sick and dying before they saw the Lord. And I imagined that when He came it would be like looking at the Baptist window: pretty as colored glass with the sun pouring through, such a shine you don't know it's getting dark. And it's been a comfort: to think of that shine taking away all the spooky feeling. But I'll wager it never happens. I'll wager at the very end a body realizes the Lord has already shown Himself. That things as they are"—her hand circles in a gesture that gathers clouds and kites and grass and Queenie pawing earth over her bone—"just what they've always seen, was seeing Him. As for me, I could leave the world with today in my eyes."

This is our last Christmas together.

Life separates us. Those who Know Best decide that I belong in a military school. And so follows a miserable succession of bugle-blowing prisons, grim reveille-ridden summer camps. I have a new home too. But it doesn't count. Home is where my friend is, and there I never go.

And there she remains, puttering around the kitchen. Alone with Queenie. Then alone. ("Buddy dear," she writes in her wild hard-to-read script, "yesterday Jim Macy's horse kicked Queenie bad. Be thankful she didn't feel much. I wrapped her in a Fine Linen sheet and rode her in the buggy down to Simpson's pasture where she can be with all her Bones. . . .") For a few Novembers she continues to bake her fruitcakes single-handed; not as many, but some: and, of course, she always sends me "the best of the batch." Also, in every letter she encloses a dime wadded in toilet paper: "See a picture show and write me the story." But gradually in her letters she tends to confuse me with her other friend, the Buddy who died in the 1880s; more and more thirteenths are not the only days she stays in bed: a morning arrives in November, a leafless birdless coming of winter morning, when she cannot rouse herself to exclaim: "Oh my, it's fruitcake weather!"

And when that happens, I know it. A message saying so merely confirms a piece of news some secret vein had already received, severing from me an irreplaceable part of myself, letting it loose like a kite on a broken string. That is why, walking across a school campus on this particular December morning, I keep searching the sky. As if I expected to see, rather like hearts, a lost pair of kites hurrying toward heaven.

To improve your luck, wear something new on Christmas Day. But not new shoes. They will hurt, and may even walk you into a catastrophe.

SUPERSTITION OF THE OLD SOUTH

207

CHRISTMAS TREES

The city had withdrawn into itself
And left at last the country to the country;
When between whirls of snow not come to lie
And whirls of foliage not yet laid, there drove
A stranger to our yard, who looked the city,
Yet did in country fashion in that there
He sat and waited till he drew us out,
A-buttoning coats, to ask him who he was.
He proved to be the city come again
To look for something it had left behind
And could not do without and keep its Christmas.
He asked if I would sell my Christmas trees;
My woods—the young fir balsams like a place
Where houses all are churches and have spires.
I hadn't thought of them as Christmas trees.
I doubt if I was tempted for a moment
To sell them off their feet to go in cars

And leave the slope behind the house all bare,
Where the sun shines now no warmer than the moon.
I'd hate to have them know it if I was.
Yet more I'd hate to hold my trees, except
As others hold theirs or refuse for them,
Beyond the time of profitable growth—
The trial by market everything must come to.
I dallied so much with the thought of selling.
Then whether from mistaken courtesy
And fear of seeming short of speech, or whether
From hope of hearing good of what was mine,
I said, "There aren't enough to be worth while."

"I could soon tell how many they would cut,
You let me look them over."

                                        "You could look.
But don't expect I'm going to let you have them."

Pasture they spring in, some in clumps too close
That lop each other of boughs, but not a few
Quite solitary and having equal boughs
All round and round. The latter he nodded "Yes" to,
Or paused to say beneath some lovelier one,
With a buyer's moderation, "That would do."
I thought so too, but wasn't there to say so.
We climbed the pasture on the south, crossed over,
And came down on the north.

                       He said, "A thousand."

"A thousand Christmas trees!—at what apiece?"

He felt some need of softening that to me:
"A thousand trees would come to thirty dollars."

Then I was certain I had never meant
To let him have them. Never show surprise!

But thirty dollars seemed so small beside
The extent of pasture I should strip, three cents
(For that was all they figured out apiece)—
Three cents so small beside the dollar friends
I should be writing to within the hour
Would pay in cities for good trees like those,
Regular vestry-trees whole Sunday Schools
Could hang enough on to pick off enough.

A thousand Christmas trees I didn't know I had!
Worth three cents more to give away than sell,
As may be shown by a simple calculation.
Too bad I couldn't lay one in a letter.
I can't help wishing I could send you one
In wishing you herewith a Merry Christmas.

                       Robert Frost

AMAHL AND THE NIGHT VISITORS
by Gian Carlo Menotti

Cast of characters:
  AMAHL—*a lame shepherd boy*
  HIS MOTHER
  KASPAR—*King bringing incense*

BALTHAZAR—*King bringing myrrh*
MELCHIOR—*King bringing gold*
PAGE—*the Kings' attendant*
SHEPHERD AND SHEPHERDESS

———

(The curtain rises. It is night. The crystal-clear winter sky is dotted with stars, the Eastern Star flaming amongst them. Outside the cottage Amahl is playing his shepherd's pipe. Within, the Mother calls.)

MOTHER: Amahl! Amahl! Time to go to bed.

AMAHL: Coming! *(Amahl does not stir.)*

MOTHER: Amahl! How long must I shout to make you obey?

AMAHL: Oh, very well. *(Amahl takes up his crutch and hobbles into the house.)*

MOTHER: What was keeping you outside?

AMAHL: Oh, Mother, you should go out and see! There's never been such a sky! Hanging over our roof there is a star as large as a window, and the star has a tail and it moves across the sky like a chariot on fire.

MOTHER: Oh! Amahl, when will you stop telling lies? All day long you wander about in a dream. Here we are with nothing to eat, not a stick of wood on the fire, not a drop of oil in the jug, and all you do is to worry your mother with fairy tales.

AMAHL: Mother, I'm not lying. Please do believe me. Come and see for yourself.

210

MOTHER: Why should I believe you? You come with a new one every day!

AMAHL: But there is a star and it has a long tail.

MOTHER: Amahl!

AMAHL: Cross my heart and hope to die.

MOTHER: Poor Amahl! Hunger has gone to your head. Unless we go begging how shall we live through tomorrow? My little son, a beggar! (*She weeps.*)

AMAHL: (*Amahl goes to her.*) Don't cry, Mother, don't worry for me. If we must go begging, a good beggar I'll be. I know sweet tunes to set people dancing. We'll walk and walk from village to town, you dressed as a gypsy and I as a clown. At noon we shall eat roast goose and sweet almonds, at night we shall sleep with the sheep and the stars. I'll play my pipes, you'll sing and you'll shout. The windows will open and people will lean out. The King will ride by and hear your loud voice and throw us some gold to stop all the noise.

MOTHER: My dreamer, good night! You're wasting the light. Kiss me good night.

AMAHL: Good night. (*Amahl goes to his pallet of straw at one side of the fireplace. The Mother secures the door, then lies down to sleep. The lights die from the room except for a faint glow through the window.*)

KASPAR, MELCHIOR, BALTHAZAR: (*The voices of the Three Kings are heard very far away.*) From far away we come and farther we must go. How far, how far, my crystal star? (*Amahl listens with astonishment to the distant singing.*) Frozen the incense in our frozen hands, heavy the gold. How far, how far, my crystal star?

(*Leaning on his crutch, Amahl hobbles over to the window. Outside appear the Three Kings: first Melchior bearing the coffer of gold, then Balthazar bearing the chalice of myrrh, and finally Kaspar bearing the urn of incense. All are preceded by the Page, carrying a rich Oriental rug and an elaborate jeweled box.*)

KASPAR, MELCHIOR, BALTHAZAR: How far, how far, my crystal star? (*The travelers approach the door of the cottage and King Melchior knocks upon the door.*)

MOTHER: Amahl! Go and see who's knocking at the door.

AMAHL: (*Amahl goes to the door.*) Mother, Mother, Mother, come with me. Outside the door there is a King with a crown.

MOTHER: What shall I do with this boy? If you don't learn to tell the truth, I'll have to spank you!

AMAHL: Mother, Mother, Mother. Come with me. If I tell you the truth, I know you won't believe me.

MOTHER: Try it for a change!

AMAHL: But you won't believe me.

MOTHER: I'll believe you if you tell me the truth.

W e three kings
of Orient are,
Bearing gifts
we traverse afar,
Field and
fountain,
Moor and
mountain,
Following
yonder star.
O star of wonder,
star of night,
Star with royal
beauty bright;
Westward leading,
Still proceeding,
Guide us to
thy perfect light!

J. H. HOPKINS, JR.

212

AMAHL: The Kings are three and one of them is black.

MOTHER: Oh! What shall I do with this boy? I'm going to the door myself and then, young man, you'll have to reckon with me! (*The Mother moves to the door. As it swings open, she beholds the Three Kings. In utter amazement, she bows to them.*)

KASPAR, MELCHIOR, BALTHAZAR: Good evening! Good evening!

BALTHAZAR: May we rest awhile in your house and warm ourselves by your fire?

MOTHER: I am a poor widow. A cold fireplace and a bed of straw are all I have to offer you. To these you are welcome.

KASPAR: Oh, thank you!

MOTHER: Come in! Come in!

(*The Mother makes way for the Kings to enter first. The Page enters first. Almost immediately King Kaspar proceeds at a stately march to one side of the fireplace. Balthazar enters and proceeds to a place beside him. Melchior is the last to take his place. Amahl watches the procession with growing wonder and excitement.*)

MELCHIOR: It is nice here.

MOTHER: I shall go and gather wood for the fire. (*The Mother goes to the door.*)

MELCHIOR: We can only stay a little while. We must not lose sight of our star.

MOTHER: Your star?

MELCHIOR: We still have a long way to go.

MOTHER: I shall be right back.

AMAHL: (*The moment his mother is gone, Amahl goes to Balthazar.*) Are you a real King?

BALTHAZAR: Yes.

AMAHL: Where is your home?

BALTHAZAR: I live in a black marble palace full of black panthers and white doves. And you, little boy, what do you do?

AMAHL: I was a shepherd; I had a flock of sheep. But my mother sold them. I had a black goat who gave me warm sweet milk. But she died of old age. But Mother says that now we shall both go begging from door to door. Won't it be fun?

BALTHAZAR: It has its points.

AMAHL: (*Pointing at the jeweled box*) And what is this?

KASPAR: This is my box. I never travel without it. In the first drawer, I keep my magic stones. One carnelian against all evil and envy. One moonstone to make you sleep. One red coral to heal your wounds. One lapis lazuli against quartern fever. One small jasper to help you find water. One small topaz to soothe your eyes. One red ruby to protect you from lightning. In the second drawer I keep my beads. Oh, how I love to play with all kinds of beads. In the third drawer, I keep licorice—black, sweet licorice. Have some. (*Amahl reaches for the candy as his mothers enters, bearing a few sticks.*)

MOTHER: Amahl, I told you not to be a nuisance.

AMAHL: But it isn't my fault! They kept asking me questions.

MOTHER: I want you to go and call the other shepherds. Tell them about our visitors and ask them to bring whatever they have in the house, as we have nothing to offer them. Hurry on!

AMAHL: Yes, Mother. (*Amahl hurries out as fast as his crutch will carry him.*)

MOTHER: (*The Mother crosses to the fireplace. Suddenly she sees the coffer of gold and the rich chalices of incense and myrrh.*) Oh, these beautiful things, and all that gold!

MELCHIOR: These are the gifts to the Child.

MOTHER: The child? Which child?

MELCHIOR: We don't know. But the Star will guide us to Him.

MOTHER: But perhaps I know him.

MELCHIOR: Have you seen a child the color of wheat, the color of dawn? His eyes are mild, His hands are those of a King, as King He was born. Incense, myrrh and gold we bring to His side, and the Eastern Star is our guide.

MOTHER: Yes, I know a child the color of wheat, the color of dawn. His eyes are mild, his hands are those of a King, as King he was born. But no one will bring

213

A Spanish legend tells that the Three Kings cross Spain each year on their way to Bethlehem and leave gifts for children who have been good. On Epiphany Eve the children put out shoes filled with hay and carrots for the camels of the Kings.

him incense or gold, though sick and poor and hungry and cold. He's my child, my son, my darling, my own.

MELCHIOR, BALTHAZAR: Have you seen a child the color of earth, the color of thorn? His eyes are sad, His hands are those of the poor, as poor He was born.

MOTHER: Yes, I know a child the color of earth, the color of thorn. His eyes are sad, his hands are those of the poor, as poor he was born. He's my child, my son, my darling, my own.

MELCHIOR: The Child we seek holds the seas and the winds on His palm.

KASPAR: The Child we seek has the moon and the stars at His feet.

BALTHAZAR: Before Him the eagle is gentle, the lion is meek.

KASPAR, MELCHIOR, BALTHAZAR: Choirs of angels hover over His roof and sing Him to sleep. He's fed by a Mother who is both Virgin and Queen. Incense, myrrh and gold we bring to His side, and the Eastern Star is our guide.

MOTHER: The child I know on his palm holds my heart. The child I know at his feet has my life. He's my son, my darling, my own, and his name is Amahl!

MOTHER: (*The call of the shepherds falls sharp and clear on the air.*) The shepherds are coming!

SHEPHERDS: All the flocks are asleep. We are going with Amahl, bringing gifts to the Kings. (*The shepherds stop in the door, struck dumb by the sight of the Kings. Amahl, however, slips in to take his place beside his mother.*)

SHEPHERDS: Oh, look! Oh, look!

MOTHER: Come in, come in! What are you afraid of? Show what you brought them.

SHEPHERD: (*The shepherd boldly marches forward and lays his gift before the Kings, then, bowing shyly, he retreats to his place.*) Olives and quinces, apples and raisins, nutmeg and myrtle, medlars and chestnuts, this is all we shepherds can offer you.

KASPAR, MELCHIOR, BALTHAZAR: Thank you kindly.

SHEPHERD: Citrons and lemons, musk and pomegranates, goat cheese and walnuts, figs and cucumbers, this is all we shepherds can offer you.

KASPAR, MELCHIOR, BALTHAZAR: Thank you kindly.

SHEPHERDS: Take them, eat them, you are welcome.

BALTHAZAR: (*Balthazar rises.*) Thank you, good friends. But now we must bid you good night. We have little time for sleep and a long journey ahead.

SHEPHERDS: (*The shepherds pass before the Kings, bowing as they depart.*) Good night, my good Kings, good night and farewell. The pale stars foretell that dawn is in sight. The night winds foretell the day will be bright. (*Having closed the door, Amahl and his mother bid the Kings good night. While the Mother prepares herself a pallet of sheepskins on the floor, Amahl seizes his opportunity to speak to King Kaspar.*)

AMAHL: Excuse me, sir. Amongst your magic stones is there . . . is there one that could cure a crippled boy? (*Kaspar does not answer. Amahl goes sadly to his pallet.*) Never mind. Good night. . . . (*The Mother and Amahl have lain down. The Kings are still sitting on the rude bench. They settle themselves to sleep leaning against each other. The Page lies at their feet, beside the rich gifts.*)

MOTHER: (*The Mother cannot take her eyes from the treasure guarded by the Page.*) All that gold! I wonder if rich people know what to do with their gold! Do they know that a house can be kept warm all day with burning logs? All

that gold! Oh, what I could do for my child with that gold! Why should it all go to a child they don't even know? They are asleep. Do I dare? If I take some they will never miss it. They won't miss it. (*Slowly she creeps across the floor.*) For my child . . . for my child. (*As the Mother touches the gold, the Page is aroused. He seizes her arm, crying out.*)

PAGE: Thief! Thief!

MELCHIOR: What is it?

PAGE: I've seen her steal some of the gold. She's a thief! Don't let her go. She's stolen the gold!

KASPAR, MELCHIOR, BALTHAZAR: Shame!

PAGE: Give it back or I'll tear it from you!

KASPAR, MELCHIOR, BALTHAZAR: Give it back! Give it back!

AMAHL: (*Amahl awakens. When he sees his mother in the hands of the Page, he

215

In Syria it is
said that the
youngest camel
of the Wise Men
was so tired when
they reached
the manger that
he fell down.
In sympathy,
the infant Christ
blessed him.
Syrian children
believe that
this animal brings
their gifts on
Epiphany. They
call him "the
Camel of Jesus."

helps himself up with his crutch and awkwardly hurls himself upon the Page.) Don't you dare! Don't you dare, ugly man, hurt my mother! I'll smash in your face! I'll knock out your teeth! *(Rushing to King Kaspar)* Oh, Mister King, don't let him hurt my mother! My mother is good. She cannot do anything wrong. I'm the one who lies, I'm the one who steals! *(At a sign from Kaspar, the Page releases the Mother. Amahl staggers toward her, sobbing.)*

MELCHIOR: Oh, woman, you may keep the gold. The Child we seek doesn't need our gold. On love, on love alone, He will build His Kingdom. His pierced hand will hold no scepter. His haloed head will wear no crown. His might will not be built on your toil. Swifter than lightning He will soon walk among us. He will bring us new life and receive our death, and the keys of His city belong to the poor. *(Turning to the other Kings)* Let us leave, my friends.

MOTHER: *(Freeing herself from Amahl's embrace, the Mother rushes after the Kings.)* Oh, no, wait. Take back your gold! For such a King I've waited all my life. And if I weren't so poor I would send a gift of my own to such a child.

AMAHL: But, Mother, let me send him my crutch. Who knows, he may need one and this I made myself. *(The Mother moves to stop him as he starts to raise the crutch. Amahl lifts the crutch. He takes one step toward the Kings, then realizes he has moved without the help of his crutch.)*

MOTHER: But you can't, you can't!

AMAHL: I walk, Mother. I walk, Mother!

BALTHAZAR, MELCHIOR, KASPAR: He walks!

MOTHER: He walks, he walks, he walks!

KASPAR, MELCHIOR, BALTHAZAR: He walks! It is a sign from the Holy Child. We must give praise to the newborn King. We must praise Him. This is a sign from God. *(Having placed the crutch in the outstretched hands of the King Kaspar, Amahl moves uncertainly. With growing confidence, Amahl begins to jump and caper about the room.)*

AMAHL: Look, Mother, I can dance, I can jump, I can run! *(Amahl stumbles.)*

MOTHER: *(She lifts Amahl from the floor.)* Please, my darling, be careful now. You must take care not to hurt yourself.

MELCHIOR, BALTHAZAR: Oh, good woman, you must not be afraid. For he is loved by the Son of God. Oh, blessed child, may I touch you? *(One by one, the Kings pass before Amahl and lay their hands upon him. Then each with his gift to the Child begins to depart.)*

AMAHL: Oh, Mother, let me go with the Kings! I want to take the crutch to the Child myself.

KASPAR, MELCHIOR, BALTHAZAR: Yes, good woman, let him come with us! We'll take good care of him, we'll bring him back on a camel's back.

MOTHER: Do you really want to go?

AMAHL: Yes, Mother.

MOTHER: Yes, I think you should go, and bring thanks to the Child yourself. What can you do with your crutch?

AMAHL: You can tie it to my back.

MOTHER: So, my darling, good-by! I shall miss you very much. Wash your ears!

AMAHL: Yes, I promise.

MOTHER: Don't tell lies!

AMAHL: No, I promise.

MOTHER: I shall miss you very much.

AMAHL: I shall miss you very much.

MELCHIOR: Are you ready?

AMAHL: Yes, I'm ready.

MELCHIOR: Let's go then.

SHEPHERDS: Come, oh, come outside. All the stars have left the sky. Oh, sweet dawn, oh, dawn of peace. (*Led by the Page, the Three Kings start their stately procession out of the cottage. Amahl rushes to his mother, bidding her good-by, then hurries to catch up with the Kings. Amahl begins to play his pipes as he goes. Outside dawn is brightening the sky. The Mother stands in the doorway of the cottage, waving to Amahl. The curtain falls slowly.*)

RATHER LATE FOR CHRISTMAS
by Mary Ellen Chase

During those confusing days before Christmas, while I wrap gifts for sisters and brothers, brothers-in-law and sisters-in-law, nephews and nieces, aunts and great-aunts, neighbors and friends, the milkman, the postman, the paper boy, the cook and the cook's children, the cleaning woman and the cleaning woman's children, I remember my grandmother, who in the twenty years I knew her wrapped Christmas gifts for no one at all. My grandmother never stood half submerged in a jungle of silver cord, gold cord, red ribbon, tinsel ribbon, white tissue paper, red tissue paper, paper marked with Aberdeens or angels. She viewed with fine scorn all such pre-Christmas frenzy. I remember her again when my January bills weigh down my desk and my disposition. My grandmother in all those years never bought a Christmas gift for anyone, although she gave many. Nor did she make her Christmas gifts by the labor of her hands, which were almost never idle.

To be sure, she spent most of her waking hours during twelve months of the year in making gifts, but they were not for Christmas. She made yards upon yards of tatting, fashioned hundreds of tea cozies, tidies, and table mats, hemstitched innumerable handkerchiefs, crocheted fine filet for pillowcases and sheets, knit countless scalloped bands of white lace for the legs of white cotton drawers, and countless stockings, gloves, mittens, scarfs, sacques, and shawls. These creations were all gifts, yet they were never given at Christmas. Instead, they were presented at odd moments to all sorts of odd and sundry persons—to the gardener, the minister's wife, a surprised boy coasting down the hill, the village schoolmistresses, the stage driver, a chance Syrian peddler, the fishman, the paperhangers, an unknown woman distributing religious literature at the back door, the sexton. Moreover, no one of my grandmother's many acquaintances ever called upon her without departing from her door richer, or at least more encumbered, than when she entered it; nor did my grandmother ever set out empty-handed to return those calls.

My grandmother's nature was essentially dramatic. She loved all sudden, surprising, unexpected things; but she loved them only if either she or God instigated them. Quite illogically she denied this privilege to others. She was distinctly irritated if anyone took her unawares either by a sudden gift or by an unexpected piece of news. She was so filled with life herself that she forever wanted to dispense rather than to receive, to initiate rather than to be initiated.

She loved sudden changes of weather, blizzards, line gales, the excitement of continuous winter cold, northern lights, falling stars; and during many years of her long and abundant life she had had her fill of such abrupt and whimsical behavior on the part of God. For she had spent much of her life at sea, where holidays were mere points in time, unprepared for, often even unnoticed, slipping upon one like all other days, recalled if wind and weather were kind, forgotten if God had other and more immediate means of attracting one's attention to His power and His might. She had spent Christmas in all kinds of strange places: off Cape Horn in a gale; running before the trades somewhere a thousand miles off Africa; in a typhoon off the Chinese coast; in the doldrums, where the twenty-fifth of December was but twenty-four still hours in a succession of motionless days; in the bitter cold of a winter storm too near the treacherous cliffs of southern Ireland for comfort or security. Small wonder that she would find it difficult, after her half-reluctant return to village life, to tie up Christmas in a neat parcel and to label it with a date.

As children we were forever asking our grandmother about those Christmases at sea.

"Didn't you give any presents at all, Grandmother? Not to the sailors or even to Grandfather?"

"The sailors," said my grandmother, "had a tot of rum all around in the dog-watch if the weather was fair. That was the sailors' present."

We always smiled over "tot." This facetious, trifling word attached to one of such enormity as "rum" in those days of temperance agitation seemed impious to say the least. "What is a tot of rum, Grandmother?"

"A tot," answered my grandmother with great dignity, "is an indeterminate quantity."

"Did the sailors sing Christmas carols when they had the tot?"

"They did not. They sang songs which no child should ever know."

"Then did you and Grandfather have no presents at all, Grandmother?"

"Whenever we got to port we had our presents; that is, if we did not forget

Give
and
spend
and
God
will
send.
OLD SAYING

A spicy pomander ball for scenting drawers and closets is made by studding a firm apple or orange with cloves, as close together as possible. The fruit is then rolled in equal parts of cinnamon and orris root and tied with a gay ribbon.

that we had had no Christmas. We had Christmas in January or even March. Christmas, children, is not a date. It is a state of mind."

Christmas to my grandmother was always a state of mind. Once she had left the sea, once she was securely on land, where the behavior of God was less exciting, she began to supplement Providence and Fate by engendering excitement in those about her. Her objection to Christmas lay in the fact that it was a day of expectation, when no one could possibly be taken by surprise. She endured it with forbearance, but she disliked it heartily.

Unlike most women of her generation, she cared not a whit for tradition or convention; but she remained to the end of her days the unwilling prey of both. Unlike most women of any generation, she scorned possessions, and she saw to it that she suffered them briefly. We knew from the beginning the fate of the gifts we annually bestowed upon her; yet we followed the admonition and example of our parents in bestowing them. From our scanty Christmas allowance of two dollars each with which to purchase presents for a family of ten, we set aside a generous portion for Grandmother's gift. She was always with us at Christmas and received our offerings without evident annoyance, knowing that what she must endure for a brief season she could triumph over in the days to come.

As we grew older and were allowed at length to select our gifts free from parental supervision, we began to face the situation precisely as it was. Instead of black silk gloves for Grandmother, we chose for her our own favorite perfumery; we substituted plain white handkerchiefs for the black-edged ones which she normally carried; a box of chocolates took the place of one of peppermints; a book called *Daily Thoughts for Daily Needs* was discarded in favor of a story by Anna Katharine Green.

My grandmother waited for a fortnight or longer after Christmas before she proffered her gifts to family, neighbors, and friends. By early January, she concluded, expectation would have vanished and satiety be forgotten; in other words, the first fine careless rapture of sudden surprise and pleasure might again be abroad in the world. She invariably chose a dull or dark day upon which to deliver her presents. Around three o'clock on some dreary afternoon was her time for setting forth. Over her coat she tied one of her stout aprons of black sateen, and in its capacious lap she cast all her own unwanted gifts—a black silk umbrella, odd bits of silver and jewelry, gloves, handkerchiefs, stockings, books, candies, Florida water, underwear, bedroom slippers, perfumeries, knickknacks of every sort; even family photographs were not excluded! Thus she started upon her rounds, returning at suppertime empty-handed and radiant.

I remember how once as children we met her thus burdened on our way home from school.

"You're rather late for Christmas, Grandmother," we ventured together.

"So, my dears, were the Three Wise Men!" she said.

The many days foretold by the Preacher for the return of bread thus cast upon the waters have in the case of my grandmother not yet elapsed. For, although she has long since gone where possessions are of no account, and where, for all we know, life is a succession of quick surprises, I receive from time to time the actual return of her Christmas gifts so freely and curiously dispensed. Only last Christmas a package revealed a silver pie knife marked with her initials, and presented to her, I remembered with a start, through the combined sacrificial resources of our entire family fully thirty years before. An accompanying note bore these words:

> Your grandmother brought this knife to my mother twenty-eight years ago as a Christmas gift. I remember how she came one rainy afternoon in January with the present in her apron. I found it recently among certain of my mother's things, and knowing your grandmother's strange ways as to Christmas gifts, I feel that honesty demands its return to you. You may be interested in this card which accompanied it.

Tied to the silver pie knife by a bit of red ribbon obviously salvaged long ago from Christmas plenty was a card inscribed on both sides. On one side was written: *To Grandmother with Christmas love from her children and grandchildren*, and on the other: *To my dear friend, Lizzie Osgood, with daily love from Eliza Ann Chase*.

UNDER THE MISTLETOE

> I did not know she'd take it so,
>   Or else I'd never dared:
> Although the bliss was worth the blow,
> I did not know she'd take it so.
> She stood beneath the mistletoe
> So long I thought she cared;
> I did not know she'd take it so,
>   Or else I'd never dared.

Countee Cullen

I HAVE NOT told you about my Christmas presents.

Mamma. Lemon colored dress and nearly six yards satin to go with it.

Papa. Morocco music-case and embroidered handkerchief.

Elmer. Daintily exquisite book of paintings and poems entitled "Heart's Ease and Happy Days." Also a pretty table with a drawer in it on which was a costly and sweet-toned telegraph instrument—a beauty. (P.S. I'd made him promise to get something simple.)

Aunt Amarala. Wine-colored plush hand-bag.

I gave Mamma a banjo covered with pale pink satin, hand-painted roses and lilacs, morning-glories under silver strings in handle, pale blue velvet round the bowl.

[She also received] about a peck of Christmas cards, the handsomest among them being one of Prang's, an immense thing, the back of which was imitation alligator-skin, and inside on one side a satin hand-painted sachet, on the other a dark rich painting with holly-berries all round it.

From the journal of Isabella Maud Rittenhouse,
Cairo, Illinois, December 1883

STUBBY PRINGLE'S CHRISTMAS

by Jack Schaefer

Hɪɢʜ ᴏɴ ᴛʜᴇ mountainside by the little line cabin in the crisp clean dusk of evening Stubby Pringle swings into saddle. He has shape of bear in the dimness, bundled thick against cold. Double socks crowd scarred boots. Leather chaps with hair out cover patched corduroy pants. Fleece-lined jacket with wear of winters on it bulges body and heavy gloves blunt fingers. Two gay red bandannas folded together fatten throat under chin. Battered hat is pulled down to sit on ears and in side pocket of jacket are rabbit-skin earmuffs he can put to use if he needs them.

Stubby Pringle swings up into saddle. He looks out and down over worlds of snow and ice and tree and rock. He spreads arms wide and they embrace whole ranges of hills. He stretches tall and hat brushes stars in sky. He is Stubby Pringle, cowhand of the Triple X, and this is his night to howl. He is Stubby Pringle, son of the wild jackass, and he is heading for the Christmas dance at the schoolhouse in the valley.

Stubby Pringle swings up and his horse stands like rock. This is the pride of his string, flop-eared ewe-necked cat-hipped strawberry roan that looks like it should have died weeks ago but has iron rods for bones and nitroglycerin for blood and can go from here to doomsday with nothing more than mouthfuls of snow for water and tufts of winter-cured bunchgrass snatched between drifts for food. It stands like rock. It knows the folly of trying to unseat Stubby. It wastes no energy in futile explosions. It knows that twenty-seven miles of hard winter going are foreordained for this evening and twenty-seven more of harder uphill return by morning. It has done this before. It is saving the dynamite under its hide for the destiny of a true cow pony which is to take its rider where he wants to go—and bring him back again.

Stubby Pringle sits his saddle and he grins into cold and distance and future full of festivity. Join me in a look at what can be seen of him despite the bundling and frosty breath vapor that soon will hang icicles on his nose. Those are careless haphazard scrambled features under the low hatbrim, about as handsome as a blue boar's snout. Not much fuzz yet on his chin. Why, shucks, is he just a boy? Don't make that mistake, though his twentieth birthday is still six weeks away. Don't make the mistake Hutch Handley made last summer when he

December,
month of holly,
pine, and balsam,
Of berries red,
of candles'
mellow light;
Of home and
fireside, laughter,
happy faces,
Of peace that
comes upon
the holy night.

FROM AN OLD CAROL

thought this was young unseasoned stuff and took to ragging Stubby and wound up with ears pinned back and upper lip split and nose mashed flat and the whole of him dumped in a rain barrel. Stubby has been taking care of himself since he was orphaned at thirteen. Stubby has been doing man's work since he was fifteen. Do you think Hardrock Harper of the Triple X would have anything but an all-around hard-proved hand up here at his farthest winter-line camp siding Old Jake Hanlon, toughest hard-bitten old cowman ever to ride range?

Stubby Pringle slips gloved hand under rump to wipe frost off the saddle. No sense letting it melt into patches of corduroy pants. He slaps right-side saddle-bag. It contains a burlap bag wrapped around a two-pound box of candy, of fancy chocolates with variegated interiors he acquired two months ago and has kept hidden from Old Jake. He slaps left-side saddlebag. It holds a burlap bag wrapped around a paper parcel that contains a close-folded piece of dress goods and a roll of pink ribbon. Interesting items, yes. They are ammunition for the campaign he has in mind to soften the affections of whichever female of the right vintage among those at the schoolhouse appeals to him most and seems most susceptible.

Stubby Pringle settles himself firmly into the saddle. He is just another of far-scattered poorly paid patched-clothes cowhands that inhabit these parts and likely marks and smells of his calling have not all been scrubbed away. He knows that. But this is his night to howl. He is Stubby Pringle, true begotten son of the wildest jackass, and he has been riding line through hell and high water and winter storms for two months without a break and he has done his share of the work and more than his share because Old Jake is getting along and slowing some and this is his night to stomp floorboards till schoolhouse shakes and kick heels up to lanterns above and whirl a willing female till she is dizzy enough to see past patched clothes to the man inside them. He wriggles toes deep into stirrups and settles himself firmly in the saddle.

"I could of et them choc'lates," says Old Jake from the cabin doorway. "They wasn't hid good," he says. "No good at all."

"An' be beat like a drum," says Stubby. "An' wrung out like a dirty dishrag."

"By who?" says Old Jake. "By a young un like you? Why, I'd of tied you in knots afore you knew what's what iffen you tried it. You're a dang-blatted young fool," he says. "A ding-busted dang-blatted fool. Riding out a night like this iffen it is Chris'mas Eve," he says. "But iffen I was your age agin, I reckon I'd be doing it too." He cackles like an old rooster. "Squeeze one of 'em for me," he says and he steps back inside and he closes the door.

Stubby Pringle is alone out there in the darkening dusk, alone with flop-eared ewe-necked cat-hipped roan that can go to the last trumpet call under

224

him and with cold of wicked winter wind around him and with twenty-seven miles of snow-dumped distance ahead of him. "Wahoo!" he yells. "Skip to my Lou!" he shouts. "Do-si-do and round about!"

He lifts reins and the roan sighs and lifts feet. At easy warming-up amble they drop over the edge of benchland where the cabin snugs into tall pines and on down the great bleak expanse of mountainside.

Stubby Pringle, spurs ajingle, jogs upslope through crusted snow. The roan, warmed through, moves strong and steady under him. Line cabin and line work

are far forgotten things back and back and up and up the mighty mass of mountain. He is Stubby Pringle, rooting tooting hard-working hard-playing cowhand of the Triple X, heading for the Christmas dance at the schoolhouse in the valley.

He tops out on one of the lower ridges. He pulls rein to give the roan a breather. He brushes an icicle off his nose. He leans forward and reaches to brush several more off sidebars of old bit in the bridle. He straightens tall. Far ahead, over top of last and lowest ridge, on into the valley, he can see tiny specks of glowing allure that are schoolhouse windows. Light and gaiety and good liquor and fluttering skirts are there. "Wahoo!" he yells. "Gals an' women an' grandmothers!" he shouts. "Raise your skirts and start askipping! I'm acoming!"

He slaps spurs to roan. It leaps like mountain lion, out and down, full into

It sifts from
leaden sieves–
It powders
all the wood.
It fills with
alabaster wool
The wrinkles
of the road–

It makes
an even face
Of mountain
and of plain–
Unbroken
forehead
from the east.
Unto the east
again.

EMILY DICKINSON

hard gallop downslope, rushing, reckless of crusted drifts and ice-coated bush branches slapping at them.

He is Stubby Pringle, born with spurs on, nursed on tarantula juice, weaned on rawhide, at home in the saddle of a hurricane in shape of horse that can race to outer edge of eternity and back, heading now for high jinks two months overdue. He is ten feet tall and the horse is gigantic, with wings, iron-boned and dynamite-fueled, soaring in forty-foot leaps down the flank of the whitened wonder of a winter world.

They slow at the bottom. They stop. They look up the rise of the last low ridge ahead. The roan paws frozen ground and snorts twin plumes of frosty vapor. Stubby reaches around to pull down fleece-lined jacket that has worked a bit up back. He pats right-side saddlebag. He pats left-side saddlebag. He lifts reins to soar up and over last low ridge.

Hold it, Stubby. What is that? Off to the right.

He listens. He has ears that can catch snitch of mouse chewing on chunk of bacon rind beyond the log wall by his bunk. He hears. Sound of axe striking wood.

What kind of dong-bonging ding-busted dang-blatted fool would be chopping wood on a night like this and on Christmas Eve and with a dance under way at the schoolhouse in the valley? What kind of chopping is this anyway? Uneven in rhythm, feeble in stroke. Trust Stubby Pringle, who has chopped wood enough for cookstove and fireplace to fill a long freight train, to know how an axe should be handled.

There. That does it. That whopping sound can only mean that the blade has hit at an angle and bounced away without biting. Some dong-bonged ding-busted dang-blatted fool is going to be cutting off some of his own toes.

He pulls the roan around to the right. He is Stubby Pringle, born to tune of bawling bulls and blatting calves, branded at birth, cowman raised and cowman to the marrow, and no true cowman rides on without stopping to check anything strange on range. Roan chomps on bit, annoyed at interruption. It remembers who is in saddle. It sighs and obeys. They move quietly in dark of night past boles of trees jet black against dim grayness of crusted snow on ground. Light shows faintly ahead. Lantern light through a small oiled-paper window.

Yes. Of course. Just where it has been for eight months now. The Henderson place. Man and woman and small girl and waist-high boy. Homesteaders. Not even fools, homesteaders. Worse than that. Out of their minds altogether. All of them. Out here anyway. Betting the government they can stave off starving for five years in exchange for one hundred sixty acres of land. Land that just might be able to support seven jackrabbits and two coyotes and nine rattlesnakes and maybe all of four thin steers to a whole section. In a good year. Home-steaders. Always out of almost everything, money and food and tools and smiles and joy of living. Everything. Except maybe hope and stubborn endurance.

Stubby Pringle nudges the reluctant roan along. In patch light from the window by a tangled pile of dead tree branches he sees a woman. Her face is gray and pinched and tired. An old stocking cap is pulled down on her head. Ragged man's jacket bumps over long woolsey dress and clogs arms as she tries to swing an axe into a good-sized branch on the ground.

Whopping sound and axe bounces and barely misses an ankle.

"Quit that!" says Stubby, sharp. He swings the roan in close. He looks down at her. She drops axe and backs away, frightened. She is ready to bolt into two-room bark-slab shack. She looks up. She sees that haphazard scrambled features under low hatbrim are crinkled in what could be a grin. She relaxes some, hand on door latch.

"Ma'am," says Stubby. "You trying to cripple yourself?" She just stares at him. "Man's work," he says. "Where's your man?"

"Inside," she says; then, quick, "He's sick."

"Bad?" says Stubby.

"Was," she says. "Doctor that was here this morning thinks he'll be all right now. Only he's almighty weak. All wobbly. Sleeps most of the time."

"Sleeps," says Stubby, indignant. "When there's wood to be chopped."

"He's been almighty tired," she says, quick, defensive. "Even afore he was took sick. Wore out." She is rubbing cold hands together, trying to warm them. "He tried," she says, proud. "Only a while ago. Couldn't even get his pants on. Just fell flat on the floor."

Stubby looks down at her. "An' you ain't tired?" he says.

"I ain't got time to be tired," she says. "Not with all I got to do."

Stubby Pringle looks off past dark boles of trees at last low ridgetop that hides valley and schoolhouse. "I reckon I could spare a bit of time," he says. "Likely they ain't much more'n started yet," he says. He looks again at the woman. He sees gray pinched face. He sees cold shivering under bumpy jacket. "Ma'am," he says. "Get on in there an' warm your gizzard some. I'll just chop you a bit of wood."

Roan stands with dropping reins, ground-tied, disgusted. It shakes head to send icicles tinkling from bit and bridle. Stopped in midst of epic run, wind-eating, mile-gobbling, iron-boned and dynamite-fueled, and for what? For silly chore of chopping.

Fifteen feet away Stubby Pringle chops wood. Moon is rising over last low

227

ridgetop and its light, filtered through trees, shines on leaping blade. He is Stubby Pringle, moonstruck maverick of the Triple X, born with axe in hands, with strength of stroke in muscles, weaned on whetstone, fed on cordwood, raised to fell whole forests. He is ten feet tall and axe is enormous in moonlight and chips fly like stormflakes of snow and blade slices through branches thick as his arm, through logs thick as his thigh.

He leans axe against a stump and he spreads arms wide and he scoops up whole cords at a time and strides to door and kicks it open. . . .

Both corners of front room by fireplace are piled full now, floor to ceiling,

good wood, stout wood, seasoned wood, wood enough for a whole wicked winter week. Chore done and done right, Stubby looks around him. Fire is burning bright and well-fed, working on warmth. Man lies on big old bed along opposite wall, blanket over, eyes closed, face gray-pale, snoring long and slow. Woman fusses with something at old woodstove. Stubby steps to doorway to back room. He pulls aside hanging cloth. Faint in dimness inside he sees two low bunks and in one, under an old quilt, a curly-headed small girl and in the other, under other old quilt, a boy who would be waist-high awake and standing. He sees them still and quiet, sleeping sound. "Cute little devils," he says.

He turns back and the woman is coming toward him, cup of coffee in hand, strong and hot and steaming. Coffee the kind to warm the throat and gizzard of chore-doing hard-chopping cowhand on a cold cold night. He takes the cup and raises it to his lips. Drains it in two gulps. "Thank you, ma'am," he says.

"That was right kindly of you." He sets cup on table. "I got to be getting along," he says. He starts toward outer door.

He stops, hand on door latch. Something is missing in two-room shack. Trust Stubby Pringle to know what. "Where's your tree?" he says. "Kids got to have a Christmas tree."

He sees the woman sink down on chair. He hears a sigh come from her. "I ain't had time to cut one," she says.

"I reckon not," says Stubby. "Man's job anyway," he says. "I'll get it for you. Won't take a minute. Then I got to be going."

He strides out. He scoops up axe and strides off, upslope some where small pines climb. He stretches tall and his legs lengthen and he towers huge among trees, swinging with ten-foot steps. He is Stubby Pringle, born an expert on Christmas trees, nursed on pine needles, weaned on pine cones, raised with an eye for size and shape and symmetry. There. A beauty. Perfect. Grown for this and for nothing else. Axe blade slices keen and swift. Tree topples. He strides back with tree on shoulder. He rips leather whangs from his saddle and lashes two pieces of wood to tree bottom, crosswise, so tree can stand upright again.

Stubby Pringle strides into shack, carrying tree. He sets it up, center of front-room floor, and it stands straight, trim and straight, perky and proud and pointed. "There you are, ma'am," he says. "Get your things out an' start decorating. I got to be going." He moves toward outer door.

He stops in outer doorway. He hears the sigh behind him. "We got no things," she says. "I was figuring to buy some but sickness took the money."

Stubby Pringle looks off at last low ridgetop hiding valley and schoolhouse. "Reckon I still got a bit of time," he says. "They'll be whooping it mighty late." He turns back, closing door. He sheds hat and gloves and bandannas and jacket. He moves about checking everything in the sparse front room. He asks for things and the woman jumps to get those few of them she has. He tells her what to do and she does. He does plenty himself. With this and with that magic wonders arrive. He is Stubby Pringle, born to poverty and hard work, weaned on nothing, fed on less, raised to make do with least possible and make the most of that. Pinto beans strung on thread brighten tree in firelight and lantern light like strings of store-bought beads. Strips of one bandanna, cut with shears from sewing box, bob in bows on branch ends like gay red flowers. Snippets of fleece from jacket lining sprinkled over tree glisten like fresh fall of snow. Miracles flow from strong blunt fingers through bits of old paper bags and dabs of flour paste into link chains and twisted small streamers and two jaunty little hats and two smart little boats with sails.

"Got to finish it right," says Stubby Pringle. From strong blunt fingers comes five-pointed star, triple thickness to make it stiff, twisted bit of old wire to hold

Choose
wisely then,
each ornament
And frosted
tinsel skein
For branches
that have
worn jewels
Of gleaming
mountain rain.
ELIZABETH–ELLAN LONG

229

In many a
bleak log cabin
On many a
rough frontier,
Christmas
was plain and
scanty
In the winter
of the year.
Yet every
childish heart
beat high,
As the twenty-
fifth drew near.

it upright. He fastens this to topmost tip of topmost bough. He wraps lone bandanna left around throat and jams battered hat on head and shrugs into now skimpy-lined jacket. "A right nice little tree," he says. "All you got to do now is get out what you got for the kids and put it under. I really got to be going." He starts toward outer door.

He stops in open doorway. He hears the sigh behind him. He knows without looking around the woman has slumped into old rocking chair. "We ain't got anything for them," she says. "Only now this tree. Which I don't mean it isn't a fine grand tree. It's more'n we'd of had 'cept for you."

Stubby Pringle stands in open doorway looking out into cold clean moonlit night. Somehow he knows without turning head two tears are sliding down thin pinched cheeks. "You go on along," she says. "They're good young uns. They know how it is. They ain't expecting a thing."

Stubby Pringle stands in open doorway looking out at last ridgetop that hides valley and schoolhouse. "All the more reason," he says soft to himself. "All the more reason something should be there when they wake." He sighs too. "I'm a dong-bonging ding-busted dang-blatted fool," he says. "But I reckon I still got a mite more time. Likely they'll be sashaying around till it's most morning."

Stubby Pringle strides on out, leaving door open. He strides back, closing door with heel behind him. In one hand he has burlap bag wrapped around paper parcel. In other hand he has squarish chunk of good pine wood. He tosses bag parcel into lap folds of woman's apron.

"Unwrap it," he says. "There's the makings for a right cute dress for the girl. Needle-and-threader like you can whip it up in no time. I'll just whittle me out a little something for the boy."

Moon is high in cold cold sky. Frosty clouds drift up there with it. Tiny flakes of snow float through upper air. Down below by a two-room shack droops a disgusted cow-pony roan, ground-tied, drooping like statue snow-crusted. It is accepting the inescapable destiny of its kind which is to wait for its rider, to conserve deep-bottomed dynamite energy, to be ready to race to the last margin of motion when waiting is done.

Inside the shack fire in fireplace cheerily gobbles wood, good wood, stout wood, seasoned wood, warming two rooms well. Man lies on bed, turned on side, curled up some, snoring slow and steady. Woman sits in rocking chair, sewing. Her head nods slow and drowsy and her eyelids sag weary but her fingers fly, stitch-stitch-stitch. A dress has shaped under her hands, small and flounced and with little puff sleeves, fine dress, fancy dress, dress for smiles and joy of living. She is sewing pink ribbon around collar and down front and into fluffy bow on back.

On a stool nearby sits Stubby Pringle, piece of good pine wood in one hand, knife in other hand, fine knife, splendid knife, all-around-accomplished knife, knife he always has with him, seven-bladed knife with four for cutting from little to big and corkscrew and can opener and screwdriver. Big cutting blade has done its work. Little cutting blade is in use now. He is Stubby Pringle, born with feel for knives in hand, weaned on emery wheel, fed on shavings, raised to whittle his way through the world. Tiny chips fly and shavings flutter. There in his hands, out of good pine wood, something is shaping. A horse. Yes. Flop-eared ewe-necked cat-hipped horse. Flop-eared head is high on ewe neck, stretched out, sniffing wind, snorting into distance. Cat hips are hunched forward, caught in crouch for forward leap. It is a horse fit to carry a waist-high boy to uttermost edge of eternity and back.

Stubby Pringle carves swift and sure. Little cutting blade makes final little cutting snitches. Yes. Tiny mottlings and markings make no mistaking. It is a strawberry roan. He closes knife and puts it in pocket. He looks up. Dress is finished in woman's lap. But woman's head has dropped down in exhaustion. She sits slumped deep in rocking chair and she too snores slow and steady.

Stubby Pringle stands up. He takes dress and puts it under tree, fine dress, fancy dress, dress waiting now for small girl to wake and wear it with smiles and joy of living. He sets wooden horse beside it, fine horse, proud horse, snorting-into-distance horse, cat hips crouched, waiting now for waist-high boy to wake and ride it around the world.

Quietly he piles wood on fire and banks ashes around to hold it for morning. Quietly he pulls on hat and wraps bandanna around and shrugs into skimpy-lined jacket. He looks at old rocking chair and tired woman slumped in it. He strides to outer door and out, leaving door open. He strides back, closing door with heel behind. He carries other burlap bag wrapped around box of candy, of fine chocolates, fancy chocolates with variegated interiors. Gently he lays this in lap of woman. Gently he takes big old shawl from wall nail and lays this over her. He stands by big old bed and looks down at snoring man. "Poor devil," he says. "Ain't fair to forget him." He takes knife from pocket, fine knife, seven-bladed knife, and lays this on blanket on bed. He picks up gloves and blows out lantern and swift as sliding moon shadow he is gone.

High high up frosty clouds scuttle across face of moon. Wind whips through topmost tips of tall pines. What is it that hurtles like hurricane far down there on upslope of last low ridge, scattering drifts, smashing through brush, snorting defiance at distance? It is flop-eared ewe-necked cat-hipped roan, iron-boned and dynamite-fueled, ramming full gallop through the dark of night. Firm in saddle is Stubby Pringle, spurs ajingle, toes atingle, out on prowl, ready to howl, heading for the dance at the schoolhouse in the valley. He is ten feet tall, great as a

F or the
neighbors came
in wagons
From half a
state away.
And the old
men brought
the banjos
They'd near
forgot to play,
While the
young folk
danced a
dos-a-dos
And clapped for
Christmas Day.

PHYLLIS MCGINLEY

232

grizzly, and the roan is gigantic, with wings, soaring upward in thirty-foot leaps. They top out and roan rears high, pawing stars out of sky, and drops down, cat hips hunched for fresh leap out and down.

Hold it, Stubby. Hold hard on reins. Do you see what is happening on out there in the valley?

Tiny lights that are schoolhouse windows are winking out. Tiny dark shapes moving about are horsemen riding off, are wagons pulling away.

M oon is dropping down the sky, haloed in frosty mist. Dark gray clouds dip and swoop around sweep of horizon. Cold winds weave rustling through ice-coated bushes and trees. What is that moving slow and lonesome up snow-covered mountainside? It is a flop-eared ewe-necked cat-hipped roan, just that, nothing more, small cow pony, worn and weary, taking its rider back to clammy bunk in cold line cabin. Slumped in saddle is Stubby Pringle, head down, shoulders sagged. He is just another of far-scattered poorly paid patched-clothes cowhands who inhabit these parts. Just that. And something more. He is the biggest thing there is in the whole wide roster of the human race. He is a man who has given of himself, of what little he has and is, to bring smiles and joy of living to others along his way.

He jogs along, slump-sagged in saddle, thinking of none of this. He is thinking of dances undanced, of floorboards unstomped, of willing women left un-whirled.

He jogs along, half asleep in saddle, and he is thinking now of bygone Christmas seasons and of a boy born to poverty and hard work and make-do poring in flicker of firelight over ragged old Christmas picture book. And suddenly he hears something. The tinkle of sleigh bells.

Sleigh bells?

Yes. I am telling this straight. He and roan are weaving through thick-clumped brush. Winds are sighing high overhead and on up the mountainside and lower down here they are whipping mists and snow flurries all around him. He can see nothing in mystic moving dimness. But he can hear. The tinkle of sleigh bells, faint but clear, ghostly but unmistakable. And suddenly he sees something. Movement off to the left. Swift as wind, glimmers only through brush and mist and whirling snow, but unmistakable again. Antlered heads high, frosty breath streaming, bodies rushing swift and silent, floating in flash of movement past, seeming to leap in air alone needing no touch of ground beneath. Reindeer? Yes. Reindeer strong and silent and fleet out of some far frozen northland marked on no map. Reindeer swooping down and leaping past and rising again and away, strong and effortless and fleeting. And with them, hard on their heels, almost lost in swirling snow mist of their passing, vague and formless but there, something big and bulky with runners like sleigh and flash of white beard whipping in wind and crack of long whip snapping.

Startled roan has seen something too. It stands rigid, head up, staring left and forward. Stubby Pringle, body atingle, stares too. Out of dark of night ahead, mingled with moan of wind, comes a long-drawn chuckle, deep deep chuckle, jolly and cheery and full of smiles and joy of living. And with it long-drawn words.

"We-e-e-l-l-l do-o-o-ne . . . pa-a-a-artner!"

Stubby Pringle shakes his head. He brushes an icicle from his nose. "An' I

didn't have a single drink," he says. "Only coffee an' can't count that. Reckon I'm getting soft in the head." But he is cowman through and through, cowman through to the marrow. He can't ride on without stopping to check anything strange on his range. He swings down and leads off to the left. He fumbles in jacket pocket and finds a match. Strikes it. Holds it cupped and bends down. There they are. Unmistakable. Reindeer tracks.

Stubby Pringle stretches up tall. Stubby Pringle swings into saddle. Roan needs no slap of spurs to unleash strength in upward surge, up up up steep mountainside. It knows. There in saddle once more is Stubby Pringle, moon-struck maverick of the Triple X, all-around hard-proved hard-honed cowhand, ten feet tall, needing horse gigantic, with wings, iron-boned and dynamite-fueled, to take him home to little line cabin and some few winks of sleep before another day's hard work. . . .

233

Stubby Pringle slips into cold clammy bunk. He wriggles vigorous to warm blanket under and blanket over.

"Was it worth all that riding?" comes voice of Old Jake Hanlon from other bunk on other wall.

"Why, sure," says Stubby. "I had me a right good time."

All right, now. Say anything you want. I know, you know, any dong-bonged ding-busted dang-blatted fool ought to know, that icicles breaking off branches can sound to drowsy ears something like sleigh bells. That blurry eyes half asleep can see strange things. That deer and elk make tracks like those of reindeer. That wind sighing and soughing and moaning and maundering down mountains and through piny treetops can sound like someone shaping words. But we could talk and talk and it would mean nothing to Stubby Pringle.

Stubby is wiser than we are. He knows, he will always know, who it was, plump and jolly and belly-bouncing, that spoke to him that night out on wind-whipped winter-worn mountainside.

"We-e-e-l-l-l do-o-o-ne . . . pa-a-a-art-ner!"

CAROLS IN THE COTSWOLDS
by Laurie Lee

Towards christmas, there was heavy snow, which raised the roads to the tops of the hedges. There were tons of the lovely stuff, plastic, pure, all-purpose, which nobody owned, which one could carve or tunnel, eat, or just throw about. It covered the hills and cut off the villages, but nobody thought of rescues; for there was hay in the barns and flour in the kitchens, the women baked bread, the cattle were fed and sheltered—we'd been cut off before, after all.

The week before Christmas, when snow seemed to lie thickest, was the moment for carol singing; and when I think back to those nights it is to the crunch of snow and to the lights of the lanterns on it. Carol singing in my village was a special tithe for the boys; the girls had little to do with it. Like haymaking, blackberrying, stone clearing, and wishing people a happy Easter, it was one of our seasonal perks.

By instinct we knew just when to begin it; a day too soon and we should have

234

been unwelcome, a day too late and we should have received lean looks from people whose bounty was already exhausted. When the true moment came, exactly balanced, we recognized it and were ready.

So as soon as the wood had been stacked in the oven to dry for the morning fire, we put on our scarves and went out through the streets, calling loudly between our hands, till the various boys who knew the signal ran out from their houses to join us. One by one they came stumbling over the snow, swinging their lanterns round their heads, shouting and coughing horribly.

"Coming carol barking then?"

We were the Church Choir, so no answer was necessary. For a year we had praised the Lord out of key, and as a reward for this service we now had the right to visit all the big houses, to sing our carols and collect our tribute.

To work them all in meant a five-mile foot journey over wild and generally snowed-up country. So the first thing we did was to plan our route; a formality, as the route never changed. All the same, we blew on our fingers and argued; and then we chose our leader. This was not binding, for we all fancied ourselves as leaders, and he who started the night in that position usually trailed home with a bloody nose.

Eight of us set out that night. There was Sixpence the Simple, who had never sung in his life (he just worked his mouth in church); the brothers Horace and Boney, who were always fighting everybody and always getting the worst of it; Clergy Green, the preaching maniac; Walt the Bully, and my two brothers. As we went down the lane other boys, from other villages, were already about the hills, bawling "Kingwenslush," and shouting through keyholes "Knock on the knocker! Ring at the bell! Give us a penny for singing so well!" They weren't an approved charity as we were, the choir; but competition was in the air.

Our first call as usual was the house of the Squire, and we trooped nervously down his drive. For light we had candles in marmalade jars suspended on loops of string, and they threw pale gleams on the towering snowdrifts that stood on each side of the drive. A blizzard was blowing but we were well wrapped up, with army puttees on our legs, woolen hats on our heads, and several scarves round our ears. As we approached the Big House across its white silent lawns, we too grew respectfully silent. The lake nearby was stiff and black, the waterfall frozen and still. We arranged ourselves shuffling round the big front door, then knocked and announced the choir.

A maid bore the tiding of our arrival away into the echoing distances of the house, and while we waited we cleared our throats noisily. Then she came back, and the door was left ajar for us, and we were bidden to begin. We brought no music; the carols were in our heads. "Let's give 'em 'Wild Shepherds,' " said Jack. We began in confusion, plunging into a wreckage of keys, of different

Villagers all, this frosty tide,
Let your doors
swing open wide,
Though wind
may follow, and
snow beside,
Yet draw us in
by your fire to bide;
Joy shall be yours
in the morning!

KENNETH GRAHAME

words and tempos; but we gathered our strength; he who sang loudest took the rest of us with him, and the carol took shape, if not sweetness.

This huge stone house, with its ivied walls, was always a mystery to us. What were those gables, those rooms and attics, those narrow windows veiled by the cedar trees? As we sang "Wild Shepherds" we craned our necks, gaping into the lamplit hall which we had never entered; staring at the muskets and untenanted chairs, the great tapestries furred by dust—until suddenly, on the stairs, we saw the old Squire himself standing and listening with his head on one side.

He didn't move until we'd finished; then slowly he tottered towards us, dropped two coins in our box with a trembling hand, scratched his name in the book we carried, gave us each a long look with his moist blind eyes, then turned away in silence. As though released from a spell we took a few sedate steps, then broke into a run for the gate. We didn't stop till we were out of the grounds. Impatient, at last, to discover the extent of his bounty, we squatted by the cow sheds, held our lanterns over the book, and saw that he had written "Two Shillings." This was quite a good start. No one of any worth in the district would dare to give us less than the Squire.

So with money in the box, we pushed on up the valley, pouring scorn on each other's performance. Confident now, we began to consider our quality and whether one carol was not better suited to us than another. Horace, Walt said, shouldn't sing at all; his voice was beginning to break. Horace disputed this and there was a brief token battle—they fought as they walked, kicking up divots of snow, then they forgot it, and Horace still sang.

Steadily we worked through the length of the valley, going from house to house, visiting the lesser and the greater gentry—the farmers, the doctors, the merchants, the majors, and other exalted persons. It was freezing hard and blowing too; yet not for a moment did we feel the cold. The snow blew into our faces, into our eyes and mouths, soaked through our puttees, got into our boots, and dripped from our woolen caps. But we did not care. The collecting box grew heavier, and the list of names in the book longer and more extravagant, each trying to outdo the other.

Mile after mile we went, fighting against the wind, falling into snowdrifts, and navigating by the lights of the houses. And yet we never saw our audience. We called at house after house; we sang in courtyards and porches, outside windows, or in the damp gloom of hallways; we heard voices from hidden rooms; we smelled rich clothes and strange hot food; we saw maids bearing in dishes or carrying away coffee cups; we received nuts, cakes, figs, preserved ginger, dates, cough drops, and money; but we never once saw our patrons. We sang, as it were, at the castle walls and, apart from the Squire, who had shown himself to prove that he was still alive, we never expected it otherwise.

As the night drew on there was trouble with Boney. "Noel," for instance, had a rousing harmony which Boney persisted in singing, and singing flat. The others forbade him to sing it at all, and Boney said he would fight us. Picking himself up he agreed we were right, then he disappeared altogether. He just turned away and walked into the snow and wouldn't answer when we called him back. Much later, as we reached a far point up the valley, somebody said "Hark!" and we stopped to listen. Far away across the fields from the distant village came the sound of a frail voice singing, singing "Noel," and singing it flat—it was Boney, branching out on his own.

We approached our last house high up on the hill, the place of Joseph the farmer. For him we had chosen a special carol, which was about the other Joseph, so that we always felt that singing it added a spicy cheek to the night. The last stretch of country to reach his farm was perhaps the most difficult of all. In these rough bare lanes, open to all winds, sheep were buried and wagons lost. Huddled together, we tramped in one another's footsteps, powdered snow blew into our screwed-up eyes, the candles burned low, some blew out altogether, and we talked loudly above the gale.

Crossing, at last, the frozen millstream—whose wheel in summer still turned a barren mechanism—we climbed up to Joseph's farm. Sheltered by trees, warm on its bed of snow, it seemed always to be like this. As always it was late; as always this was our final call. The snow had a fine crust upon it, and the old trees sparkled like tinsel. We grouped ourselves round the farmhouse porch. The sky cleared, and broad streams of stars ran down over the valley and away to Wales. On Slad's white slopes, seen through the black sticks of its woods, some red lamps still burned in the windows.

Everything was quiet; everywhere there was the faint crackling silence of the winter night. We started singing, and we were all moved by the words and the sudden trueness of our voices. Pure, very clear, and breathless we sang:

> *"As Joseph was a-walking*
> *He heard an angel sing;*
> *'This night shall be the birth-time*
> *Of Christ the Heavenly King.*

> *" 'He neither shall be borned*
> *In Housen nor in hall,*
> *Nor in a place of paradise*
> *But in an ox's stall. . . .' "*

And two thousand Christmases became real to us then; the houses, the halls, the places of paradise had all been visited; the stars were bright to guide the Kings through the snow; and across the farmyard we could hear the beasts in their stalls. We were given roast apples and hot mince pies, in our nostrils were spices like myrrh, and in our wooden box, as we headed back for the village, there were golden gifts for all.

CHRISTMAS TREE

little tree
little silent Christmas tree
you are so little
you are more like a flower

who found you in the green forest
and were you very sorry to come away?
see   i will comfort you
because you smell so sweetly

i will kiss your cool bark
and hug you safe and tight
just as your mother would,
only don't be afraid

look   the spangles
that sleep all the year in a dark box
dreaming of being taken out and allowed to shine,
the balls the chains red and gold the fluffy threads,

put up your little arms
and i'll give them all to you to hold
every finger shall have its ring
and there won't be a single place dark or unhappy

then when you're quite dressed
you'll stand in the window for everyone to see
and how they'll stare!
oh but you'll be very proud

and my little sister and i will take hands
and looking up at our beautiful tree
we'll dance and sing
"Noel Noel"

e. e. cummings

CHRISTMAS CLOSES A GULF
by Moss Hart

Barnett Hart, Moss's father;

Moss with his grandfather

I<small>T WAS THE</small> Christmas after my aunt had left the house, and since it was she who always supplied the tree and the presents for my brother and myself, this first Christmas without her was a bleak and empty one. I remember that I was more or less reconciled to it, because my father had worked only spasmodically throughout the year. Two of our rooms were vacant of boarders and my mother was doing her marketing farther and farther away from our neighborhood. This was always a sign that we were dangerously close to rock bottom, and each time it occurred I came to dread it more. It was one of the vicious landmarks of poverty that I had come to know well and the one I hated most. . . .

Obviously Christmas was out of the question—we were barely staying alive. On Christmas Eve my father was very silent during the evening meal. Then he surprised and startled me by turning to me and saying, "Let's take a walk." He had never suggested such a thing before, and moreover, it was a very cold winter's night. I was even more surprised when he said as we left the house, "Let's go down to One Hundred Forty-ninth Street and Westchester Avenue." My heart leaped within me. That was the section where all the big stores were, where at Christmastime open pushcarts full of toys stood packed end-to-end for blocks at a stretch. On other Christmas Eves I had often gone there with my aunt, and from our tour of the carts she had gathered what I wanted the most. My father had known of this, and I joyously concluded that his walk could mean only one thing—he was going to buy me a Christmas present.

On the walk down I was beside myself with delight and an inner relief. It had been a bad year for me, that year of my aunt's going, and I wanted a Christmas present terribly—not a present merely, but a symbol, a token of some sort. I needed some sign from my father or mother that they knew what I was going through and cared for me as much as my aunt and my grandfather did. I am sure they were giving me what mute signs they could, but I did not see them. The idea that my father had managed a Christmas present for me in spite of everything filled me with a sudden peace and lightness of heart I had not known in months.

We hurried on, our heads bent against the wind, to the cluster of lights ahead that was 149th Street and Westchester Avenue, and those lights seemed to me the brightest lights I had ever seen. Tugging at my father's coat, I started down the line of pushcarts. There were all kinds of things I wanted, but since nothing had been said by my father about buying a present, I would merely pause before a pushcart to say, with as much control as I could muster, "Look at that chemistry set!" or, "There's a stamp album!" or, "Look at the printing press!" Each time my father would pause and ask the pushcart man the price. Then without a word we would move on to the next pushcart. Once or twice he would pick up a toy of some kind and look at it and then at me, as if to suggest this might be something I might like, but I was ten years old and a good deal beyond just a toy; my heart was set on a chemistry set or a printing press. There they were on every pushcart we stopped at, but the price was always the same and soon I looked up and saw we were nearing the end of the line. Only two or three pushcarts remained. My father looked up, too, and I heard him jingle some coins in his pocket. In a flash I knew it all. He'd gotten together about seventy-five cents to buy me a Christmas present, and he hadn't dared to say so in case there was nothing to be had for so small a sum.

As I looked up at him I saw a look of despair and disappointment in his eyes that brought me closer to him than I had ever been in my life. I wanted to throw my arms around him and say, "It doesn't matter . . . I understand . . . this is better than a chemistry set or a printing press. . . . I love you." But instead we stood shivering beside each other for a moment—then turned away from the last two pushcarts and started silently back home. I don't know why the words remained choked up within me. I didn't even take his hand on the way home, nor did he take mine. We were not on that basis. Nor did I ever tell him how close to him I felt that night—that for a little while the concrete wall between father and son had crumbled away and I knew that we were two lonely people struggling to reach each other.

I came close to telling him many years later, but again the moment passed. Again it was Christmas and I was on my way to visit him in Florida. My father was a bright and blooming ninety-one years of age now and I arrived in Florida with my wife to spend Christmas and New Year's with him. On Christmas Eve we sat in his living room, and while my wife chatted with his nurse and companion, I sat on a sofa across the room with my father, showing him the pictures of his two grandchildren. Suddenly I felt his hand slip into mine. It was the first time in our lives that either of us had ever touched the other. No words were spoken and I went right on turning the pages of the picture album, but my hand remained over his. A few years before I might have withdrawn mine after a moment or two, but now my hand remained; nor did I tell him what I was thinking and feeling. The moment was enough. It had taken forty years for the gulf that separated us to close.

A Christmas Alphabet

by
Marion Conger

A is for Angels, Appearing on high, proclaiming glad news from a clear midnight sky. **B** is Balthazar, Black King from afar, who journeyed to Bethlehem led by a star, Bearing gifts to the **C**hild born that first Christmas day and laid in a Cradle on Cushions of hay. **D**'s for the Dolls of which little girls Dream, **E** for an Eggnog with nutmeg and cream. **F** is a Fir tree made Festive and bright by candles a Family has gathered to light, by silvery **G**arlands and Gewgaws of Gold, and all that its fragrant Green branches can hold of Gingerbread babies and cranberry strings and other most Gorgeously Glittering things. **H** is for Holly wreaths decking the Halls, and Hemlock boughs Hung on the living-room walls. **I** is for Ice skaters racing together, on Indigo ponds in Icicle weather. **J** is the Jewel-colored Jellies and Jams served with turkeys and geese and with clove-studded hams. **K** is Kris Kringle, whose cheeks are like cherries, and the magical Knapsack of Khaki he carries, full of Kites and Kaleidoscopes, Kerchiefs and Kittens, and stuffed Kangaroos and gay Knitted mittens. **L** is for Logs that are Laid on the hearth to burn when the winter sweeps out of the north.

M is for Misty-eyed Maidens and Misses who stand 'neath the Mistletoe waiting for kisses. **N** is for Nuts with a Nutcracker handy. **O** is for Oranges and Oodles of candy. **P** is Plum Puddings with hard sauce on top, and Pies made of Pumpkin, and Popcorn to Pop. **Q** is a warm patchwork Quilt on a bed. **R** is for Ribbons of Raspberry Red. **S** is for Sleighs and for Sleds and for Skis, Skimming over the Snow with the greatest of ease. **T** is for Tops, and for all of the Toys, like Trumpets and Tom- toms, that make a fine noise. **U** is a Useful, Uninteresting box of Umbrellas and Underwear, mufflers and socks. **V** is a Vigorous reindeer named Vixen who, with Dancer and Prancer and Donder and Blitzen, flies around the **W** orld like the down of a thistle When Saint Nick cracks his Whip and gives them a Whistle. **X** is for Xmas cards come by the dozens from aunts and from uncles, from friends and from cousins. **Y** is a Yule candle lighted each Year, and the Yawning of Youngsters as bedtime draws near. **Z** is a Zebra with shoe-button eyes, peeking out of a stocking in happy surprise, and looking as if—if he could— he would say, "Merry Christmas to all, and to all a good day!"

SIGNOR SANTA

by Jo Pagano

The whole blame, says my mother, lies on my father's *stubborn insistence* that he play Santa Claus. If he had taken her advice in the first place and minded his own business, everything would have turned out differently; as it was . . .

"But what was I to do?" cries my father. "*Corpo di Bacco!* Why lay all the blame on me? It was not my idea in the beginning. Gianpaolo himself suggested it. With my stomach, said he, I would make an admirable Santa Claus—and I thought, for the sake of the occasion . . ."

And so on and so forth. Nevertheless, in all fairness, I do not think it just to lay the whole blame for what happened on my father. Certainly he acted from the best of motives—that much cannot be denied; but can the same be said of Signor Simone? In this there are those of us who are inclined to take my father's view of the matter; indeed, we are inclined to feel that if ever the last detail of all that bewildering tangle of cross-purposes which went to make up that fateful Christmas Eve were finally unearthed and laid fair and square before an impartial jury, Signor Simone would not have a leg left to stand on. On the other hand, there is also, without doubt, a certain amount of reasonableness in the position taken by my mother—that is, that my father would have been much better off if, in the first place, he had gracefully withdrawn and let Signor Simone go ahead and *be* Santa Claus, since his heart seemed so set on it; still, can one exactly blame my father? After all, why *should* he have given in? Who did Signor Simone think he was anyway? Simply because he was Gianpaolo's wife's second cousin . . .

But let us not anticipate. To begin at the beginning:

It was a couple of weeks before Christmas that we first learned of the great gathering which our *paesanos*, the Maccaluccis, were planning on having that Christmas Eve. (May God help us someday to forget it, as my mother wailed afterward.) The celebration was to have a dual function, for not only were we to gather in humble memory of the Holy One, we were also to give honor to Erminio, the Maccaluccis' second son, who was returning for his Christmas vacation from the seminary where he was studying to become a priest. They were going to have a great celebration—cards, music, dancing, as well as the traditional Christmas Eve supper, and they had invited all of their friends.

244

Gianpaolo grew very excited as he told us about it. Like all peasant Italians, he had a devout respect for holidays and formal occasions of any description, especially those of a churchly origin, and if necessary he would have mortgaged his house in order to celebrate this Christmas in a fitting manner—but fortunately such a drastic measure was not necessary. As usual, it was my father who provided the necessary finances—fifty dollars, to be exact. ("He must think you really *are* Santa Claus," said my mother.) But to proceed:

All, no doubt, would have gone without mishap, had it not been for the unexpected arrival, some ten days or so before Christmas, of Mrs. Maccalucci's second cousin, Silvestro Simone. (Accursed be his name!) He was an imposing individual, matching, in fleshly bulk, the two hundred odd pounds with which Heaven (and my mother's spaghetti) had adorned my father; he had a face like a beefsteak, a voice like a steamroller, and a huge belly which seemed almost too much for the rest of him to carry around. This man, this contemptible, loathsome scoundrel, had worked alongside my father and Gianpaolo in the Colorado coal mines of their youth, but it had been nearly thirty years since he and my father had seen each other. ("Could he not have made it thirty more?" wailed my mother.) During this time, much water, as the old saw has it, had flowed under many bridges; the passing years had carried my father and Gianpaolo many miles from those dark tunnels beneath the earth in which they had spent their first years in this country. These same years had carried Signor Simone many miles from the coal mines also, but in a different direction; for, while Gianpaolo and my father, imitating the course of the sun, had traveled westward, arriving, by successive stages, in California, Simone had journeyed east. He had been married (as we were to hear a dozen times from his own lips) three times; he had had six children by his first wife, four by his second, and eight by his last. ("By God, Luigi, I bet you can't beat *that* record!" he roared to my father.) During these years he had been in one business after another—saloonkeeper, restaurant owner, hotel proprietor; and he had wound up in Boston (where he had spent the past six years) as the proprietor of a fancy Italian grocery.

So much for a few brief facts about this reprehensible individual. Would any of us have resented him on the basis, so to speak, of himself? In all fairness, I must say *I do not think so.* We did not begrudge him his money, the diamond-studded elk's tooth that dangled from his stomach, the fancy Italian grocery (which from his description must have put to shame the Grand Central Terminal); certainly he could have had a dozen wives and fifty children for all we cared about it. What then? Just this—*we did not like his manner.* As my father so succinctly put it, who did Simone think he was anyway? He moved in on Gianpaolo, accompanied by his wife and the four youngest of their eight children,

It was a European custom to paint nuts silver or gold and hang them on the Christmas tree. Sometimes a verse or tiny manger scene would be put in a hollowed-out walnut that had been broken in half and hinged on one side so that it would open and close.

We bring in
the holly, the
ivy, the pine;
The spruce and
the hemlock
together we twine;
With evergreen
branches our
wall we array;
For keeping of
Christmas our
high holiday.

OLD ENGLISH SONG

246

without warning, without apology, seeming to think that the mere fact of his presence was sufficient to put the Maccaluccis in a very ecstasy of appreciation; he ate their food, drank their wine, slept like a king in the paternal bed (which, for want of another, Mr. and Mrs. Maccalucci had had to give up to the Simones, themselves sleeping on a mattress in the attic); and he did not offer to buy even an ice-cream cone for the children! And in the morning, when the children were waiting in line to get to the bathroom, he—but let us not go into that; suffice it to say that never, in all of our collective experience, had we run across anyone with such a positive genius for making himself offensive.

Does this not make understandable, then, my father's attitude in the matter? Had it been anyone but Simone (as my father himself will vehemently tell you), he would have withdrawn courteously at the first indication of a misunderstanding as to who was to play Santa Claus. But for nearly a week—that is to say, ever since the Simones had popped in from Boston for their "visit"—we had been hearing reports, from Gianpaolo and Mrs. Maccalucci, about his patronizing behavior; and therefore when, at dinner the Sunday before Christmas (to which the Maccaluccis had invited us in order to meet their houseguests), Simone gave indication that he himself had intentions of playing Santa Claus at the celebration, we were more than prepared to resent his presumptuousness.

Long before he proclaimed his intention, however, my father had had more than enough of Signor Simone. He had never liked him, even back in the old days (as he later confessed), but in spite of this dislike, which he had almost forgotten, and which had been revived by the reports Gianpaolo had been relaying to us regarding his guest's behavior, he had looked forward to seeing Simone again, to reminisce about the days of their youth, to discuss old friends, old experiences which they had had in common—this was the spirit in which, with my mother and me, he had gone to the Maccaluccis' for dinner, prepared to ignore the ancient dislike and to meet Simone as an old friend, found again after many years of parting, with whom he could drink a glass of wine for the sake of the old times. And did Simone make such an agreeable reunion possible? Did he, indeed? *I will present only the simple facts.* Would you like to know the first remark he made to my father as we entered the house?

"Luigi Altieri!" he roared, pumping my father's hand and nearly knocking him down with a terrific blow in the small of his back. "You alive after all these years?" This, the greeting he gave to my father; and to my mother?

"Rosa, Rosa!" said he, as though reproachfully. "You still? But how have you been able to endure each other?" And then he laughed, and threw his massive arms about her. "But how fat you've become!" he cried. *"Per Dio,* I should never have known you!"

My father, trying to recover his breath, which had been knocked out of his lungs by the pounding Simone had given him, coughed, sputtered, wheezed; my mother extended one cheek for the kiss which Simone straightaway implanted on it through his mustache.

"And this young man?" said Simone, fixing a curious eye upon me. "Your son, no doubt?"

"This is Robert, my youngest," said my mother coldly. "He is an artist."

"But no!" he said, his features expanding; and he clasped my hand in a grip that made my toes quiver. "An artist! Well, don't worry, I won't tell anyone!" he cried, and opening his mouth he let loose an extraordinary sound that seemed

to begin in the innermost depths of that remarkable stomach and thence to billow up through his lungs and out of his throat like the mounting roar of a flood-burst; he laughed, chortled, groaned; the diamond elk's tooth quivered; tears came to his eyes, and he slapped his stomach with his hands.

Was it then so humorous? We all stared; my mother coughed discreetly behind her handkerchief; I drew myself up, and—

But no matter.

Such was our introduction to this monster, but unfortunately our acquaintance did not end there; we had come to the Maccaluccis' for dinner, and to dinner we stayed. Meanwhile, we met Mrs. Simone, a pale, ferret-eyed wisp of a woman, and the Simone children, two boys, two girls, the oldest ten, the youngest five; Mr. and Mrs. Maccalucci hovered around us anxiously, took

our hats and coats, pulled out chairs, poured some wine; and at last we sat down to dinner.

In the meantime, Simone plied my father with questions: how had he fared during all these years?

"One thing is sure; you haven't starved!" he said, glancing jocularly at my father's stomach. "Do you have so many friends, then?"

My father laughed politely and muttered something behind his mustache; and at that moment the spaghetti arrived.

"Ah!" said Simone, tucking his napkin into his collar contentedly; and forthwith proceeded to heap a good half of the platter onto his own plate.

Midway through the meal the talk turned to the forthcoming Christmas celebration, and then it was that Simone made the remark which, like a lighted match tossed carelessly into a haystack, started everything.

"I have been told," said he to my father in Italian, "that you are planning to play Santa Claus for the children?" And, before my father could answer, "That will have to be changed," said he (precisely, as my father remarked afterward, as though he *owned* the place). "For the past five years I have played Santa Claus for my children, and," said he (waving his fork in the air), "they would not know you, they would think you were an impostor—"

"But, my good friend . . ." began my father courteously, glancing timidly toward Gianpaolo, whose face had turned blood red.

"And besides," Simone continued obliviously, "you have not got the figure for it. Look!" he cried, pounding his stomach. "You should see what a Santa Claus I make—ain't that so?" he added in sudden English to his wife.

At this point Gianpaolo, who had been making an ill-concealed attempt to disguise his mounting anger, exploded into action.

"Eet'sa too late!" he said, so excited that he too lapsed into English, which language, for some reason, he invariably used when he wished to be emphatic. "Eet'sa too late!" he repeated, and then, finding he could not go on without resorting to his native tongue, he let forth a torrent of voluble Italian. The plans had all been made, he explained heatedly. It was impossible to change them now!

But why? Simone demanded. What difference did it make? It made lots of difference! said Gianpaolo. The plans had been made, and made they must stay. *It was too late to change them!* At this point a gleam came into Simone's eyes. And what of his children? he demanded. How would they feel to see an unfamiliar Santa Claus? That could not be helped, said Gianpaolo, his own eyes glinting; Simone's were not the only children who would be present; *did Simone by any chance think the celebration was being given for his special benefit?*

"*Sangue de la Madonna!*" bellowed Simone, crashing his fist against the table. "What do you mean by that?"

248

Gianpaolo leaped up from his chair, quivering with fury. Simone rose like a great shaggy bear to meet him.

"Stop!" cried my father, getting between them. What nonsense! he added. He would gladly withdraw in favor of Simone.

Not for one moment, said Gianpaolo, looking venomously at Simone. *The plans had been made, and made they must stay!*

Simone shrugged and sat down again; finally Gianpaolo resumed his seat, and we went on with the dinner as though nothing had happened.

The question of who was to play Santa Claus at the celebration was not mentioned again, but once or twice I caught Simone giving furtive glances both to Gianpaolo and to my father. Ah, had we but known what lay behind those glances!

But we did not know. The following afternoon my father (despite the warnings of my mother that he had better mind his own business) went downtown, as per arrangement, and rented himself a resplendent Santa Claus outfit; and so the great day arrived.

It was not yet five o'clock when we approached the Maccaluccis' that fateful Christmas Eve, but already darkness had fallen. It had been drizzling all afternoon, and the streets were filled with puddles.

Long before we got to the house itself we heard the sounds of the gathering; the windows were ablaze with light, and we could hear singing and laughter, the lilting strains of an accordion, the strum of guitars. They had put holly wreaths and silver crosses in the windows, and through the panes we could see the shadowy forms of people moving about.

My father hid the box containing his Santa Claus outfit in the back of the car, and we went up the steps and into the house. There, in the small living room, dining room, and kitchen, upward of fifty people were gathered. There was a huge fire roaring in the living-room fireplace, and underneath the Christmas tree stood a miniature manger, complete with the infant Christ, the Virgin Mother, and the Three Wise Men of Bethlehem, all in tiny figures of wax; the walls and ceiling were festooned with ribbons of colored paper and the tip of the tree was crowned with a gleaming star. As Gianpaolo proudly told us, no expense had been spared to make the celebration a magnificent one; he had invited all his friends and their children, and the tables groaned beneath the pitchers of wine, and the house was filled with the tantalizing odors of the feast which the women were preparing.

In the midst of all this sat, in lordly fashion, Simone, ensconced in the most comfortable chair in the house, a goblet of wine in one huge hand; he nodded to us coolly as we entered, and I thought I saw a peculiar gleam, as though of calculation, come into his eyes as we went past him into the bedroom to dispose of our hats and coats.

Our arrival had interrupted the music and singing, but as soon as we had greeted the assembled guests and paid our respects to Erminio, who, since he was one day to be a priest, was treated with considerable awe by the rest, we found places and joined in the festivities. The accordionist and guitar players formed, as it were, a hub, from which all the other activity radiated; almost all joined in the singing, and we heard again and again the familiar melodies of the land from which we had stemmed—*"O Sole Mio," "Ciribiribin," "Santa Lucia"*—

folk songs, too, the songs of the field and the plow, deep in the memories of the oldest present; my father beamed and swayed and shouted; my mother nodded her head with a faraway look in her eyes. . . .

As it neared time to eat, the gathering became increasingly exuberant; the wine flowed more and more freely, faces became flushed, voices grew louder; the musicians perspired and struggled with their instruments and the house rocked to the sound of stamping feet and clapping hands. In the midst of all this, it was announced that the feast was ready, and in a few moments great steaming platters were brought in and laid upon the tables set in the living and dining rooms.

In obedience to the Catholic custom, there was no meat. The main courses were spaghetti with a savory sauce composed of olive oil flavored with garlic, parsley, and ground hot peppers; a dozen different kinds of fish, fried peppers in oil, olives, three or four kinds of salads, roasted chestnuts, a dozen varieties of Italian pastry drenched in honey, dates, dried figs, fresh grapes and apples and oranges. . . .

For upward of two hours we sat and gorged ourselves, while the flickering candles grew shorter and shorter, and the wind lashed the rain against the windows, and the logs crackled in the fireplace. Gallon after gallon of wine had been consumed, and by the time the feast was over there was not an adult present, at least among the men, who remained sober.

And what of Simone, during all this? He ate and drank as much as any four people present, making slanderous remarks, all the while, regarding the food: the spaghetti had not been salted enough, the fish was undercooked, the olives were dry. . . . Several times it looked as though Gianpaolo, who was seated opposite him at the table, were on the point of throwing some of the cutlery in his direction; but nothing, fortunately, happened, and the meal was concluded without mishap.

As soon as we had finished, the tables were cleared of everything save the fresh fruit, the nuts, and the wine, and the festivities recommenced. In obedience to the Italian custom, the plans were to eat, drink, and make merry all the night long, then go in a troop to early-morning Mass, then return for the Christmas Day dinner.

Those who wished could catch an hour or two of sleep in the meantime, but usually there were few, aside from some of the oldest, who slept; the festivities by tradition usually continued without letup from the afternoon of Christmas Eve on through Christmas Day.

"Is the sleigh, sir, put away, sir, In the barn beside the deer?" "Yes, I'm going to get it ready To use again next year."

It was now approaching ten o'clock, but the exuberance had not abated. The men played cards, shouting and slapping their hands on the table as they brought the cards down; the women busied themselves washing the dishes and cleaning up the kitchen; some of the younger couples danced. And through all this the children ran about playing games, shouting, crying, throwing candies and cookies at each other . . . frantic mothers scurried about, trying to control their offspring . . . an argument or two developed amongst the cardplayers . . . someone spilled a pitcher of wine on the floor. . . . Yes, everything was progressing beautifully.

And then the fateful hour of midnight approached.

The plans, which my father and his *paesano* had gone over carefully a hundred times, were as follows: a few minutes before midnight my father was to take his Santa Claus outfit and go out in the back to the garage. Here a great sack had been hidden, filled with presents for the children. In the house, meanwhile, the children were to be herded into the living room, around the Christmas tree.

"And the
pack, dear,
is it back, dear?"
"Yes. It's empty
of its toys,
And tomorrow
I'll start filling it,
For next year's
girls and boys."

ROWENA BENNETT

Promptly at the stroke of midnight my father was to appear, dressed as Santa Claus, the sack of presents slung over his shoulder.

These, the plans; and what happened?

Fifteen minutes or so before midnight, my father and his *paesano* exchanged a knowing glance. My father coughed, glanced at the children blandly, then, motioning to me to follow him, he got up from the table and went out the front door. We got the box with the Santa Claus suit from the car, then went around the house and to the back, where Gianpaolo was waiting for us in the garage. In a few minutes we had helped my father change into the Santa Claus suit, with its red coat and pantaloons; he stood up proudly and stroked the white whiskers which enveloped his ruddy face like a cloud.

"Well, how do I look?" he demanded.

But he looked magnificent! Gianpaolo reassured him, in a very ecstasy of enthusiasm; he straightened the coat, patted my father's stomach, tucked one sagging corner of the trousers into the boots. Magnificent, magnificent! he repeated. And now for the presents, he added, turning to a canvas which had been laid over some jugs in one corner of the garage, where the sack of presents had been hidden. He lifted the canvas—and then it was that we gained our first inkling that all was not to happen, this fateful eve, as planned. *The sack with the presents had disappeared.*

"Sangue de la Madonna!" Gianpaolo ejaculated, wrinkling his forehead in agony, and staring at the blank space beneath the canvas. He tore the canvas off frantically and began to search among the jugs, throwing them this way and that wildly.

But what was the matter? asked my father courteously.

Matter! said Gianpaolo. The presents—*someone had stolen them!*

What? said my father. But that was impossible!

At that moment, from the direction of the house, we heard a familiar voice calling our *paesano's* name.

"Gianpaolo, Gianpaolo!"

We rushed out into the yard. Mrs. Maccalucci was running toward us, her hair flying wildly in the drizzling rain.

"What's-a-matter?" cried her husband.

"Simone!" she gasped, then began to wail some more and wring her hands. Gianpaolo grabbed her by the shoulders and shook her.

"What's-a-matter?" he repeated.

Simone had stolen the presents and, dressed in a Santa Claus suit of his own, was even now preparing to give them out to the children!

"Corpo di Bacco!" bellowed Gianpaolo, and, pushing her aside, he ran toward the house, followed by my father and me. We rushed up the back steps,

through the kitchen, through the dining room, into the living room—and sure enough, there he was, surrounded by the awestruck children, dressed in a resplendent red Santa Claus suit, complete with whiskers and all.

"*Simone!*" screamed Gianpaolo.

And do you know what Simone did? *He turned and looked at us blandly!*

"*Che fai*, what are you doing?" stuttered Gianpaolo, so beside himself he could hardly talk.

"I am giving the children their presents," retorted Simone suavely.

"You? You?" cried Gianpaolo; then, "Monster!" he cried, and, leaping for-

ward on his short bandy-legs, he swung his fist against Simone's jaw. Simone ducked, and with a push of one huge paw knocked Gianpaolo to the floor. My father stared at his undersized friend, where he lay on the floor, then turned to Simone.

"So!" he said; and without another word he leaped upon his friend's assailant. The women screamed, the children whimpered and wailed, the other male guests began milling around excitedly; and in the middle of all this my father and Simone groaned, flailed, tugged.

Suddenly my father dealt Simone a resounding smack that knocked him into the fireplace. He bellowed and struggled to regain his feet; but the flames leaped over him and his whiskers caught fire.

"*Mamma mia!*" he screamed. "Help, help!"

From victorious antagonist my father turned abruptly to the role of rescuer;

he reached forward and pulled Simone upright, slapping at the whiskers to put the fire out. Simone, however, apparently mistook these friendly blows as the signal of a new attack; he hit back; they began to wrestle; suddenly my father's own whiskers caught fire.

They released each other and began dancing around, pulling at their smoldering whiskers. Someone threw a pitcher of wine over them; then all at once there was a scream:

"Fire! Fire!"

The paper festoons had caught flame; in a moment the fire had swept to the curtains and the ceiling; pandemonium broke loose. Hysterical mothers grabbed for their children; the men rushed back and forth from the kitchen frantically, bearing buckets and pans of water; someone put in a call for the fire wagon.

From this point on so many things happened at once it is impossible to relate them with any pretense of order; the fire wagons arrived with much clanging of bells and screaming of sirens, and a great crowd of people collected in the street. We had already put out the fire, however, and presently the engines departed.

Meanwhile a couple of police patrol cars arrived on the scene, and to these worthy guardians of the public morale much explanation had to be given before they could be persuaded not to herd "the whole damn bunch" of us down to the station house.

Simone, upon orders of his erstwhile host, packed his clothes (still maintaining stubbornly that it was all a misunderstanding, that his intentions had been the most honorable), and, accompanied by his wife and children, departed in a huff for a hotel; then the guests, one by one, began to leave.

At the last, none were left save the Maccaluccis and their own children, my mother and father, and me. My mother and Mrs. Maccalucci were weeping; we sat desolately amidst, as it were, the ruins, and surveyed the charred walls and ceiling, the water-drenched furniture, the sorry remains of the magnificent Christmas tree.

"*Per l'amore di Dio!*" wailed Gianpaolo. "Cousin or no cousin—if I ever see him again I'll kill him!"

At that moment there was the sound of someone coming up the front steps, then entering the house.

"But who can that be?" muttered Gianpaolo, and, mumbling to himself, he started to rise.

Yes! We saw the countenance and figure of Simone (carrying an umbrella archly) appear in the doorway.

He stood and looked at us all haughtily.

"Excuse me," he said coldly. "I forgot my shaving brush."

Gianpaolo stared at him; then suddenly he let out a scream, and, picking up a long knife from the table, he started after Simone. Simone stared at the knife, paled, dropped the umbrella, then, whirling around, started pell-mell down the steps, with Gianpaolo hard after him.

These, then, are the simple facts of the case. In conclusion it may be added that Gianpaolo received thirty days for attempted assault with a deadly weapon; Simone, on the other hand, went scot-free, and even now, no doubt, is back in that magnificent Italian grocery in Boston, safely barricaded behind his salami and cheese. Is this, then, justice? On top of all that, my father had to foot the bill for the damages—one hundred and six dollars and eighty cents, to be exact. It is such things that make my mother bitter. If my father had not been so *stubbornly insistent* in the first place, says she, all might have turned out differently; as it was— But enough; we shall leave it for the reader to judge.

A LARGE CHRISTMAS
by Lillian Smith

WE WERE NOT ALONE in being poor. Times were hard in the South—much harder for most than for us, as our father often reminded us. Our region was deep in a depression long before the rest of the country felt it—indeed, it had never had real prosperity since the Civil War—only spotty surges of easy money. But even the bank did not know—and it knew plenty—how little money we managed on those years. It got worse instead of better as time passed. And there came a winter when my younger sister and I, who were in Baltimore preparing ourselves to be a great pianist (me) and a great actress (her), felt we were needed at home. We had been supporting ourselves in our schools, but even so, we felt the parents needed us.

It was our barter year: Dad would take eggs to town, swap them for flour or cornmeal or coffee, and do it so casually that nobody suspected it was necessary. They thought he was so proud of his wife's Leghorns that he wanted to show their achievements to his friends at the stores. Eggs from the hens, three pigs which he had raised, milk and butter from the cow, beans he grew and dried, and apples from a few old trees already on the property—that was about

255

it. It was enough. For Mother could take cornmeal, mix it with flour, add soda and buttermilk and melted butter, a dab of sugar and salt, and present us with the best hot cakes in the world. Her gravy made of drippings from fried side meat, with flour and milk added and crushed black pepper, would have pleased Escoffier or any other great cook. And when things got too dull, my sister and I would hitch up the two feisty mules to the wagon and go for as wild a ride as one wanted over rough clay winter roads.

Nevertheless, the two of us had agreed to skip Christmas. You don't always have to have Christmas, we kept saying to each other. Of course not, the other would answer.

We had forgotten our father.

In that year of austerity, he invited the chain gang to have Christmas dinner with us. The prisoners were working the state roads, staying in two shabby red railroad cars on a siding. Our father visited them as he visited "all his neighbors." That night, after he returned from a three-hour visit with the men, we heard him tell Mother about it. She knew what was coming. "Bad place to be living," he said. "Terrible! Not fit for animals much less—" He sighed. "Well, there's more misery in the world than even I know; and a lot of it is unnecessary. That's the wrong part of it, it's unnecessary." He looked in his wife's dark eyes. She waited. "Mama," he said softly, "how about having them out here for Christmas? Wouldn't that be good?" A long silence. Then Mother quietly agreed. Dad walked to town—we had no car—to tell the foreman he would like to have the prisoners and guards come to Christmas dinner.

"All of them?" asked the chain-gang foreman.

"We couldn't hardly leave any of the boys out, could we?"

Close to noon on Christmas Day we saw them coming down the road: forty-eight men in stripes, with their guards. They came up the hill and headed for the house, a few laughing, talking, others grim and suspicious. All had come, white and Negro. We had helped Mother make two caramel cakes and twelve sweet-potato pies and a wonderful backbone-and-rice dish (which Mother, born on the coast, called pilau); and there were hot rolls and Brunswick stew, and a washtub full of apples which our father had polished in front of the fire on Christmas Eve. It would be a splendid dinner, he told Mother, who looked a bit wan, probably wondering what we would eat in January.

While we pulled out Mother's best china—piecing out with the famous heirloom fish plates—our father went from man to man shaking hands, and soon they were talking freely with him, and everybody was laughing at his funny— and sometimes on the rare side—stories. And then, there was a hush, and we in the kitchen heard Dad's voice lifted up: *"And it came to pass in those days—"*

Mother stayed with the oven. The two of us eased to the porch. Dad was standing there, reading from St. Luke. The day was warm and sunny and the forty-eight men and their guards were sitting on the grass. Two guards with guns in their hands leaned against trees. Eight of the men were lifers; six of them, in pairs, had their inside legs locked together; ten were killers (one had bashed in his grandma's head); two had robbed banks, three had stolen cars, one had burned down his neighbor's house and barn after an argument, one had raped a girl—all were listening to the old old words.

When my father closed the Bible, he gravely said he hoped their families were having a good Christmas, he hoped all was well "back home." Then he smiled and grew hearty. "Now boys," he said, "eat plenty and have a good time. We're proud to have you today. We would have been a little lonely if you hadn't come. Now let's have a Merry Christmas."

The men laughed. It began with the Negroes, who quickly caught the wonderful absurdity, it spread to the whites and finally all were laughing and muttering Merry Christmas, half deriding, half meaning it, and my father laughed with them, for he was never unaware of the absurd which he seemed deliberately, sometimes, to whistle into his life.

They were our guests, and our father moved among them with grace and ease. He asked them about their families, telling them a little about his. One young man talked earnestly in a low voice. I heard my father say, "Son, that's mighty bad. We'll see if we can't do something about it." (Later he did.)

When Mother said she was ready, our father asked "Son," who was one of the killers, to go help "my wife, won't you, with the heavy things." And the young man said he'd be mighty glad to. The one in for raping and another for robbing a bank said they'd be pleased to help, too, and they went in. My sister and I followed, not feeling as casual as we hoped we looked. But when two guards moved toward the door my father peremptorily stopped them with, "The boys will be all right." And "the boys" were. They came back in a few minutes bearing great pots and pans to a serving table we had set up on the porch. My sister and I served the plates. The murderer and his two friends passed them to the men. Afterward, the rapist and two bank robbers and the arsonist said they'd be real pleased to wash up the dishes. But we told them nobody should wash dishes on Christmas—just have a good time.

That evening, after our guests had gone back to their quarters on the railroad siding, we sat by the fire. The parents looked tired. Dad went out for another hickory log to "keep us through the night," laid it in the deep fireplace, scratched the coals, sat down in his easy chair by the lamp. Mother said she had a letter from the eldest daughter, in China—would Papa read it? It was full of cheer,

B etter is a
dinner of herbs
where love is,
than a stalled ox
and hatred
therewith.

PROVERBS 15:17

as such letters are likely to be. We sat quietly talking of her family, of their work with a religious organization, of China's persisting troubles after the 1911 revolution.

We were quiet after that. Just rested together. Dad glanced through a book or two that his sons had sent him. Then the old look of having something to say to his children settled on his face. He began slowly:

"We've been through some pretty hard times, lately, and I've been proud of my family. Some folks can take prosperity and can't take poverty; some can take being poor and lose their heads when money comes. I want my children to accept it all; the good and the bad, for that is what life is. It can't be wholly good; it won't be wholly bad." He looked at our mother, sitting there, tired but gently involved. "Those men, today—they've made mistakes. Sure. But I have too. Bigger ones maybe than theirs. And you will. You are not likely to commit a crime but you may become blind and refuse to see what you should look at, and that can be worse than a crime. Don't forget that. Never look down on a man. Never. If you can't look him straight in the eyes, then what's wrong is with you." He glanced at the letter from the eldest sister. "The world is changing fast. Folks get hurt and make terrible mistakes at such times. But the one I hope you won't make is to cling to my generation's sins. You'll have plenty of your own, remember. Changing things is mighty risky, but not changing things is worse—that is, if you can think of something better to change to. . . . Mama, believe I'll go to bed. You about ready?"

On the stairs he stopped. "But I don't mean, Sister, you got to get radical." He laughed. His voice dropped to the soft tones he used with his younger children. "We had a good Christmas, didn't we?" He followed our mother up the stairs.

My younger sister and I looked in the fire, dreaming about a future we could not know and didn't want to talk about. After a long silence, we succumbed to a little do-you-remember about the Christmases of our childhood. And soon we were laughing about how Father used to organize us for the shaking of the pecan trees, and how later round the hearth we cracked the nuts for fruitcakes and chewy syrup candy, and the firecrackers and Roman candles we Southerners saved for Christmas, and the excitement and terror of hog killings on frosty dawns, and the sausages our grandmother made for the special Christmas breakfast, with just enough red pepper and sage. . . .

And now the fire in front of us was blurring.

My sister said softly, "It was a large Christmas."

"Which one?"

"All of them," she whispered.

NEW RELATIONS AND DUTIES
by Frederick Douglass

My TERM OF SERVICE with Edward Covey expired on Christmas Day, 1834. I gladly enough left him, although he was by this time as gentle as a lamb. My home for the year 1835 was already secured, my next master selected. There was always more or less excitement about the changing hands, but determined to fight my way, I had become somewhat reckless and cared little into whose hands I fell. The report got abroad that I was hard to whip; that I was guilty of kicking back, and that, though generally a good-natured Negro, I sometimes "got the devil in me." These sayings were rife in Talbot County and distinguished me among my servile brethren. Slaves would sometimes fight with each other, and even die at each other's hands, but there were very few who were not held in awe by a white man. Trained from the cradle up to think and feel that their masters were superiors, and invested with a sort of sacredness, there were few who could rise above the control which that sentiment exercised. I had freed myself from it, and the thing was known. One bad sheep will spoil a whole flock. I was a bad sheep. I hated slavery, slaveholders, and all pertaining to them; and I did not fail to inspire others with the same feeling wherever and whenever opportunity was presented. This made me a marked lad among the slaves, and a suspected one among slaveholders. A knowledge also of my ability to read and write got pretty widely spread, which was very much against me.

The days between Christmas Day and New Year's were allowed the slaves as holidays. During these days all regular work was suspended, and there was nothing to do but keep fires and look after the stock. We regarded this time as our own by the grace of our masters, and we therefore used it or abused it as we pleased. Those who had families at a distance were expected to visit

At midnight
on Christmas Eve
the animals in the
barns sink to their
knees and turn
toward Bethlehem.
They also speak
to each other about
the good season
and its meaning.
But if you try to
eavesdrop on them,
you may die.

SUPERSTITION OF THE OLD SOUTH

them and spend with them the entire week. The younger slaves or the un-married ones were expected to see to the animals and attend to incidental duties at home. The holidays were variously spent. The sober, thinking, industrious ones would employ themselves in manufacturing corn brooms, mats, horse collars, and baskets, and some of these were very well made. Another class spent their time in hunting opossums, coons, rabbits, and other game. But the majority spent the holidays in sports, ball playing, wrestling, boxing, running, footraces, dancing, and drinking whiskey; and this latter mode was generally most agreeable to their masters. A slave who would work during the holidays was thought by his master undeserving of holidays. There was in this simple act of continued work an accusation against slaves, and a slave could not help thinking that if he made three dollars during the holidays he might make three hundred during the year. Not to be drunk during the holidays was disgraceful.

The fiddling, dancing, and "jubilee beating" was carried on in all directions. This latter performance was strictly southern. It supplied the place of violin or other musical instruments and was played so easily that almost every farm had its "Juba" beater. The performer improvised as he beat the instrument, marking the words as he sang so as to have them fall pat with the movement of his hands. Once in a while among a mass of nonsense and wild frolic, a sharp hit was given to the meanness of slaveholders.

Take the following for example:

> We raise de wheat,
> Dey gib us de corn:
> We bake de bread,
> Dey gib us de crust;
> We sif de meal,
> Dey gib us de huss;
>
> We peel de meat,
> Dey gib us de skin;
> And dat's de way
> Dey take us in . . .

This is not a bad summary of the palpable injustice and fraud of slavery, giving, as it does, to the lazy and idle the comforts which God designed should be given solely to the honest laborer. But to the holidays. Judging from my own observation and experience, I believe those holidays were among the most effective means in the hands of slaveholders of keeping down the spirit of in-surrection among the slaves.

CAROL OF
THE BROWN KING

Of the three Wise Men
Who came to the King,
One was a brown man,
So they sing.

Of the three Wise Men
Who followed the Star,
One was a brown king
From afar.

They brought fine gifts
Of spices and gold
In jeweled boxes
Of beauty untold.

Unto His humble
Manger they came
And bowed their heads
In Jesus' name.

Three Wise Men,
One dark like me—
Part of His
Nativity.

Langston Hughes

261

'Twas in the moon of wintertime
   When all the birds had fled,
That Mighty Gitchi Manitou
   Sent angel - choirs instead;
Before their light the stars grew dim,
   and wond'ring hunters heard the hymn—
Jesus your King is born, Jesus is born,
   In excelsis gloria.

Within a lodge of broken bark
   The tender Babe was found,
A ragged robe of rabbit skin
   enwrapp'd His beauty round;
But as the hunter braves drew nigh,
   The angel song rang loud and high—
Jesus your King is born, Jesus is born,
   In excelsis gloria.

The earliest moon of wintertime
   Is not so round and fair
As was the ring of glory on
   The helpless Infant there.
The Chiefs from far before Him knelt
   With gifts of fox and beaver pelt—
Jesus your King is born, Jesus is born,
   In excelsis gloria.

O children of the forest free,
   O sons of Manitou,
The Holy Child of earth and Heav'n
   Is born to day for you.
Come kneel before the radiant Boy,
   Who brings you beauty, peace and joy—
Jesus your King is born, Jesus is born,
   In excelsis gloria.

English interpretation by J. E. Middleton

CHRISTMAS MORNING

by Frank O'Connor

I NEVER REALLY LIKED my brother, Sonny. From the time he was a baby he was always the mother's pet and always chasing her to tell her what mischief I was up to. Mind you, I was usually up to something. Until I was nine or ten I was never much good at school, and I really believe it was to spite me that he was so smart at his books. He seemed to know by instinct that this was what Mother had set her heart on, and you might almost say he spelled himself into her favor.

"Mummy," he'd say, "will I call Larry in to his t-e-a?" or: "Mummy, the k-e-t-e-l is boiling," and, of course, when he was wrong she'd correct him, and next time he'd have it right and there would be no standing him. "Mummy," he'd say, "aren't I a good speller?" Cripes, we could all be good spellers if we went on like that!

Mind you, it wasn't that I was stupid. Far from it. I was just restless and not able to fix my mind for long on any one thing. I'd do the lessons for the year before, or the lessons for the year after: what I couldn't stand were the lessons we were supposed to be doing at the time. In the evenings I used to go out and play with the Doherty gang. Not, again, that I was rough, but I liked the excitement, and for the life of me I couldn't see what attracted Mother about education.

"Can't you do your lessons first and play after?" she'd say, getting white with indignation. "You ought to be ashamed of yourself that your baby brother can read better than you!"

She didn't seem to understand that I wasn't, because there didn't seem to me to be anything particularly praiseworthy about reading, and it struck me as an occupation better suited to a sissy kid like Sonny.

263

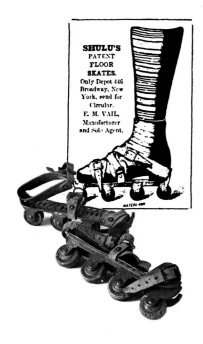

"The dear knows what will become of you," she'd say. "If only you'd stick to your books you might be something good like a clerk or an engineer."

"I'll be a clerk, Mummy," Sonny would say smugly.

"Who wants to be an old clerk?" I'd say, just to annoy him. "I'm going to be a soldier."

"The dear knows, I'm afraid that's all you'll ever be fit for," she would add with a sigh.

I couldn't help feeling at times that she wasn't all there. As if there was anything better a fellow could be!

Coming on to Christmas, with the days getting shorter and the shopping crowds bigger, I began to think of all the things I might get from Santa Claus. The Dohertys said there was no Santa Claus, only what your father and mother gave you, but the Dohertys were a rough class of children you wouldn't expect Santa to come to anyway. I was scouting round for whatever information I could pick up about him, but there didn't seem to be much. I was no hand with a pen, but if a letter would do any good I was ready to chance writing to him. I had plenty of initiative and was always writing off for free samples and prospectuses.

"Ah, I don't know will he come at all this year," Mother said with a worried air. "He has enough to do looking after good boys who mind their lessons without bothering about the rest."

"He only comes to good spellers, Mummy," said Sonny. "Isn't that right?"

"He comes to any little boy who does his best, whether he's a good speller or not," Mother said firmly.

Well, I did my best. God knows I did! It wasn't my fault if, four days before the holidays, Flogger Dawley gave us sums we couldn't do, and Peter Doherty and myself had to play hooky. It wasn't for love of it, for, take it from me, December is no month for playing hooky, and we spent most of our time sheltering from the rain in a store on the quays. The only mistake we made was imagining we could keep it up till the holidays without being spotted. That showed real lack of foresight.

Of course, Flogger Dawley noticed and sent home word to know what was keeping me. When I came in on the third day the mother gave me a look I'll never forget, and said: "Your dinner is there." She was too full to talk. When I tried to explain to her about Flogger Dawley and the sums she brushed it aside and said: "You have no word." I saw then it wasn't the fact that I'd been playing hooky she minded but the lies, though I still didn't see how you could play hooky without lying. She didn't speak to me for days. And even then I couldn't make out what she saw in education, or why she wouldn't let me grow up naturally like anyone else.

To make things worse, it stuffed Sonny up more than ever. He had the air of one saying: "I don't know what they'd do without me in this blooming house." He stood at the front door, leaning against the jamb with his hands in his trouser pockets, trying to make himself look like Father, and shouted to the other kids so that he could be heard all over the road. "Larry isn't allowed to go out. He played hooky with Peter Doherty and me mother isn't talking to him."

And at night, when we were in bed, he kept it up.

"Santa Claus won't bring you anything this year, aha!"

"Of course he will," I said.

"How do you know?"

"Why wouldn't he?"

"Because you played hooky with Doherty. I wouldn't play with them Doherty fellows."

"You wouldn't be allowed to."

"I wouldn't play with them. They're no class. They had the bobbies up at the house."

"And how would Santa know I played hooky with Peter Doherty?" I growled, losing patience with the little prig.

"Of course he'd know. Mummy would tell him."

"And how could Mummy tell him and he up at the North Pole? Poor Ireland, she's rearing them yet! 'Tis easy seen you're only an old baby."

"I'm not a baby, and I can spell better than you, and Santa won't bring you anything."

"We'll see whether he will or not," I said sarcastically, letting on to be quite confident about it.

But, to tell the God's truth, I wasn't confident at all. You could never tell what powers these superhuman chaps would have of knowing what you were up to. And I had a bad conscience about skipping school because I'd never before seen the mother like that.

That was the night I decided that the only sensible thing to do was to see Santa myself and explain to him. Being a man, he'd probably understand. In those days I was a good-looking kid and had a way with me when I liked. I had only to smile nicely at one old gent on the North Mall to get a penny from him, and I felt if only I could get Santa by himself I could do the same with him and maybe get something worthwhile from him. I wanted a model railway.

I started to practice lying awake, counting five hundred and then a thousand, and trying to hear first eleven, then midnight, from Shandon. I felt sure Santa would be round by midnight, seeing that he'd be coming from the north, and would have the whole of the South Side to do afterward. In some ways I was very farsighted. The only trouble was the things I was farsighted about.

In Ireland
candles are
set in the
windows on
Christmas Eve
to light the
Christ Child
on His way.
And only a
woman
named Mary
may snuff
out the church
candles on
Christmas Day.

I was so wrapped up in my own calculations that I had little attention to spare for Mother's difficulties. Sonny and I used to go to town with her, and while she was shopping we stood outside a toy shop in the North Main Street, arguing about what we'd like for Christmas.

On Christmas Eve when Father came home from work and gave her the house-keeping money, she stood looking at it doubtfully while her face grew white.

"Well?" he snapped, getting angry. "What's wrong with that?"

"What's wrong with it?" she muttered. "On Christmas Eve!"

"Well," he asked truculently, sticking his hands in his trouser pockets as though to guard what was left, "do you think I get more because it's Christmas?"

"Lord God," she muttered distractedly. "And not a bit of cake in the house, nor a candle, nor anything!"

"All right," he shouted, beginning to stamp. "How much will the candle be?"

"Ah, for pity's sake," she cried, "will you give me the money and not argue like that before the children? Do you think I'll leave them with nothing on the one day of the year?"

"Bad luck to you and your children!" he snarled. "Am I to be slaving from one year's end to another for you to be throwing it away on toys? Here," he added, tossing two silver coins on the table, "that's all you're going to get, so make the most of it."

"I suppose the publicans will get the rest," she said bitterly.

Later she went into town, but did not take us and returned with a lot of parcels, including the Christmas candle. We waited for Father to come home to his tea, but he didn't, so we had our own tea and a slice of Christmas cake each, and then Mother put Sonny on a chair with the holy-water stoup to sprinkle the candle, and when he lit it she said: "The light of heaven to our souls." I could see she was upset because Father wasn't there—it should be the oldest and the youngest. When we hung up our stockings at bedtime he was still out.

Then began the hardest couple of hours I ever put in. I was ever so sleepy but afraid of losing the model railway, so I lay for a while, making up things to say to Santa when he came. They varied in tone from frivolous to grave, for some old gents like kids to be modest and well-spoken, while others prefer them with spirit. When I had rehearsed them all I tried to wake Sonny to keep me company, but that kid slept like the dead.

Eleven struck from Shandon, and soon after I heard the latch, but it was only Father coming home.

"Hello, little girl," he said, letting on to be surprised at finding Mother waiting up for him, and then broke into a self-conscious giggle. "What is keeping you up so late?"

"Do you want your supper?" she asked shortly.

266

"Ah, no, no," he replied. "I had a bit of pig's cheek at Daneen's on my way home (Daneen was my uncle). I'm very fond of a bit of pig's cheek. . . . My goodness, is it that late?" he exclaimed, letting on to be astonished. "If I knew that I'd have gone to the North Chapel for midnight Mass. I'd like to hear the *Adeste* again. That's a hymn I'm very fond of—a most touching hymn."

Then he began to hum it falsetto.

"*Adeste fideles*
Solus domus dagus—"

Father was very fond of Latin hymns, particularly when he had a drop in, but as he had no notion of the words he made them up as he went along, and this always drove Mother mad.

"Ah, you disgust me!" she said in a scalded voice, and closed the bedroom door behind her. Father laughed as if he thought it a great joke; and he struck a match to light his pipe and for a while puffed at it noisily. The light under the door dimmed and went out but he continued to sing emotionally.

"*Dixie medearo*
Jutum tonum tantum
Venite adoremus—"

He had it all wrong but the effect was the same on me. To save my life I couldn't keep awake.

Coming on to dawn, I woke with the feeling that something dreadful had happened. The whole house was quiet, and the little bedroom that looked out on the foot and a half of backyard was pitch-dark. It was only when I glanced at the window that I saw how all the silver had drained out of the sky. I jumped out of bed to feel my stocking, well knowing that the worst had happened. Santa had come while I was asleep, and gone away with an entirely false impression of me, because all he had left me was some sort of book, folded up, a pen and pencil, and a tuppenny bag of sweets. For a while I was too stunned even to think. A fellow who was able to drive over rooftops and climb down chimneys without getting stuck—God, wouldn't you think he'd know better?

Then I began to wonder what that foxy boy, Sonny, had. I went to his side of the bed and felt his stocking. For all his spelling and sucking he hadn't done so much better, because, apart from a bag of sweets like mine, all Santa had left him was a popgun, one that fired a cork on a piece of string and which you could get in any shop for sixpence.

All the same, the fact remained that it was a gun, and a gun was better than a

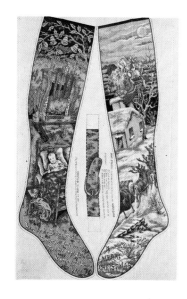

book any day of the week. The Dohertys had a gang, and the gang fought the Strawberry Lane kids who tried to play football on our road. That gun would be very useful to me in many ways, while it would be lost on Sonny who wouldn't be allowed to play with the gang, even if he wanted to.

Then I got the inspiration, as it seemed to me, direct from heaven. Suppose I took the gun and gave Sonny the book! Sonny would never be any good in the gang: he was fond of spelling, and a studious child like him could learn a lot of spellings from a book like mine. As he hadn't seen Santa any more than I had, what he hadn't seen wouldn't grieve him. I was doing no harm to anyone; in fact, if Sonny only knew, I was doing him a good turn which he might have cause to thank me for later. That was one thing I was always keen on; doing good turns. Perhaps this was Santa's intention the whole time and he had merely become confused between us. It was a mistake that might happen to anyone. So I put the book, the pencil, and the pen into Sonny's stocking and the popgun into my own, and returned to bed and slept again. As I say, in those days I had plenty of initiative.

It was Sonny who woke me, shaking me to tell me that Santa had come and left me a gun. I let on to be surprised and rather disappointed in the gun, and to divert his mind from it made him show me his picture book, and told him it was much better than what Santa brought me.

As I knew, that kid was prepared to believe anything, and nothing would do him then but to take the presents in to show Father and Mother. This was a bad moment for me. After the way she had behaved about my lying, I distrusted Mother, though I had the consolation of believing that the only person who could contradict me was now somewhere up by the North Pole. That gave me a certain confidence, so Sonny and I burst in with our presents, shouting: "Look what Santa Claus brought!"

Father and Mother woke, and Mother smiled, but only for an instant. As she looked at me her face changed. I knew that look; I knew it only too well. It was the same she had worn the day I came home from playing hooky, when she said I had no word.

"Larry," she said in a low voice, "where did you get that gun?"

"Santa left it in my stocking, Mummy," I said, trying to put on an injured air, though it baffled me how she guessed that he hadn't. "He did, honest."

"You stole it from that poor child's stocking while he was asleep," she said, her voice quivering with indignation. "Larry, Larry, how could you be so mean?"

"Now, now, now," Father said deprecatingly, " 'tis Christmas morning."

"Ah," she said with real passion, "it's easy it comes to you. Do you think I want my son to grow up a liar and a thief?"

"Ah, what thief, woman?" he said testily. "Have sense, can't you?" He was

268

as cross if you interrupted him in his benevolent moods as if they were of the other sort, and this one was probably exacerbated by a feeling of guilt for his behavior of the night before. "Here, Larry," he said, reaching out for the money on the bedside table, "here's sixpence for you and one for Sonny. Mind you don't lose it now!"

But I looked at Mother and saw what was in her eyes. I burst out crying, threw the popgun on the floor, and ran bawling out of the house before anyone on the road was awake. I rushed up the lane behind the house and threw myself on the wet grass.

I understood it all, and it was almost more than I could bear; that there was no Santa Claus, as the Dohertys said, only Mother trying to scrape together a few pence from the housekeeping; that Father was mean and common and a drunkard, and that she had been relying on me to raise her out of the misery of the life she was leading. And I knew that the look in her eyes was the fear that, like my father, I should turn out to be mean and common and a drunkard.

After that morning, I think my childhood was at an end.

George Washington himself prepared this list
of presents he planned to give to his five-year-old stepson,
Jackie, and his three-year-old stepdaughter,
Patsy, on Christmas Day, 1759.

A bird on Bellows
A Cuckoo
A turnabout Parrot
A Grocers Shop
An Aviary
A Prussian Dragoon
A Man Smoakg
A Tunbridge Tea Sett
3 Neat Tunbridge Toys
A Neat Book fash Tea Chest
A box best Household Stuff
A straw Patch box w. a Glass
A neat dress'd Wax Baby

FRANCIE NOLAN'S CHRISTMAS TREE
by Betty Smith

CHRISTMAS WAS a charmed time in Brooklyn in 1912.

The spruce trees began coming into Francie Nolan's neighborhood the week before Christmas. Their branches were corded to make shipping easier. Vendors rented space on the curb before a store and stretched a rope from pole to pole and leaned the trees against it. All day they walked up and down this one-sided avenue of aromatic leaning trees, blowing on stiff ungloved fingers. And the air was cold and still, and full of the pine smell and the smell of tangerines which appeared in the stores only at Christmastime and the mean street was truly wonderful for a little while.

There was a cruel custom in the neighborhood. At midnight on the Eve of our dear Saviour's birth, the kids gathered where there were unsold trees. There was a saying that if you waited until then, you wouldn't have to buy a tree; that "they'd chuck 'em at you." This was literally true. The man threw each tree in turn, starting with the biggest. Kids volunteered to stand up against the throwing. If a boy didn't fall down under the impact, the tree was his. If he fell, he forfeited his chance at winning a tree. Only the roughest boys and some of the young men elected to be hit by the big trees. The others waited shrewdly until a tree came up that they could stand against. The littlest kids waited for the tiny, foot-high trees and shrieked in delight when they won one.

On the Christmas Eve when Francie was ten and her brother, Neeley, nine, Mama consented to let them go down and have their first try for a tree. Francie had picked out her tree earlier in the day. She had stood near it all afternoon and evening praying that no one would buy it. To her joy, it was still there at midnight. It was ten feet tall and its price was so high that no one could afford to buy it. Its branches were bound with new white rope and it came to a sure pure point at the top.

The man took this tree out first. Before Francie could speak up, a neighborhood bully, a boy of eighteen known as Punky Perkins, stepped forward and ordered the man to chuck the tree at him. The man hated the way Punky was so confident. He looked around and asked, "Anybody else wanna take a chanct on it?"

Francie stepped forward. "Me, Mister."

A spurt of derisive laughter came from the tree man. The kids snickered. A few adults who had gathered to watch the fun guffawed. "Aw g'wan. You're too little," the tree man objected.

"Me and my brother—we're not too little together."

She pulled Neeley forward. The man looked at them—a thin girl of ten with starveling hollows in her cheeks but with the chin still baby-round. He looked at the little boy with his fair hair and round blue eyes—Neeley Nolan, all innocence and trust.

"Two ain't fair," yelped Punky.

"Shut your lousy trap," advised the man, who held all power in that hour. "These here kids is got nerve. Stand back, the rest of youse. These kids is goin' to have a show at this tree."

The others made a wavering lane, a human funnel with Francie and her brother making the small end of it. The big man at the other end flexed his great arms to throw the great tree. He noticed how tiny the children looked at the end of the short lane. For the split part of a moment, the tree thrower went through a kind of Gethsemane.

Oh, Jesus Christ, his soul agonized, why don't I just give 'em the tree and say Merry Christmas? I can't sell it no more this year and it won't keep till next year. The kids watched him solemnly as he stood there in his moment of thought. But then, he rationalized, if I did that, all the others would expect to get 'em handed to 'em. And next year, nobody a-tall would buy a tree off of me. I ain't a big enough man to give this tree away for nothin'. No, I gotta think of myself and my own kids. He finally came to his conclusion. Oh, what the hell! Them two kids is gotta live in this world. They *got* to learn to give and to take punishment. As he threw the tree with all his strength, his heart wailed out, It's a rotten, lousy world!

Francie saw the tree leave his hands. The whole world stood still as something dark and monstrous came through the air. There was nothing but pungent darkness and something that grew and grew as it rushed at her. She staggered as the tree hit them. Neeley went to his knees but she pulled him up fiercely before he could go down. There was a mighty swishing sound as the tree settled. Every-

271

Now gay trees rise
Before your eyes,
Abloom with
tempting cheer;
Blithe voices sing,
And blithe bells ring
For Christmastide
is here.

FROM AN OLD CAROL

272

thing was dark, green and prickly. Then she felt a sharp pain at the side of her head where the trunk of the tree had hit her. She felt Neeley trembling.

When some of the older boys pulled the tree away, they found Francie and her brother standing upright, hand in hand. Blood was coming from scratches on Neeley's face. He looked more like a baby than ever with his bewildered blue eyes, and the fairness of his skin made more noticeable because of the clear red blood. But they were smiling. Had they not won the biggest tree in the neighborhood? Some of the boys hollered, "Hooray!" A few adults clapped. The tree man eulogized them by screaming, "And now get the hell out of here with your tree."

Such phrases could mean many things according to the tone used in saying them. So Francie smiled tremulously at the kind man. She knew that he was really saying, "Good-by—God bless you."

It wasn't easy dragging that tree home. They were handicapped by a boy who ran alongside yelping, "Free ride! All aboard!" who'd jump on and make them drag him along. But he got sick of the game eventually and went away.

In a way, it was good that it took them so long to get the tree home. It made their triumph more drawn out. Francie glowed when a lady said, "I never saw such a big tree!" The cop on their corner stopped them, examined the tree, and solemnly offered to buy it for fifteen cents if they'd deliver it to his home. Francie nearly burst with pride although she knew he was joking.

They had to call to Papa to help them get the tree up the narrow stairs. Papa came running down. His amazement at the size of the tree was flattering. He pretended to believe that it wasn't theirs. Francie had a lot of fun convincing him although she knew all the while that the whole thing was make-believe. Papa pulled in front and Francie and Neeley pushed in back and they began forcing the big tree up the two narrow flights of stairs. Papa started singing, not caring that it was rather late at night. He sang "Holy Night." The narrow walls took up his clear sweet voice, held it for a breath and gave it back with doubled sweetness. Doors creaked open and families gathered on the landings, pleased and amazed at something unexpected being added to that moment of their lives.

Francie saw the Tynmore sisters, who gave piano lessons, standing together in their doorway, their gray hair in crimpers, and ruffled, starched nightgowns showing under their voluminous wrappers. They added their thin poignant voices to Papa's. Floss Gaddis, her mother and her brother, Henny, who was dying of consumption, stood in their doorway. Henny was crying and when Papa saw him he let the song trail off; he thought maybe it made Henny too sad.

Flossie was in a Klondike-dance-hall-girl costume waiting for an escort to take her to a masquerade ball which started soon after midnight. More to make Henny smile than anything else, Papa said, "Floss, we got no angel for the top of this Christmas tree. How about you obliging?"

Floss was all ready to make a smart-alecky reply, but there was something about the big proud tree, the beaming children and the rare goodwill of the neighbors that changed her mind. All she said was, "Gee, ain't you the kidder, Mr. Nolan."

They set the tree up in the front room after Mama had spread a sheet to protect the carpet from falling pine needles. The tree stood in a big tin bucket with broken bricks to hold it upright. When the rope was cut away, the branches spread out to fill the room. They draped over the piano and some of the chairs stood among the branches. There was no money to buy decorations or lights. But the great tree standing there was enough. The room was cold. It was a poor year, that one—too poor for them to buy the extra coal for the front-room stove. The room smelled cold and clean and aromatic.

Every day, during the week the tree stood there, Francie put on her sweater and stocking cap and went in and sat under the tree. She sat there and enjoyed the smell and the dark greenness of it.

Oh, the mystery of a great tree, a prisoner in a tin wash bucket in a tenement front room!

From *A Tree Grows in Brooklyn*

THE BALLAD OF BEFANA
An Epiphany Legend

Befana the Housewife, scrubbing her pane,
Saw three old sages ride down the lane,
Saw three gray travelers pass her door—
Gaspar, Balthazar, Melchior.

"Where journey you, sirs?" she asked of them.
Balthazar answered, "To Bethlehem,

For we have news of a marvelous thing.
Born in a stable is Christ the King."

"Give Him my welcome!"
Then Gaspar smiled,
"Come with us, mistress, to greet the Child."

"Oh, happily, happily would I fare,
Were my dusting through and I'd polished the stair."

Old Melchior leaned on his saddle horn.
"Then send but a gift to the small Newborn."

"Oh, gladly, gladly I'd send Him one,
Were the hearthstone swept and my weaving done.

"As soon as ever I've baked my bread,
I'll fetch Him a pillow for His head,
And a coverlet too," Befana said.

"When the rooms are aired and the linen dry,
I'll look at the Babe."
But the Three rode by.

She worked for a day and a night and a day,
Then, gifts in her hands, took up her way.
But she never could find where the Christ Child lay.

And still she wanders at Christmastide,
Houseless, whose house was all her pride,

Whose heart was tardy, whose gifts were late;
Wanders, and knocks at every gate,
Crying, "Good people, the bells begin!
Put off your toiling and let love in."

Phyllis McGinley

CHRISTMAS MEDITATION OF A YOUNG STUDENT

NIGHT HAS FALLEN; the clear, bright stars are sparkling in the cold air; noisy, strident voices rise to my ear from the city, voices of the revelers of this world who celebrate with merrymaking the poverty of their Saviour. Around me in their rooms my companions are asleep, and I am still wakeful, thinking of the mystery of Bethlehem.

Come, come, Jesus, I await you.

Mary and Joseph, knowing the hour is near, are turned away by the townsfolk and go out into the fields to look for a shelter. I am a poor shepherd; I have only a wretched stable, a small manger, some wisps of straw. I offer all these to you, be pleased to come into my poor hovel. I offer you my heart; my soul is poor and bare of virtues, the straws of so many imperfections will prick you and make you weep—but oh, my Lord, what can you expect? This little is all I have. I am touched by your poverty, I am moved to tears, but I have nothing better to offer you. Jesus, honor my soul with your presence, adorn it with your graces. Burn this straw and change it into a soft couch for your most holy body.

Jesus, I am here waiting for your coming. Wicked men have driven you out, and the wind is like ice. I am a poor man, but I will warm you as well as I can. At least be pleased that I wish to welcome you warmly, to love you and sacrifice myself for you.

But in your own way you are rich, and you see my needs. You are a flame of charity, and you will purge my heart of all that is not your own most holy Heart. You are uncreated holiness, and you will fill me with those graces which give new life to my soul. Oh, Jesus, come, I have so much to tell you, so many sorrows to confide, so many desires, so many promises and so many hopes.

I want to adore you, to kiss you on the brow, oh tiny Jesus, to give myself to you once more, forever. Come, my Jesus, delay no longer, come, be my guest.

Alas! It is already late, I am overcome with sleep and my pen slips from my fingers. Let me sleep a little, oh Jesus, while your Mother and St. Joseph are preparing the room.

I will lie down to rest here, in the fresh night air. As soon as you come, the splendor of your light will dazzle my eyes. Your angels will awaken me with sweet hymns of glory and peace, and I shall run forward with joy to welcome you and to offer you my own poor gifts, my home, all the little I have. I will worship you and show you all my love with the other shepherds who have joined me, and with the angels of Heaven, singing hymns of glory to your loving heart.

*These moving words were written on Christmas Eve, 1902,
by a young Italian named Angelo Giuseppe Roncalli who was studying for
the priesthood in Rome. Two years later he graduated as a
doctor in theology and was ordained. The world now remembers him
as the widely beloved Pope John XXIII.*

Christmas
Around the World

Christmas
Around the World

IN WESTERN SAMOA, in the warm, flower-scented dawn, clocks are striking six. Christmas Day has begun. At this same moment it is seven a.m. in wintry Alaska, where children tumble from warm beds to see what Santa Claus has left them. Along the east coast of the United States it is noon. Families are gathering at laden tables, where golden-skinned turkeys wait to be carved. And in England other families are sitting down to late afternoon tea. Already dusk has fallen in the Holy Land, where it is seven p.m. The first stars have appeared in the sky, another Christmas is drawing to its close.

In every time zone Christ's birthday is celebrated. The ways of celebration, the legends and folklore of the season, vary, as will be seen on the following pages. They have, however, much in common. The gifts, the foods, the languages in which carols are sung, the sources of radiance, the religious ceremonies, differ only in detail. Everywhere there is some form of giving, feasting and song. Everywhere there is light. Everywhere—for at least this day—peace and goodwill prevail among men.

Germany-Austria

Many of the world's cherished Christmas traditions stem from Germany, a land steeped in the lore of the season. In Europe from time immemorial evergreen trees had been brought into homes during the northern winter as symbols of unending life, but it was here, in the Black Forest, that they were first used as a part of Christmas. Here, too, when Alsace was German, the fragrant firs and spruces were first decorated with sparkling glass balls and garlands of tinsel.

Marzipan, lebkuchen, springerle, stollen and other mouth-watering holiday treats are of German origin. And the colorful German Advent calendars with little windows to open for each day of the season are a delight to children everywhere. It is with Advent that the German Christmas begins. Then an evergreen wreath with four candles is hung in many houses, and every Sunday until Christmas Eve one candle is lighted.

The season in Teutonic countries has a history of darkness, too. Evil spirits were once said to roam free at this holy time. So on Knocking Night, the last Thursday before Christmas, mummers in grotesque costumes went from house to house, knocking at doors, rattling cans and cowbells, and cracking whips to drive the spirits away.

Even old Father Christmas, himself a kindly bearer of gifts, was once believed to travel with frightening masked companions who doled out switches and punishment to naughty children. And today, in Austria, good Saint Nicholas parades through the streets in full bishop's regalia, followed by a band of *Buttenmandln*. Clothed all in straw and wearing fur masks, they pounce upon and squeeze the young people they meet.

New Year's Eve, with its free-flowing wine and beer, its dancing and street parades, brings the holidays to an exuberant end.

280

1

2

4   5

7

1: The Bavarian village at Kochel at Christmastime. 2: Buttenmandln, wrapped in straw and wearing frightening masks, catch and squeeze young people. 3: The church of Maria Gern, built in 1709, near Berchtesgaden in the Bavarian Alps. 4: Baked dough figure of a man in Tyrolean dress. 5: A decorated Christmas biscuit. 6: The Christmas market in front of the modern town hall, Stuttgart, Germany. 7: One of the "monsters" who come to frighten away evil spirits on the first three Thursdays of December in the Salzburg region, Austria.

6

ITALY

THE ITALIANS HAVE a female Santa Claus called the Lady Befana, who distributes gifts on Epiphany while children roam the streets blowing paper trumpets. Legend has it that when Christ was born the shepherds told her of the wondrous happening and the guiding star, but she delayed setting out. Every Christmas since, she has wandered in search of the Holy Child, leaving gifts at each house in the hope that He might be within. Like Santa Claus, she comes down the chimney.

One of the most colorful Christmas customs is that of the pipers, or *pifferai*. During Advent shepherds, attired in sheepskin trousers, flaming red vests and broad-brimmed hats with red tassels and white peacock feathers, march into the towns from the outlying districts. They carry bagpipes, reeds and oboes, on which they play sweet music before each shrine to the Holy Child. They pause, too, before carpenter shops in honor of Joseph. Often they are invited into homes, where they sing old carols and folk songs.

The Urn of Fate is a gay and suspenseful part of Christmas. A large ornamental bowl brimming over with wrapped gifts, it contains many empty boxes. Each person takes his turn at reaching into the bowl, and many are likely to draw blanks before getting a real present.

The *Ceppo* was the early Italian equivalent of the Christmas tree. Made of cardboard and three or four laths or canes, it was pyramidal in shape, about three feet high, with shelves rising to three or four levels. At the top of the pyramid was placed a pine cone or a puppet. Wax candles were lit along the cane sides of the pyramid, and at the lowest level an Infant Jesus made of wax or plaster lay in a cradle surrounded by shepherds, saints and angels. The shelves above held candy, fruit and small presents.

1

2

3

4

5

6

1: Woman dressed as the Befana
sits before her cottage, collecting
offerings for the Red Cross. 2: Pipers
from outlying villages gather on
the Via Frattina, Rome. 3: "Santa Claus"
poses with a child and a man who wears
the typical costume of Cagliari,
Sardinia. 4: At the top of the famous
Spanish Steps, Romans view a
crèche in a background which depicts
Rome in the sixteenth century.
5: A Christmas feast including noodle
torte, prosciutto and panettone.
6: Ceppo with gifts and manger scene.

283

FRANCE

ALONG THE BROAD boulevards of Paris, shopwindows are resplendent in December with dolls, toys and animated figures. Throughout France small painted clay figures made in Provence and called *santons*, "little saints," are sold. Some are miniatures of the Holy Family to place in a crèche; others are figurines of butchers, bakers, policemen and priests to be given as playthings.

Almost every home has its crèche. In rural areas the children gather laurel, holly, stones and moss from the woods for its decoration. Grown-ups go to the woods, too, to bring home the Yule log. On Christmas Eve a glass of wine is poured over the log before it is ignited, and a late supper, to be eaten after midnight Mass, may be cooked over the blaze. In cities, where fireplaces are infrequent, the tradition is kept by eating cakes shaped like logs and covered with chocolate icing to resemble tree bark. Then the children hang up stockings or set out shoes for Father Christmas to fill. Adult gift-giving comes later, on New Year's Day.

A colorful custom in some regions is the Christmas Eve procession to church. Young people dressed as shepherds and shepherdesses march through the streets beating drums and playing wind instruments, their way lighted by men bearing torches. And in the vaulted splendor of Gothic cathedrals, just at midnight, organs and choirs, often accompanied by bells, harps and flutes, raise the triumphant strains of "*Adeste Fideles.*"

On Epiphany *gâteaux des rois*, or kings' cakes, are baked to honor the Magi. These are round, "plentifully daubed with almond paste," and each contains a coin, a bean or a small favor. The person who finds the prize in his piece is given a paper crown and named king or queen for the day. Everyone must obey the new ruler's commands during the games and dances that follow.

284

1

2

3

5

6

1: *Father Christmas painted on the window of a Paris bistro.* 2: *Small trees and evergreen garlands adorn the façade of a celebrated restaurant.* 3: *A shepherd carries a beribboned lamb at Christmas Eve Mass as part of a traditional ceremony at Les Baux in Provence.* 4: *Always beautiful, the Champs Élysées is especially dazzling at Christmastime.* 5: *A chocolate-covered Yule log and other holiday confections in the window of a patisserie.* 6: *A Provençal santon maker shown with one of his creations.*

4

285

SWEDEN

In Sweden Christmas is the holiday of holidays, the star and jewel of the northern year. From the gaudily lit streets and markets of Stockholm to each tiny snow-covered hamlet, Christmas is a play of contrasts—bright light amid winter darkness, pagan customs mingled with Christian ritual. Here, in heathen times, it was believed that at Christmas the dead returned to earth, so food and drink were set out for them. Today the children set out food for Santa Claus.

In the long midwinter darkness any light is welcome, so the making of candles is a high point of the Christmas celebration. And on Saint Lucia's Day, December thirteenth, a young girl clad in white with a crown of candles on her hair, followed by other young people carrying burning candles, awakens sleeping families at dawn to offer them wheat cakes and coffee. Many people believe that she represents the revered Lucia of ancient Syracuse, who had her eyes put out for refusing to renounce her Christian faith. In villages throughout the land young girls vie each year for the honor of portraying her.

Even more colorful is the procession of the Star Boys, which reenacts the journey of the Three Kings to Bethlehem. As they go about the towns singing, they are followed by strangely costumed figures, most notably Judas with his purse.

There is always great feasting. The Christmas pig and the Christmas beer symbolize fecundity; and, according to old tradition, the manner in which the dough of the Christmas cake rises portends whether or not a good year is in prospect.

On December thirty-first a vigil is held at many churches, with prayers at the stroke of twelve. Then large parties are held in restaurants and halls while the young stream through the streets and the church bells ring in the New Year.

1

2

3

4

5

6

1: *As Christmas Day dawns, families travel in torchlit sleighs to church services.* 2: *The snow-covered Christmas market at Stortorget, Stockholm.* 3: *A young girl dressed as Saint Lucia, sometimes called the Queen of Light.* 4: *Holiday baked goods include pastries, fruitcakes, decorated cookies and muffins.* 5: *Julotta, the early Christmas service, in northern Sweden.* 6: *The famous Scandinavian smorgasbord of cheeses, breads, salads and meats.*

287

Spain

FROM THE SNOWBOUND villages of Catalonia to the sun-drenched province of Cadiz, Christmas in Spain is a time of devout and beautiful religious ceremonies. The observances begin on December eighth, which is the Feast of the Immaculate Conception. After Vespers on that day the stately Dance of the Sixes is performed in the magnificent cathedral of Seville. Despite the dance's name, the origin of which is lost in the mists of antiquity, ten boys are trained under ecclesiastical direction to participate. Dressed in plumed hats and lace-trimmed suits of pale blue satin, like royal pages of a bygone era, they go through intricate, ritualistic steps before the altar to the accompaniment of clicking castanets.

In cathedrals, in country churches and in most homes, manger scenes known as *Nacimientos* are centers of devotion. Carved *Nacimiento* figures appear in the shops in early December, and are sold along with Christmas evergreens on the steps of the great cathedral in Barcelona. Many families gather around their household *Nacimientos* every evening during Christmas week to sing carols, and children shake tinkling tambourines as they dance for the Christ Child.

There are special holiday foods, of course, such as *dulces de almendra,* or sweet almond pastries. Elaborate cards bearing greetings are distributed by tradesmen to their patrons. And the rich give food and clothing to the poor for, according to time-honored tradition, good luck will come only to those who are generous during this season of peace and goodwill.

It is not until January sixth that the children receive their gifts, which are said to be left by the Magi passing through on their way to Bethlehem. On that day, too, elaborate parades honoring the Three Kings are held in the big cities.

288

1

2

3

4

5

7

1: *A crèche at the San Rafael Orphanage for disabled children in Madrid.* 2: *The Dance of the Sixes being performed in the cathedral at Seville.* 3: *A market stall displaying Christmas toys and ornaments in the Plaza Mayor, Madrid.* 4, 5: *Turn-of-the-century commercial greeting cards, sent by a cobbler and a barber.* 6: *Table laden with holiday foods, including turkey, eels and almonds.* 7: *A stall where crèche figures are sold in the Plaza Mayor.*

6

POLAND

WITH THE APPEARANCE of the first star on Christmas Eve, the daylong fast of the Polish *Wigilia* is ended and families gather around the table to honor the Holy Child.

Before the traditional supper is served, the father of the house breaks the *Oplateki*, or Christmas wafers, which are marked with Nativity scenes and have been blessed by the Church. He then distributes the pieces to all who are present as tokens of friendship and peace.

The meal that follows has twelve courses, one for each Apostle. It is always meatless, consisting generally of borsch, fish, cabbage, mushrooms, almonds, and pastries made with poppy seed and honey. The hospitable Poles have a saying: "Our hearts are open to stranger, kith and kin." And so an extra place is set for anyone who might come knocking at the door.

In commemoration of the birds and beasts who gathered at the Manger, children dressed as storks, bears, or characters from the Nativity go from house to house singing carols. They are rewarded with gifts of food.

In many homes sheaves of wheat or other grain from the harvest are placed in the four corners of the principal room on Christmas Eve. Straw is spread on the floor and even under the white cloth on the dining table as a reminder of the Manger. On Christmas Eve, too, there are Poles, Ukrainians and other Slavic people who put their children to sleep on beds of straw or hay in imitation of the newborn Christ.

The great midnight Mass in Poland is called *Pasterka*, the Mass of the Shepherds. And on this most sacred of nights, according to legend, those whose lives have been pure and blameless may see in the winter sky, where the heavens have parted, a vision of Jacob's ladder.

1

2

3

4

6

5

7

1: Painted wooden pull toy depicting
Laykonik, the first Tatar prince in
Poland. 2: A band of musicians rides
through the streets of Kraków advertising
gifts for sale in a department store and
wishing everyone happy holidays.
3: A wooden church near Zakopane in
the Carpathian Mountains. 4: The stately
Slovacki Theatre in Kraków. 5: There are
few decorations but many enthusiastic
shoppers in Kraków. 6: Crèche from the
Kraków annual competition, covered
with tinfoil. 7: An intricate paper cutting
used as a Christmas decoration.

291

The Holy Land

CHRISTMAS IN THE Middle East is a time of contrasts, of the mingling of East and West, of ancient and modern. Nowhere is this more apparent than in Jerusalem, the capital city of Israel, and a holy city for three of the world's major faiths—Christianity, Judaism and Islam. In Jerusalem at Christmastime, pilgrims from the world over mingle with resident Jews and Arabs as they seek out the special services conducted by the thirty Christian denominations located in the city. This is also the season of the Jewish holy days of Hanukkah, and the lunar cycle sometimes causes a Muslim holiday to fall during Christmas week. Then decorations are even more dazzling, stores even more crowded.

Just a few miles to the south of Jerusalem lies the "little town of Bethlehem," where the contrasts are even more striking. Despite the busloads of camera-carrying tourists that arrive each year for Christmas week, Bethlehem retains an Eastern, almost Biblical atmosphere. Mosques stand in tranquil harmony with Christian churches, and the sound of muezzins chanting their prayers blends with the plainsong echoing from the cathedrals. Though jet planes roar past overhead, packladen donkeys still pick their way through the narrow streets; and veiled women dressed in such robes as Mary might have worn rub elbows with visitors in sundresses or slacks.

Standing on the spot where, according to legend, Jesus was laid in a manger, the Church of the Nativity is the central focus of all Christianity as the holy night draws nigh. Services from the Church are televised and broadcast throughout the world. But outside the town are olive groves where trees planted before the birth of Christ still flourish. And in the surrounding fields, shepherds still watch their flocks by night—a timeless reminder of that first, wondrous Christmas Eve.

292

3

1: In the fields a shepherd in traditional robes stands guard over his flock. 2: An Arab student choir singing ancient Christmas songs at the YMCA in East Jerusalem. 3: A view of Bethlehem with its mosques and churches outlined against the surrounding hills. 4: A small band accompanies carolers on a street in Bethlehem. 5: A Greek pilgrim lights candles for Christmas in Bethlehem. These devoted worshippers, who travel from Greece to Israel for the sacred event, commemorate the birth of Jesus according to the Julian calendar, two weeks later than it is celebrated in the West.

5

4

293

Great Britain

CHRISTMAS COMES TO Great Britain with the pealing of many bells. They ring from the towers of famous abbeys and the belfries of small rural churches. In Dewsbury, Yorkshire, the Devil's Knell or Old Lad's Passing has, for the greater part of seven hundred years, been solemnly tolled for the last hour of Christmas Eve, a warning to the Prince of Evil that he will die when the Prince of Peace is born. Then at midnight, here and throughout England, the bells begin a joyous music that announces the blessed birth. In some areas handbell ringers still walk the wintry streets.

Carolers gather around communal Christmas trees on village greens and raise their voices at candlelit church services. Their music is especially beautiful in Wales, where communal singing is an important part of everyday life. Here young men used to escort the minister to predawn services, lighting his way with fiery torches. Then, after the prayers and sermon, the congregation would sing psalms and hymns until daybreak.

Christmas itself is a day of family gaiety—and of feasting on turkey with roast potatoes, mince pies and plum puddings. At dinner or at tea, tables are decorated with paper hats, whistles and crackers (or snappers) containing riddles, fortunes and little gifts.

In Scotland, however, the most elaborate festivities are saved for Hogmanay, or New Year's. In some parts of Angus the old year is burned out with enormous bonfires around which the people dance. And at Stonehaven processions are held in which balls of flaming tallow-coated rope are swung about on the ends of long cords. Outside the Tron Church in Edinburgh crowds gather to wait for midnight. When the hour strikes, those in Highland dress toss their bonnets into the air and dance reels to the wild music of bagpipes.

294

1

2

3

4

5

7

6

1: Lincoln Cathedral, in Lincolnshire, viewed across snow-covered rooftops. 2: Choirboys singing Christmas hymns at King's College Chapel in Cambridge. 3: Village carolers in front of the Black Horse Pub in Buckinghamshire. 4, 5: Special-issue postage stamps brighten the holiday mail. 6: Oxford Street, London, decorated with garlands and lights. 7: Plum pudding, the traditional English Christmas dessert.

MEXICO

DECEMBER IS THE month when the flame-colored, star-shaped flower of the poinsettia bursts into bloom throughout Mexico. Known as *flor de Nochebuena*, flower of Holy Night, it is that nation's gift to the rest of the world. It also symbolizes Mexico's rich blend of the festive and devout at Christmastime.

Starting early in December, the marketplaces fill up with flowers, baskets, toys, and figures of the Holy Family. Produce booths are stocked with cakes, cheeses and fruits, while Indians stream into the cities from outlying districts bringing wares of leather, clay and wood. And everywhere—in doorways and arches—are the *piñatas*, earthenware bowls decorated with brightly colored paper.

Beginning on December sixteenth a novena known as the *posada* is held. *Posada* means inn. The ceremony itself is a nightly reenactment of the trials of the Holy Family as they sought shelter in Bethlehem. For nine days the children of each house go from room to room asking for shelter and being refused. In one room a beautifully decorated altar has been set up, and a crèche with an empty crib. In this crib, on Christmas Eve, the children place a figure of the Christ Child.

Afterward they roam the streets breaking the *piñatas*. Blindfolded, each child is given a chance to hit a *piñata* with a long stick. When finally the jar is broken, a profusion of peanuts, fruits and candy showers down.

The important holiday meal, served late on Christmas Eve, usually includes fried sweet puffs with brown-sugar syrup, known as *buñuelos*, and *capirotada*, a Mexican bread pudding.

The Feast of Epiphany is celebrated in Mexican churches with soaring music and thousands of lighted candles, expressing adoration of the Christ Child and joy at His birth.

296

1

2

3

1: During the Christmas season balloons of all shapes and colors are sold in Mexico City. 2: A young man breaking open a piñata.
3: A woman and man portraying Mary and Joseph are carried in a procession to the church in the small town of Tepoztlán.
4: Gay figures of a clown, giraffe and horse for sale in a piñata store.
5: Musicians and native foods in a festive Mexico City restaurant at Christmastime.

5

4

297

CHRISTMAS IN MY COUNTRY

The Christian Children's Fund of Richmond, Virginia, is a nonprofit organization dedicated to serving the needs of children worldwide through person-to-person assistance programs. It sponsors an annual art competition open to children under fifteen years of age. One contest theme was "Christmas in My Country." Here are some of the winners from among the thousands of entries submitted, with a short commentary by each young artist. The pictures have been shown in the Metropolitan Museum of Art in New York City.

Michiko Kokubo, age five, Tokyo, Japan: "This picture shows a dinosaur celebrating Christmas holding balloons."

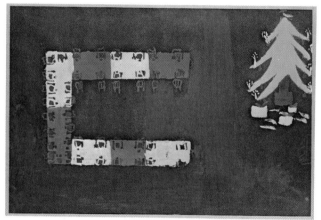

Christian Guilhof, age twelve, Crest, France: "My drawing represents the dining room, with its Christmas fir tree and tables ready for the meal."

Chen Yih Chi, age ten, Yilan, Taiwan: "In my picture Santa Claus is looking for his reindeer to start."

José Roman, age fourteen, Valdepeñas, Spain: "My picture is of Christmas in my home village. People enjoy themselves the best they can. Some go to church, others go to the public house to eat and drink, and others gather with their kindred."

Winston Postoak, age fourteen, Hartshorne, Oklahoma, winner of the first prize: "My picture shows
a trading-post meeting for Pueblo Indian ceremonial to celebrate Christmas."

Chung Chan Soo, age thirteen, Kwangju, Korea:
"A wish for gift from Santa."

Klaus Wolkenstein, age twelve, Berlin, Germany: "On my picture we see
a church at Christmas Eve in the mountains. Many people are going
to the church. On the place before the church a Christmas tree is standing
with burning candles. Children have built snowmen. It begins to
become dark. At the windows we see decorated Christmas trees."

Nunzia Falco, age thirteen, Naples, Italy: "Although we celebrate Christmas on the twenty-fifth of December as the birthday of Jesus, with carols and the service in the chapel, we in Italy give our presents at Epiphany. It is a wonderful day when the children wake up and find presents that the Befana has left. She is a kind witch who flies on her broomstick taking gifts in a sack and dropping them down the chimney."

ACKNOWLEDGMENTS

Except as noted below, biblical quotations are from the Reader's Digest edition of the King James Version. Page 43, lines 1-2, 10-13, 15-20; 44, lines 39-42; 46, lines 25-26; 49, lines 26-29; 53, lines 9-12: quotations are from The Jerusalem Bible, © 1966 by Darton, Longman & Todd, Ltd., and Doubleday & Company, Inc. Used by permission of the publishers. Page 71: *Home for Christmas* by Elizabeth Bowen is from *The Family Christmas Book*, © 1957 by Prentice-Hall, Inc. Used by permission of the author and Curtis Brown, Ltd. Page 73: *The Holy Night* is from *Christ Legends* by Selma Lagerlöf, translated by Velma Swanston Howard, copyright 1908 by Holt, Rinehart and Winston, Inc., copyright 1936 by Velma Swanston Howard. Used by permission of Holt, Rinehart and Winston, Inc. Page 76: *Star of the Nativity* is from *The Poems of Doctor Zhivago* by Boris Pasternak, translation © 1971 by Eugene M. Kayden. Used by arrangement with The Kent State University Press. Page 79: *The Ox and the Ass at the Manger*, translated by Enid McLeod, is from *Selected Writings of Jules Supervielle*, © 1967 by New Directions Publishing Corporation. Minor changes in original text made with the approval of the publisher. Used by permission of New Directions Publishing Corporation. Page 95: *Why the Chimes Rang*, copyright 1906, 1908, 1924, 1945 by The Bobbs-Merrill Company, Inc., is by Raymond MacDonald Alden. Used by permission of The Bobbs-Merrill Company, Inc. Page 98: *Christmas in Maine*, copyright 1941 by Robert P. Tristram Coffin, is used as abridged by permission of the Estate of Robert P. Tristram Coffin. Page 103: *A Letter from Santa Claus* is from *My Father, Mark Twain* by Clara Clemens Gabrilowitsch, copyright 1931 by Clara Clemens Gabrilowitsch, © renewed by Clara Clemens Samossoud. Used by permission of Harper & Row, Publishers, Inc. Page 108: *My First Christmas Tree*, copyright 1911 by The Curtis Publishing Company, is by Hamlin Garland. Used by permission of Isabel Garland Lord and Constance Garland Doyle. Page 113: *The Gift of the Magi* by O. Henry is used by permission of Doubleday & Company, Inc. Page 118: *The Christmas of the Phonograph Records* is from *The Christmas of the Phonograph Records: A Recollection* by Mari Sandoz, © 1966 by the Estate of Mari Sandoz. Used by permission of the University of Nebraska Press and A. M. Heath & Co., Ltd. Page 127: *Velvet Shoes*, copyright 1921, renewed 1949 by William Rose Benét, is from *Collected Poems of Elinor Wylie*. Used by permission of Alfred A. Knopf, Inc. Page 137: *To Springvale for Christmas* by Zona Gale is used by permission of the Zona Gale Breese Trust. Page 143: *Christmas Day at Sea* is from *Tales of Hearsay, and Last Essays* by Joseph Conrad. Used by permission of J. M. Dent & Sons Ltd. and the Trustees of the Joseph Conrad Estate. Page 145: *December* is from *That's Why*, copyright 1946 by Aileen Fisher. Used by permission of Aileen Fisher. Page 197: *A Christmas Memory*, © 1956 by Truman Capote, is from *Breakfast at Tiffany's* by Truman Capote. Used by permission of Random House, Inc., and Hamish Hamilton Ltd. Page 202, line 22: words from the song "Alexander's Ragtime Band" by Irving Berlin, copyright 1911 by Irving Berlin, copyright renewed, are used by permission of Irving Berlin Music Corporation. Page 202, line 22: words from the song "The Darktown Strutters Ball," W/M: Shelton Brooks, copyright 1917, renewed 1945, are used by permission of Leo Feist Inc. Page 202, line 29: words from the song "Show Me the Way to Go Home" are used by permission of Campbell Connelly & Co. Ltd. Page 208: *Christmas Trees* is from *The Poetry of Robert Frost*, edited by Edward Connery Lathem, copyright 1916, © 1969 by Holt, Rinehart and Winston, Inc., copyright 1944 by Robert Frost. Used by permission of Holt, Rinehart and Winston, Inc., and Jonathan Cape Limited. Page 210: *Amahl and the Night Visitors*, copyright 1951, 1952 by G. Schirmer, Inc., international copyright secured, is by Gian Carlo Menotti. Used by permission of G. Schirmer, Inc. Page 218: *Rather Late for Christmas*, first published in *Vogue*, copyright 1942 by Condé Nast Publications, Inc., is by Mary Ellen Chase. Used by permission of the author. Page 221: *Under the Mistletoe* is from *Copper Sun* by Countee Cullen, copyright 1927 by Harper & Row, Publishers, Inc., copyright 1955 by Ida M. Cullen. Used by permission of Harper & Row, Publishers, Inc. Page 223: *Stubby Pringle's Christmas* is from *The Collected Stories of Jack Schaefer*, © 1966 by Jack Schaefer. Used by permission of Houghton Mifflin Company and A. D. Peters and Company. Page 234: *Carols in the Cotswolds* is from *The Edge of Day*, © 1959 by Laurie Lee. Used by permission of the author, William Morrow & Company, Inc., and The Hogarth Press, Ltd. Page 238: *Christmas Tree*, © 1972 by the Estate of Marion M. Cummings, is a private Christmas card poem by e.e. cummings, and is from the Berg Collection, New York Public Library. Page 239: *Christmas Closes a Gulf* is from *Act One* by Moss Hart, © 1959 by Catherine Carlisle Hart and Joseph M. Hyman, Trustees. Used by permission of Random House, Inc. Page

244: *Signor Santa*, copyright 1935 by The Atlantic Monthly Company, is used by permission of William Morris Agency, Inc. Page 255: *A Large Christmas* is from *Memory of a Large Christmas*, © 1961, 1962 by Lillian Smith. Used by permission of W. W. Norton & Company, Inc., and the Estate of Lillian E. Smith. Page 261: *Carol of the Brown King*, © 1958 by The Crisis Publishing Company, Inc., is by Langston Hughes. Used by permission of Harold Ober Associates Inc. Page 262: *Jesous Ahatonhia*, English interpretation by J. E. Middleton, is used by permission of copyright owner, The Frederick Harris Music Co. Limited, and Alfred Lengnick & Co., Ltd. Page 263: *Christmas Morning*, copyright 1946 by Frank O'Connor, is from *The Stories of Frank O'Connor*. Used by permission of Alfred A. Knopf, Inc., and A. D. Peters and Company. The story originally appeared in *The New Yorker*. Page 270: *Francie Nolan's Christmas Tree* is from *A Tree Grows in Brooklyn*, copyright 1943, 1947 by Betty Smith. Used by permission of Harper & Row, Publishers, Inc., and William Heinemann Ltd. Page 273: *The Ballad of Befana* is from *Merry Christmas, Happy New Year*, © 1957 by Phyllis McGinley. Used by permission of the author, The Viking Press, Inc., and A. P. Watt & Son. Page 275: *Christmas Meditation of a Young Student* is from *Journal of a Soul* by Pope John XXIII, © 1965 by Geoffrey Chapman, Ltd., and translated by Dorothy White. Used by permission of McGraw-Hill Book Company, Geoffrey Chapman, Ltd., and Palm Publishers, Ltd.

MARGINALIA
Page 96: from *Now Every Child* in *Poems for Children*, copyright 1951 by Eleanor Farjeon. Used by permission of J. B. Lippincott Company and Harold Ober Associates Inc. Page

99: *Sleigh Bells at Night* in *Summer Green* by Elizabeth Coatsworth, copyright 1948 by Macmillan Publishing Co., Inc. Used by permission of Macmillan Publishing Co., Inc. Page 122: from *The Christmas Long Ago* in *Joyful Poems for Children* by James Whitcomb Riley, copyright 1944 by Lesley Payne, copyright 1941, 1946, © 1960 by Lesley Payne, Elizabeth Eitel Miesse and Edmund H. Eitel. Used by permission of The Bobbs-Merrill Company, Inc. Page 142: *Christmas Chant*, copyright 1949 by The Curtis Publishing Company, is by Isabel Shaw. Used by permission of the author. Pages 152, 154: from *In the Week When Christmas Comes* in *Poems for Children*, copyright 1951 by Eleanor Farjeon. Used by permission of J. B. Lippincott Company and Harold Ober Associates Inc. Page 157: from *Christmas Singing* by Elsie Williams Chandler in *St. Nicholas Magazine*, copyright 1929 by The Century Company. Used by permission of Appleton-Century-Crofts, Educational Division, Meredith Corporation. Pages 193, 194: from *The Open Door*, © 1957 by Helen Keller. Used by permission of Doubleday & Company, Inc. Pages 199, 200, 202, 204, 206, 207, 260: *Superstitions of the Old South* are based on material in *The Southern Christmas Book*, © 1958 by Harnett T. Kane. Used by permission of David McKay Company, Inc. Page 229: *Choose Wisely Then, Each Ornament* by Elizabeth-Ellan Long in *Christmas Idea Book*, copyright 1953 by Dorothy Biddle and Dorothea Blom. Pages 230, 232: from *The Western Country* in *Mince Pie and Mistletoe*, © 1959, 1961 by Phyllis McGinley. Used by permission of J. B. Lippincott Company and Curtis Brown, Ltd. Pages 248, 251, 252: *Conversation between Mr. and Mrs. Santa Claus*, copyright 1947 by The Curtis Publishing Company, is by Rowena Bennett. Used by permission of the author.

ILLUSTRATION CREDITS

Page 10: The Michael Friedsam Collection, 1931, The Metropolitan Museum of Art, New York. Pages 13, 21 (top), 86: The Loretta Hines Howard Collection, 1964, The Metropolitan Museum of Art; photos by Lee Boltin. Pages 14, 24: The National Gallery, London. Pages 15, 22, 23, 29: photos from Scala. Page 16: Galleria Sabauda, Turin; photo from Scala. Page 17: Pieve San Stefano, Carmignano; photo from Scala. Pages 18, 19, 49: Museo Arte de Cataluña, Barcelona; photos from Oronoz Madrid. Page 20: The Art Institute of Chicago, Gift of Charles Deering; photo from Joseph Martin/Scala. Pages 21 (bottom), 26 (top and bottom), 28, 32 (top and bottom), 34, 41, 43 (bottom), 54, 55, 56, 59 (top), 63 (bottom), 82, 94: The Pierpont Morgan Library, New York. Pages 25, 27, 30, 66: Uffizi, Florence; photos from Scala. Page 31: Giraudon/Lauros. Page 33: Francis Brunel. Pages 35, 65: Rijksmuseum, Amsterdam. Pages 36, 43 (top): The British Museum, London. Pages 38, 292, 293 (top left, bottom): Aramco World Magazine. Page 40: Bodleian Library, Oxford. Page 45: The Victoria and Albert Museum, London; photo by Michael Holford. Page 46: The Cloisters Collection, The Metropolitan Museum of Art. Page 47: Alte Pinakothek, Munich; photo from Scala. Page 48: Santa Maria

Fuoris Portas, Castelsepio; photo from Scala. Page 50: Rapho Guillumette/Georg Gerster. Page 51: Museo Arte de Cataluña; photo from Scala. Page 52: Baptistry, Florence; photo from Scala. Page 53: Magnum Photos, Inc./Erich Lessing. Page 57: National Museum, Naples; photo by Federico Arborio Mella. Page 59 (bottom): Casanatense Library, Rome; photo from Scala. Page 60: The National Portrait Gallery, London. Page 61: photo by John Freeman & Co. Page 63 (top): Kunsthistorisches Museum, Vienna. Page 67: Archives of Cooperative Lutheranism, New York. Page 68: Musée des Beaux-Artes, Rennes; photo from Scala. Pages 70, 163, 170, 196, 235: Radio Times Hulton Picture Library. Page 73: Stepan Dabakjan, Christian Children's Fund, Inc.; photo by Ernest Coppolino. Pages 74, 75: Fronval. Pages 76, 77, 78: Karen Pellaton. Pages 80, 85, 88, 91: Katharine Dodge. Page 92: Francis Dupuy, Christian Children's Fund, Inc.; photo by Ernest Coppolino. Page 96: from Magic of a People; photos by Charles and Ray Eames. Pages 98, 109 (top), 123, 141, 245, 246, 248, 251, 252, 267, 272: The Cousley Collections; photos by Ernest Coppolino. Pages 100, 101, 102, 116, 118, 121, 122, 124, 126, 138 (bottom), 140, 157, 168, 236, 256, 260, 264, 265: The Cousley Collections; photos by Martin Glanzman. Page 103: Mark Twain Memorial; photo by Ernest Coppolino. Pages 105-107: manuscript of 'Twas the Night Before Christmas by Clement C. Moore from The New-York Historical Society. Page 105: photo by Henry Ries. Page 107: Sidney Strange Antiques Exchange; portrait from Dictionary of American Portraits, Dover Publications, Inc., 1967, photo by Henry Ries. Page 108: Poestenkill, New York: Winter by Joseph H. Hidley, Abby Aldrich Rockefeller Folk Art Collection, Williamsburg, Virginia. Pages 226, 227, 259, 269: Abby Aldrich Rockefeller Folk Art Collection. Pages 109 (bottom), 254: The Jerry Smith Collections; photos courtesy of Hallmark Cards Incorporated. Pages 110, 114, 165: Culver Pictures, Inc. Page 111: collections of Kit Robbins and John Noble. Page 112: The Granger Collection. Page 113: Leo and Diane Dillon. Page 115: from Good Housekeeping, December 1916, copyright 1916 by Hearst Corporation; reproduced by permission. Pages 117, 195, 258: Hallmark Cards Incorporated. Page 119: copyright 1905 by The New York Times Company; reprinted by permission. Pages 120, 125, 270: Ib Ohlsson. Page 127: Kenneth Hine. Pages 128, 130, 132, 135: Jerry Pinkney. Page 136: Nathaniel Currier, from The Twelve Days of Christmas by Miles and John Hadfield, Cassell & Company Ltd. Pages 136, 149, 262, 280, 282, 284, 286, 288, 290, 294, 296: calligraphy and lettering by Hal Fiedler. Pages 143, 219, 221, 273: The Fine Arts Collection of The Seamen's Bank for Savings; photos by William Sonntag. Pages 145, 146, 147, 148: Harald Sund. Pages 150, 159, 167, 175, 185, 192: Robert Shore. Page 152: by permission of Lords Gallery. Page 155: courtesy of The Victoria and Albert Museum. Pages 156, 161, 173, 176: from A Christmas Carol by Charles Dickens, 1916, 1956, published by arrangement with the Arthur Rackham Estate;

reproduced by permission of J. B. Lippincott Company and William Heinemann Ltd. Pages 172, 182, 190: John Leech, from the Oxford Illustrated Dickens Edition of Christmas Books, published by Oxford University Press. Page 179: George Cruikshank. Page 183: by permission of B. Weinreb & Douwina Ltd. Page 186: Phiz. Page 191: courtesy of Pollocks Toy Museum, London. Pages 198, 199, 200, 201, 202, 203, 204, 205, 206: Darrell Sweet. Page 207: The Barbara Johnson Collection, Museum of American Folk Art, New York. Pages 208-209: Nita Engle. Pages 210, 213, 215, 217: Ray Ameijide. Page 218: Hoosick Falls in Winter by Grandma Moses, 1944, © 1970 by Grandma Moses Properties, Inc., New York, Abby Aldrich Rockefeller Folk Art Collection. Page 222: Night Before Christmas by Grandma Moses, 1960, © Grandma Moses Properties, Inc., New York; from The Night Before Christmas, Random House, Inc. Page 224: The Boss Has a Young 'Un by George Phippen, courtesy of the George Phippen Gallery and Mr. and Mrs. Paul Dennis. Pages 225, 228, 233: Walter Ferro. Pages 229, 283 (bottom right): from The Trees of Christmas, © 1969 by Abingdon Press. Page 231: Sears, Roebuck and Co. and Crown Publishers, Inc.; photo by William Sonntag. Pages 234, 268: courtesy of The New-York Historical Society. Page 238: The Christmas Tree, from a painting by E. Osborn, 1864, A Book of Christmas by William Sansom, Weidenfeld & Nicolson Ltd., 1968. Page 239: courtesy of Mrs. Moss Hart. Pages 241, 242, 243: Margaret Cusack. Pages 247, 250, 253: Sandford Kossin. Page 261: Oscar Liebman. Page 263: Lew McCance. Pages 275, 276: Isa Barnett. Page 278: from Family Circle. Page 280 (top): German National Tourist Office. Pages 280 (bottom), 281 (top left): Ernst Baumann, Bad Reichenhall. Page 281 (top center, top right, bottom left): Landesbildstelle Württemberg, Stuttgart. Page 281 (bottom right): H. Sager, Salzburg-Aigen. Pages 282 (top, bottom), 283 (top left, top right): Roma's Press Photo/Velio Cioni. Page 283 (bottom left): Masera. Page 284 (top): Rapho/Belzeaux. Page 284 (bottom): Rapho/Doisneau. Page 285 (top left): Phedon-Salou. Page 285 (top right): Fotogram/Édouard Berne. Page 285 (bottom left): Atlas-Photo/G. Boutin. Page 285 (bottom right): Kay Lawson. Pages 286 (top, bottom), 287 (top left, bottom left): N. Göran Algård. Page 287 (top right): IMS/Kjill Nilsson. Page 287 (bottom right): IMS/Stig Grip. Pages 288 (top), 289 (top left, bottom left, bottom right): Algár. Page 288 (bottom): Lara. Page 289 (top center, top right): Sanchez Martinez. Pages 290 (top), 291 (top right, bottom right): Claus Hansmann. Pages 290 (middle, bottom), 291 (top left, bottom left): The Quo Vadis Society of the Kosciuszko Foundation/Andrew Rudzinski. Page 293 (top right): Alon Reininger/Frederic Lewis, Inc. Pages 294 (top), 295 (top left, bottom left): British Tourist Authority. Pages 294 (bottom), 295 (bottom right): Photo Trends. Page 295 (top center, top right): The Post Office, Great Britain. Pages 296 (top, bottom), 297 (top left, bottom left): Stoppelman. Page 297 (bottom right): DPI/Ruiko. Pages 298, 299, 300: Christian Children's Fund.